Dead Hands

Dead Hands

FICTIONS OF AGENCY,
RENAISSANCE TO MODERN

KATHERINE ROWE

STANFORD UNIVERSITY PRESS

Stanford, California 1999

Stanford University Press
Stanford, California
© 1999 by the Board of Trustees of the Leland Stanford Junior University

Printed in the United States of America
CIP data appear at the end of the book

Contents

Illustrations

Preface

Toward the beginning of Emily Brontë's *Wuthering Heights*, the narrator, Lockwood, wakes from a nightmare to hear a teasing, insistent scratch on his window. Thinking a tree branch is brushing the lattice, he breaks the pane. "Stretching an arm out to seize the importunate branch," he closes his hand "on the fingers of a little, ice-cold hand!":

> The intense horror of nightmare came over me; I tried to draw back my arm, but the hand clung to it, and a most melancholy voice sobbed,
> "Let me in—let me in!"
> —Terror made me cruel; and, finding it useless to attempt shaking the creature off, I pulled its wrist on to the broken pane, and rubbed it to and fro till the blood ran down and soaked the bed-clothes: still it wailed, "Let me in!" and maintained its tenacious gripe, almost maddening me with fear.[1]

This is a riveting moment, memorable years after reading the novel. But it is also oddly opaque. It introduces the ghost of Catherine

Earnshaw and sets up familiar themes of haunting and intrusion, but it has no plot consequences. Likewise, Lockwood's intense horror—the vivid details of cutting her wrist and his blood-soaked bed-clothes, which suggest that something more than Cathy's ghost has come home to him—seems to have no aim; the novel becomes less and less interested in its narrator. Finally, two things make the hand itself especially peculiar. First is the sudden shift of grip: Lockwood grabs the hand first, only to find it suddenly clutching him. Second is the free-floating way it haunts: by rights, Heathcliff or his family should be the ones haunted, as they are throughout the rest of the novel. But in this early scene it seems that any person, including the reader, might find himself or herself the object of Cathy's terrifying desire. What gives the sudden grip of her disembodied hand such disproportionate force and affect?

The purpose of this study is to suggest some answers to this question by tracing the literary and intellectual history of this device: the severed, disembodied, or ghostly hand. Brontë and the other Gothic writers who popularized this figure invoke a literary tradition that goes back to early modern drama and that draws on a broad and eclectic field of manual iconography: from religious imagery, sixteenth-century medical anatomies, emblem books, witch-craft, and folklore to the popular metaphors of nineteenth-century industrialism, contemporary labor movements, and forensic science. The images and gestures that thread through these different traditions—betrothal rings, daggers, hands from the clouds, clasped hands, occult hands of glory, laboring hands, legal mortmain, palmistry, phantom limbs, and fingerprints—suggest the breadth of reference brought into play in this device.

Within these disparate fields, the figure of the dead hand represents a specific set of intellectual concerns: the relationship between human intentions or will—collective and individual—and meaningful action in the world. Across Western philosophical writings, particularly in the Aristotelian tradition, the hand is the pre-eminent bodily metaphor for human action. And indeed, it is the chief exemplar of the vexed belief that preoccupies both Marxist and analytic philosophies of action. In both of these philosophies (though with different consequences), what makes us feel that we can and do act as individuals, with purpose and effect, is the common human experience of being in our own bodies, moving about in the world. Dead hands challenge and complicate this "common sense" logic of kinetic self-possession, both as a full account of bodily experience and as an ahistorical given. They punctuate states of partial attention and volition, like Lockwood's waking nightmare. They embody an urgent but aimless sense of purpose like the insistent hand at his window. They disrupt the familiar connections between cause and effect that permit us to attribute and interpret actions. And they stage sudden reversals of control—like Cathy's icy clutch—that direct us to the disabling, dependent, and self-alienating experiences of the acting self.

By tracing the dynamic history of this device—as it develops on the Elizabethan and Jacobean stage convention and later blossoms in Gothic fiction—this study advances a comparatist reading of early modern and modern concerns about the nature of action and its relation to interiority, authority, and identity. For the *sense* of the self as a source of effectual, meaningful action has its own history. The modern notion of the body as proper to the self, inhabited and owned by the self, develops with the Anglo-American political philosophy of possessive individualism in the seventeenth century. Dead hands describe the margins of this political tradition: in early modern fictions that define the self in terms of performance, rather than property; and in modern fictions that question the role bodily experience plays in ratifying social and legal definitions of person. Thus, the purpose of this study is not to amplify the well-traveled debates between positivist and materialist accounts of human action: that we shape events and the social institutions we live in or that these produce our subjectivity effects. I aim instead to outline the history of the way bodily performance—in particular, the exemplary performance of the hands—has been used to ratify or challenge the concept of autonomous human agency. My question is not, "Does the perception that we inhabit bodies that act on the world confer a real or a false consciousness of self?" But rather, "How did our current conceptions of subordinate and autonomous agency, and their dependence on bodily evidence and experience, evolve?" The spine of this study, then, can best be described as a conceptual history, or historical epistemology—what Lorraine Daston calls "the history of the categories that structure our thought, pattern our arguments and proofs, and certify our standards for explanation."[2] The pattern traced here is the explanatory role manual action and manual activity play in our changing ideas about human agency.

The body of this study, by contrast, remains an analysis of the literary devices animated by these ideas. To track a literary convention through very different cultures and genres requires a mixed approach, one that describes the convention's formal shape and situates it historically at the same time. Thus, Chapters 1 and 4 map out the formal structure of the device as it is used in early modern and modern fiction respectively: first in the context of Renaissance anatomies and later in terms of the Gothic tradition. These are the two periods in which the figure of a severed hand gets its most rhetorically intense and elaborate literary expression—migrating into new genres and annexing new institutional and disciplinary material. Accordingly, Chapters 2, 3, and 5 explore what motivates formal innovation in these two periods: concerns about effectual political agency, and the changing nature of duty and service articulated in Jacobean drama; and the changing conditions of labor and social identity explored in nineteenth-century fiction. Readers will notice the absence of a chapter focused in the eighteenth century, which might have drawn tighter genealogical links between the early and later modern periods. But the discontinuous arc of this narrative is deliberate. It facilitates a particular kind of double vision: allowing us to read for formal connections between the early modern and modern versions of this device, while sharpening the conceptual contrasts between the apparently similar terms that animate it.

Finally, I do not aim to write an encyclopedic study of the literary uses of the hand. The variety and breadth of manual imagery in Western literature make that impossible. The narrower focus of *Dead Hands* is to demonstrate what makes the figure of a severed or disembodied hand a coherent literary convention and to describe the major shifts in its form and aesthetic—as it answers the very different conceptual demands of these different periods. For this reason, I have followed the device into Continental literatures only where the Anglo-American tradition directly draws on them, as in the case of Renaissance emblem books and medical anatomies and Anglo-Continental witchcraft traditions. And I do not treat the rich non-Western imagery of iconic hands, like the Arabic *khamsa* (or "hand of Fatima"), for these have their own complex cultural history. I hope that readers with many interests and fields of expertise will turn to the chapters closest to the material with which they work and find a model for interpreting the device that best suits their own reading.

Readings of the body shaped by a single part produce no more or less true a reading of a body general than others. But they do more clearly remind us of the heterogeneity of the terms with which Western thought invents corporeality and physical experience. By directing attention to the hand, this book supports a broader claim about the study of the figurative and corporeal body: "the body" as a site of cultural fiction making brings together various, sometimes contradictory, spheres of reference, fictional strategies, and values. The body imagined in relation to its hand is shaped by those fictions and faculties particular to the hand: the principle of rational organization; the capacity to express, manufacture, and possess; and the dependencies of mutual labor and layered agency. What explains the attraction of the figure of the hand, at different historical moments—in different languages, media, and literary genres—to this cluster of conceptual problems? To the extent that this question can be answered, its answers are at once organic and social. The powerful legacy of scholastic philosophy sustains Aristotelian ideas about the ontological nature of the hand and its relation to action from the Renaissance through nineteenth- and twentieth-century philosophy. At the same time, the transformations of early modern economic life profoundly changed the significance of those Aristotelian claims for later periods.

Together with interpretive tradition and material history, the natural qualities of the hand itself—in its relation to the brain and body—also contribute to its long association with problems of human action. The human vocal system offers a limited set of phonemes, differently intoned, combined, and selected as meaningful (or not) in different languages and at different moments. Similarly, the neuromechanical structure of the hand provides the basic somatic units that facilitate and shape social, intellectual, and philosophical invention. We point, grasp or release, cup or spread the fingers, and so on; and these motions vary their meaning situationally, culturally, and over time. Furthermore, the gestures, habits, and practices that incorporate these motions shape the plastic brain as much as the brain controls them. The mutually determining relation between language use and brain development has become a truism of cognitive science. Recently, neuroscience has extended this recognition to manual activity, describing the interaction between biology and culture in the hand as both an evolutionary and individual adaptive process.[3] What the hand and brain do especially well together, because of the hand's remarkable range of motor function, is develop "novel behaviors or adaptive strategies . . . to meet unpredictable demands presented by the particular environment encountered by each individual."[4] The trope of the severed hand foregrounds this primary, cognitive and motor encounter between unpredictable environment and adaptive innovation. At once severed and vital, it symbolizes both possession and dispossession of those faculties that master unpredictable events. And it has a long history of serving this paradoxical symbolic function. The significance of such encounters, individual and collective, is a matter of culture and history working on an apparent constant—the hand or hands we have here. The fictions explored below illuminate the dynamic nature of that constant, and what we grant ourselves and others on account of it. They test the ontological certainties attributed to and figured by the mobile, instrumental hand—extending a skeptical invitation to "look closer" at common sense vocabularies of bodily experience.

Portions of this book have appeared elsewhere in somewhat different form. An early version of Chapter 1 appeared in *The Body in Parts* (edited by David Hillman and Carla Mazzio [New York: Routledge, 1997]. It is reprinted here by permission of Routledge

Press. Chapter 2 first appeared in *Shakespeare Quarterly* (fall 1994); it is reprinted by permission of *Shakespeare Quarterly*. The Mellon foundation provided generous support for the year in which I began work on this subject. A fellowship from the Morse fund at Yale University helped see it to completion. A grant from the Madge Miller Research Fund at Bryn Mawr College assisted in production. I am indebted to the staff at Printed Media, the Office of Public Affairs, and the Latent Finger Print Division of the Federal Bureau of Investigation, U. S. Department of Justice, for help in fingerprint research. Margaret Powell offered invaluable assistance tracking down obscure severed hands at Sterling Library and elsewhere, as did Nathan Costa and Andrew Zurcher.

This book has grown in part from systematic research and reading, in part from the contributions of friends and colleagues quick to offer their favorite examples for analysis. Among others who have lent their hands along the way, I owe special debts to the generosity and insight of Douglas Bruster, Elizabeth Heckendorn Cook, Jenine Dallal, Carolyn Dever, Heather Dubrow, Elizabeth Fowler, Kevis Goodman, Laura Green, David Hillman, Heather James, Suzanne Keen, Laura King, Frances MacDonnell, Lawrence Manley, Carla Mazzio, Elizabeth Meade, John Norman, Annabel Patterson, David Quint, Joseph Roach, Kathryn Schwarz, Alan Trachtenberg, Blakey Vermeule, Luke Wilson, Sarah Winter, and Elizabeth Wolf. They tested early my ability to write with rigor out of my field as well as in it. Philip Fisher, Marjorie Garber, and Roland Greene guided this study from its inception with astuteness and patience. The generous and exacting commentary of two readers for Stanford University Press—Lowell Gallagher and Jacques Lezra—clarified my vision. Finally, the steady, if occasionally bemused support of my family sustained this work in more ways than I can say.

Without Bruce Jacobson this book would not have been written. It is dedicated to him, and in memory of Jean Dickinson Potter and Sylvia Altman Jacobson, who helped me begin.

Dead Hands

Essentialism, Agency, and the Exemplary Hand

> All the work of the hand is rooted in thinking. Therefore think-
> ing itself is man's simplest, and for that reason hardest, handwork,
> if it would be properly accomplished.
>
> —Heidegger, *What Is Called Thinking?*

In the history of writing about the hand, there are at least two kinds of books: encyclopedic works that gather every known reference to this part of the body and studies of its significant place in specific disciplines. *Chirologia . . . Chironomia* (1644), by the English physician and scholar John Bulwer, offers a good illustration of both. Bulwer advertised this work, an anatomy of the natural and rhetorical gestures of the hand, in terms that have been repeated over the following centuries by writers interested in this part of the body: *Chirologia* offers "profitable hints to such ingenious spirits who desire to understand the mysterious properties of so admirable and important a piece of themselves."[1] Having hooked all virtuous, curious, and introspective readers, he describes his Baconian method. He will comprehensively survey the disciplines:

> I shall annex consultations with nature, affording a gloss of their causes. And for the further embellishing thereof, I shall enrich most points of expression with examples both of sacred and profane authority, more especially drawn from poets and historians. . . . I shall lay claim to all metaphors, proverbial translations or usurpations, and all kind of symbolical elegancies taken and borrowed from gestures of the body. (Bulwer, 6)

To this he adds an ethnographic view, including "the civil rights, and ceremonious customs and fashions of diverse nations in their national expressions by gesture, with the personal properties and genuine habits [of] particular men." And finally, he promises to reduce this varied material—"being but as so many several lines that meet in an angle, and touch at this point"—to its "fountain and common parent the body of men" (6).

Every century or so another book on hands pursues similar encyclopedic designs: attempting to collect every commonplace and idiom that refers to the hand, finding this part of the body a key to all Western mythologies and registering the real appeal of such exhilarating intellectual essentialism.[2] More frequently, the disparate subjects brought together in *Chirologia* have been pursued separately in books that meditate on the significance of the hand in the context of specific disciplines. To give a few recent examples: the medical study of the hand, begun by the early anatomists that Bulwer read, is now a distinct, surgical subdiscipline.[3] The analysis of manual gesture, taken up by later rhetoricians, remains lively in the works of modern sociolinguists. Bulwer's interest in physiognomy and the passions—the forerunners of psychology—adumbrates works as diverse as Charles Bell's essays on anatomy and Alphonse Bertillon's forensic phrenology.[4] Marc Le Bot's *La Main de dieu, la main du diable* returns to the aesthetic traditions that supplied much of the material for *Chirologia*; in "The Handle," George Simmel describes the mixture of practical and aesthetic categories that also preoccupies Bulwer.[5] Robert Hertz's seminal study of the social meanings of right- and left-handedness works out the anthropological method latent in Bulwer's interest in the "ceremonious customs and fashions" of nations.[6]

This study is neither kind of "hand" book, though it sometimes crosses into their territory. Instead, it plumbs a specific imaginative task that attracts writers of literature to the figure of the hand: the task of exploring and defining meaningful human action. When Western literature addresses questions of agency with critical or skeptical intent, it frequently turns to a peculiar trope: the figure of a severed or disembodied hand. From Jacobean stage props to nineteenth-century ghost stories, this figure sustains a long tradition in Senecan and Gothic fiction. Its roots in Anglo-American literature are as old as Grendel's claw, torn off by Beowulf and hung at the roofbeam of Heorot. Its popular influences are as current as Captain Hook's hook in *Peter Pan* and "Thing" in *The Addams Family*. Canonical examples include the infamous scene in Shakespeare's *Titus Andronicus*, in which Lavinia carries her father's severed hand offstage in her mouth; Cathy's ghostly hand, creeping in at the window at the beginning of *Wuthering Heights*; Adam Smith's "invisible hand" of a providential economy; the "Dead Hand" of Casaubon's will, which haunts the fifth book of *Middlemarch*; and the nightmare hand that lies gently across Ishmael's counterpane, early in *Moby Dick*. These disparate works all employ versions of the device I call (after Eliot) the "dead hand."

With its close focus on the body part most often associated with intentional, effective action, the trope of manual dismemberment brings to attention the fraught ties between spirit and body, between persons, and between persons and things that constitute agency relations. The familiar example of Grendel's arm illustrates the way this trope presents these different ties and unravels them. Grendel's trophy arm symbolizes the connection between heroic action and gift exchange that sustains Anglo-Saxon community in *Beowulf*. Communal security in the poem depends on excluding alien hands from the scenes of exchange that bind the Geats together: the gift-seat and hall where rings are exchanged and drinking cups pass from hand to hand. When Grendel plunders his way up to Hrothgar's throne, he nearly destroys the *comitatus* at Heorot, and his dismembered arm signifies the triumph of the Geats over that threat. Yet it also brings Grendel's mother back to avenge his death, in a manner that parodies earlier gift exchanges and reanimates the poem's "restless spirit" of feud. Like the other important gifts in the poem (rings, swords, Wealtheow's necklace), the arm signifies the gift ties that empower individual and communal action, while also encoding the inherent weaknesses and dangers of those ties.

At the heart of this trope is the perception of the hand as a separate piece of the body, linked to it by metonymy or synecdoche. Whereas philosophers since Aristotle have seen the hand as the special embodiment of the human ability to manufacture and control the material world, dismemberment relocates this part in that material, instrumental world. Dead hands come to resemble the accessories, tools, and marks they leave behind: as powerful an instrument, but as loosely held as those. Wandering or ghostly, they symbolize the loss, theft, or withering of an individual's capacity to act with real political or personal effect. And their tenuous, prosthetic affiliation to the body raises questions about whether the powers they embody are in fact proper to any person. Thus, when Beowulf breaks the bone-locks in Grendel's shoulder, he exposes the paradoxically fragile bonds that invigorate his own hands "with the strength of thirty men." The dissolution of those bonds with the passage of time is the topic of the rest of the poem, but it is predicted in the haunting symbol of that dislocated claw.

The range of anatomical terms used to describe Grendel's limb raises an important rhetorical and logical issue for this study. In Anglo-Saxon, Grendel's severed limb is termed variously *hond* ("hand"), *earm ond eaxle* ("arm and shoulder"), *Grendles grape* ("Grendel's grasp"), and *feondes fingras* ("the foe's fingers"). The narrator describes the monstrous hand vividly, emphasizing its steely, instrumental nature: at the end of each finger are nail beds "likest to steel" (*style gelicost*), with frightfully hard "hand-spurs" or claws (*handsporu*). Thus, in *Beowulf*, as in Renaissance anatomies, the term "hand" comprises both the five-fingered extremity at the end of an arm, and the whole limb from the shoulder down. I use the phrase "dead hand" in the spirit of this etymology. Fictional accounts of severed hands vary as to where they break bone-locks, inscribe a cut, or set a limit on the pursuit of causal and intentional sequences. Sometimes they mark separation very close to the body, sometimes at the farthest extreme—assimilating the hand to the traces it leaves, as in the case of handwriting and fingerprints. The central interest of this study is the different explanations of action served by the trope of dismemberment, wherever it is applied to this bodily instrument.

Anatomical Explanations of Agency

The use of the hand in explanations of human action has a long history in Anglo-American thought. The classical source of this topos is Aristotle's assertion in *De partibus animalium* that the hand is the "instrument of instruments." By the early modern period this definition was widely available in translations of Galen's *On the Usefulness of the Parts of the Body (De usu partium)*, which summarizes the double sense of Aristotle's phrase. First, Galen explains, the hand is the supreme example *of* all instruments and tools:

> [It is] of all instruments the most variously serviceable. For the hand is talon, hoof, and horn at will. So too it is spear and sword, and whatsoever other weapon or instrument you please; for all these can it be from its power of grasping and holding them all. In harmony with this varied office is the form which nature has contrived for it.[8]

And second, it is a tool that uses tools, "the instrument *for* all instruments" (my emphasis):

> Now, just as man's body is bare of weapons, so is his soul destitute of skills. Therefore, to compensate for the nakedness of his body, he received hands, and for his soul's lack of skill, reason, by means of which he arms his body in every way. . . . For though the hand is no one particular instrument, it is the instrument for all instruments because it is formed by Nature to receive them all, and similarly, although reason is no one of the arts in particular, it would be an art for the arts because it is naturally disposed to take them all unto itself. Hence man, the only one of all the animals having an art for arts in his soul, should logically have an instrument for instruments in his body. (Galen, 71)

From this double definition, several ideas follow, and we hear echoes of them every time the hand serves an exemplary role in Western philosophy. First, the hand demonstrates the difference between human and animal bodies and proves the superiority of the former. Its uniquely human qualities are what Heidegger evokes throughout his work, from his analysis of being and presence to his lectures on thinking.[9] Second, the hand is linked by analogy as well as physiology to the faculty of reason: it is the instrument of reason and its material counterpart. By extension, it comes to exemplify the rational order of the body, perfect in part and whole. As Galen tells us, this part is "in every respect so constituted that it would not have been better had it been made differently" (Galen, 72). In this way, the hand can serve as both a figurative and material starting place for epistemologies as diverse as the "Argument from Design" and Wittgenstein's *On Certainty*.[10]

Third, hands are distinguished by their capacity for willed, effective action. This is most evident in their ability to grasp:

> Since the work performed by the hand is grasping, and it would never be able to grasp anything if it were without motion (for then it would not be different at all from a dead hand or one made of stone), it is clear that the part of it most important for its action will be that which is found to be the cause of its motion. Since, indeed, I have shown, that all voluntary motions (those of the hand are of course voluntary) are performed by muscles, the muscles of the hand would be the most important instrument of its motion. (Galen, 81)

As the instrument of reason and volition, the muscular hand bridges the gap between spiritual and material motions. It was obvious to Aristotle, as it is to us now, that not all the motions of the hand are purposeful or intentional. But the voluntary nature of manual gesture remains a familiar commonplace in the philosophy of action. So much so, that even when a philosopher like John Passmore argues against reducing human behavior to the models provided by the body, he turns immediately to the example of hand signals.[11] Signaling, signing one's name, switching on a light—and the even more popular example of lifting an arm—are the favorite topoi of contemporary analytic philosophers, as they seek to refine the basic dichotomies of classical philosophy: between action and movement, doing and suffering, explanations of purpose and explanations of cause.[12]

Most importantly, Aristotle's seminal phrase, "instrument of instruments," defines the hand as both an object and a body part: it inhabits a liminal space between the object world (the world of tools and weapons it employs) and (as the physical metaphor for those instruments) the world of interiority, intentions, and inventions—of the self. Moving between these two worlds, it embodies a dynamic relation between intention and act, naturalizing the capacity for fundamental kinds of action in the human form. What is most striking about this relation is the necessary distance it maintains between volitions and the material actions they command. This is not simply a Cartesian distance that makes the hand the end of a sequence of mechanical links—but a difference located in and symbolized by the hand. Augustine's famous account of violent self-division in the *Confessions* gives an eloquent example of the way this difference functions in philosophical analyses of the will. He describes his struggle to submit to God in terms of physical prowess and disability, making a remarkable analogy between spiritual response and motor control:

> I was frantic, overcome by violent anger with myself for not accepting your will and entering into your covenant. . . . During this agony of indecision I performed many bodily actions, things which a man cannot always do, even if he wills to do them. If he has lost his limbs, or is bound hand and foot, or if his body is weakened by illness or under some other handicap, there are things which he cannot do. I tore my hair and hammered my forehead with my fists; I locked my fingers and hugged my knees; and I did all this because I made an act of will to do it. But I might have had the will to do it and yet not have done it, if my limbs had been unable to move in compliance with my will. I performed all these actions, in which the will and the power to act are not the same. Yet I did not do that one thing which I should have been far, far better pleased to do than all the rest and could have done so at once, as soon as I had the will to do it, because as soon as I had the will to do so, I should have willed it wholeheartedly. For in this case, the power to act was the same as the will. To will it was to do it. Yet I did not do it.[13]

The inability to will oneself to accept God's will marks the difference between acts of faith and other kinds of acts. Paradoxically, for Augustine, the successful performance of an act requires and is produced in the distance between the will to do that act and its material instrument:

> The mind commands the hand to move and is so readily obeyed that the order can scarcely be distinguished from its execution. Yet the mind is mind and the hand is part of the body. But when the mind

commands the mind to make an act of will, these two are one and the
same and yet the order is not obeyed.[14]

Augustine solves the paradox by conceiving a double will: "So there
are two wills in us, because neither by itself is the whole will, and
each possesses what the other lacks" (*Confessions*, 8.9).

The self-divisions figured in the trope of the dead hand derive
from this central feature of thinking about willful action. But
fictional dismemberments literalize the Augustinian double will—
typically in grotesque or absurd ways—so that the hand and the rest
of the body act at odds. "Hand" books like Bulwer's follow the
anatomists by celebrating the superiority of the hand over other
parts of the body. They vaunt this part of the body, which lends itself to more commonplaces, adages, and idioms than any other;
which serves in more social and political rituals; which yields more
artistic and civil enterprises; which communicates more forcefully
and widely across different cultures. Dead hand stories, by contrast,
test such confident claims by dismembering the metaphors they are
couched in: hands can pull out the tongue, strangle the head, and
cut off the privates if they offend. Worse, hands can also cut *themselves* off rebelliously, escaping the dominion of brain and soul,
effectively setting Augustine's double will at cross-purposes. In this
way, the grotesquery of Senecan and Gothic fiction, which often
appears gratuitous, offers a serious challenge to the central place of
volition and sufferance in accounts of the acting self. The urgent
moments in dead hand stories come when hands act spasmodically,
spontaneously, contrarily, or as if charmed.

The practice of literalizing figurative qualities of the hand reflects both the anatomical sources of this trope and its grotesque aesthetic. But its interesting effect is to make the conceptual grounding
of volition in the body particularly conspicuous. Dead hand stories
illuminate the reflex of physical essentialism. Indeed, it is in part the
conceptual turn to accounts of bodily experience, particularly
motor control, that organizes this trope as a field and makes it recognizably the same, from one historical moment to the next. Or
rather, it is the impulse to make this conceptual turn visible, and call
it into question, that the device serves consistently, in many differ-

ent periods. Elaine Scarry has described the function of this kind of essentialism in the classic literature of consent, which returns over and over to the central paradox that Augustine wrestles with: what does it mean to willfully submit to the will of another, and how is such a contradiction effected and lived? Across the discourses of medicine, political philosophy, and marriage law—which generate the familiar forms of this question for modern readers—Scarry anatomizes the way the body anchors consent: "The body is, first, the thing protected by consent; second, the lever across which rights are generated and political self-authorization is achieved; third, the agent and expression of consent and hence the site of the performative; and fourth and finally, a ratifying power."[15] Looking closely at the philosophy of volition in which theories of consent are elaborated, Scarry finds a second transformation within, and in response to, this essentializing reflex. "Once the volitional is located in the material, the material is now itself reconceived as artifactual; it is perceived as a made thing and described in the idiom of creation and invention" (Scarry, 85). Scarry calls this double impulse—first to ground volition in the body and then to reimagine the body as a made thing—the "two-part structure of perception" that shapes the essentialist thinking of many different discourses.

The trope of the dead hand dramatizes this double impulse at the heart of our interactions with the material world. That impulse is implicit in Aristotle's definition of a body part that is also an instrument. But the dead hand estranges the conventional intimacies between persons and things that shape human identity. And it exposes unacknowledged ones. Thus, for example, the familiar pointing hands from the margins of medieval manuscripts carry an overplus of directive intention, urging us to "mark this text, look here, take this to heart." But the purely instrumental, orthographic form of this direction generates no sense of dissonance or surprise. The reader reads these *maniculae* in terms of the conventional relationship between the writing hand and the written text: writing translates thoughts into material forms that have a life of their own that is not necessarily uncanny. But when wandering or ghostly hands like "Thing" strike a pose that recalls these manuscript hands, or write their own mischievous letters or forge signatures, they make these conventions strange. When severed hands enter the world of things in ways that evoke contexts other than writing—warfare, witchcraft, gift giving, service—the intimate dependence of self and artifact that they represent is even more pronounced.

On the scale of visceral responses to this interdependence, Scarry's writing ranks among the most confident. "If our artifacts do not act on us, there is no point in having made them. We make material artifacts in order to interiorize them: we make things so they will in turn remake us, revising the interior of embodied consciousness" (Scarry, 97).[16] With some exceptions, dead-hand stories express more suspicion and unease about the way the world of things might turn on the self to remake it. The body is reconceived as artifactual in this fiction in one of two ways, but both are profoundly self-alienating. Either it is maneuvered directly into the world of things—made into a stage prop, charmed like a witch's "Hand of Glory," or supplemented prosthetically like an amputee, or the experience of being in a body is itself radically reconceived: our sense of the body as a thing proper to the self, inhabited by the self, turns out to be as much a consequence of cultural fiction as physiological fact. This is the damaging experience of W. W. Jacobs's unwary factory worker, incorporated into his machinery, and Mark Twain's American slaves, inventoried in their owner's estate.

When the hand transforms itself from an instrument of human creation to a constructed thing, it raises questions about the final power of the body to ratify expressions of the self like consent. Indeed it is the ratifying gestures of the hand—bestowing authority, denoting sufferance, confirming agreement, conferring unique identity—that equivocate most troublingly in this tradition. Shakespeare's infamous spectacle of Titus's hand in Lavinia's mouth makes us uncomfortable for precisely this reason. Lavinia's exit evokes the contemporary iconography of just Empire, as if her injuries sanction the family's right to revenge itself and rule Rome. Yet she is on the way to death at her father's hand—and, as we are reminded vividly when the severed hand takes the place of her missing tongue—she cannot say whether she consents to be made such an instrument or to be used this way.

It is clear from this example that the two-part structure of perception dramatized by dead hands does political and social, as well as conceptual, work. The vehicle for this work is the distinctive motion or mobility of disembodied hands; as props they circulate the stage, as ghosts they circle the market or the house, as forensic evidence they travel from the study to the courtroom to the files. In all these instances, they evoke the venerable association of physical motions with political agency. The classical works of English political philosophy, from John of Salisbury's influential *Policraticus* (1159) to Thomas Hobbes's *Leviathan* (1651) conceive of political volition in terms of physical motion. Internal motions like digestion and external ones like defense are the central conceits of the allegory of the body politic and ground its operations in natural law. Voluntary motions in particular enact the central conditions of political identity. But these change as political theory and practice change: at different moments such conditions may be freedom, dependence, subjection to the monarch, market, or master, and so on.[17] Across different periods, the trope of the dead hand undermines the force of the body to generate political rights and authority in this way. And again, it is precisely the unexpected mobility of the hand that communicates this challenge. Thus, in the *Policraticus* for example, hands tender active but sometimes wayward service as the figurative deputies and officers of the body politic. It is this service that is put in question by the severed and charmed hands of Elizabethan and Jacobean drama. Similarly, the creeping hands of Gothic fiction, which alienate their own labor and return from the grave, satirize the notions of economic self-determination and social progress that dominate Anglo-American political thinking in the nineteenth century.

When the body serves as "the lever across which rights are generated and political *self*-authorization is achieved," that is because it is reconceived as property. This reconception is the heart of the political theory of possessive individualism that informs the "two-part perception" Scarry describes. And it is against the backdrop of the development of this theory in social and political life that the trope of the dead hand evolves. C. B. Macpherson describes the emergence in seventeenth-century English political philosophy of the idea of the individual as "essentially the proprietor of his own person or capacities." The influence of this idea on later economic and political thought is as broad as it is proverbial, but its early progress can be quickly summarized. Hobbes's definition of human beings as "self-moving and self-directing systems of matter," who must paradoxically submit to the compulsion of the market, gave way to Locke's famous definition of the individual as a proprietor of his own, partially alienable person.[18] "Though the earth and all inferior creatures be common to all men, yet every man has a property in his own person. This no body has any right to but himself. The labour of his body, and the work of his hands, we may say, are properly his."[19]

The examples of dead hands offered so far, which typify the central changes in the way the trope is used, bracket these recognitions—in both the skeptical and the historical senses of the word. The distance between intention and effects symbolized by the mobility of the instrumental hand raises persistent questions: Who owns the actions and effects of this hand? To what body is it proper? Their answers, as I have suggested, are usually contrarian. Dead hands articulate what might be called the dispossessive conditions of identity, in which the body, its alienable parts, and even its voluntary motions fail to ratify the rights, authority, or propriety of the self. The different implications of these questions at different historical moments divide this study into two parts. The first three chapters trace developments in the notions of personal action and volition—specifically the concept of a person as an agent or "doer"—that precede the works of Hobbes and Locke and are to some degree displaced by them. The last two mark the period after which the theory of individual freedom founded in possession was naturalized in institutional form. The changes that take place in the life of this trope—when it blossoms into a small narrative genre in the mid-nineteenth century, and later when it is adapted to racial, forensic, and bureaucratic fictions of identity in America—register the contradictions of a notion of individual freedom founded in possession. Again and again, with different inflections, dead hand stories pose the Augustinian problem of what it means to alienate some part of the self by submitting it—in faith, marriage, service, or sale—to another. And they ask at what cost this submission succeeds.

The Literary History of the Dead Hand

The kinds of questions articulated by the dead hand are shared by writers from the early modern to the modern period: When is a given intervention in the world meaningful? Who is properly the principal and who the accessory in a corporate action? What binds the one to the other? What does it feel like to find oneself the instrument of another's will? What are the conditions of moral responsibility for an action? But the ways these questions are set up change as new social forms and technologies challenge prevailing ideas about the nature and conditions of human action. As I have said, the distinctive feature of the ghostly, dismembered, and wandering hands in Anglo-American literature is to record such challenges and investigate them. The literary history of this trope takes its most dynamic turns during two periods of intense innovation in such relations: the late sixteenth and early seventeenth centuries in England and the nineteenth and early twentieth centuries in England and America.

At the end of the sixteenth century, early religious iconography of the hand came together with anatomical explanations of willful action to produce the complex visual and textual symbol of a dismembered, dissected hand. This intersection is the topic of Chapter 1. As an abstraction, the anatomical hand embodies the essential human capacity for creation and action defined by Aristotle. As the instrument and object of analysis, it is invested, surprisingly, with several agencies: those of the anatomist, the corpse, and the divine Creator working together to illuminate the design of the body—but also potentially in conflict. The paradox of multiple agencies competing in a single instrument in this way translated well to the contemporary stage, as Chapters 2 and 3 demonstrate. Senecan revenge tragedies like Shakespeare's *Titus Andronicus* brought such anatomical commonplaces to the stage to explore the developing notion of the "agent": a category of person who acts for another.

The word "agent" entered common English use in this period, according to the OED, identifying such secondaries as deputy, steward, factor, and dealer. It emerged as a general category for these disparate roles at the same time that the conditions, obligations, and rights of such roles in England were urgently questioned. Contemporary dictionary entries suggest that the authority of the agent is perceived as a vexed issue quite early in the seventeenth century. John Rider's *Bibliotecha Scholastica* (1589) defines the term simply in the phrase "an Agent or doer." And John Minsheu's magisterial dictionary of technical terms for commerce and government, *Ductoris in Linguas* (1617), expands a little with "An Agent, a Dealer or Factor." But John Bullokar's *English Expositor* (1616) and Henry Cockeram's *English Dictionarie* (1623) introduce the possibility of illicit contrivance that goes against the principal authority, with "a doer, or meddler in a matter." The analysis of such meddling took place across a variety of spheres in this period, reflecting what the historian Henry Sumner Maine described as a profound shift from a status to a contract society. The problem of how to contain and regulate the relation between principal and agent, of how to know whose will is performed in any given act, preoccupied legal, commercial, and political theory in the early and mid-seventeenth century.[20] But the intense conflicts raised by the changing role of the agent in this period are illustrated most vividly in the theater. The Machiavellian servants and intelligencers of plays like Webster's *The Duchess of Malfi* repeatedly engage in dubious contracts, symbolized and cemented in uneasy set-pieces of ritual handclasp. These stage handclasps disrupt the lines of moral responsibility and legal obligation they are meant to establish. And they register the mixed and often conflicting loyalties—to duty defined by status and duty determined by voluntary obligation—that mark the shifts of early contractualism.[21]

Testing the principles of rational self-interest and voluntary obligation, Jacobean servants and intelligencers also signal a progressive inward movement of the concept of the agent. They set the stage for the notion of agency-for-the-self that seventeenth-century possessive individualism required. But by establishing human ac-

tions as the natural property of the political self, the work of
Hobbes and Locke laid the conceptual groundwork for conflicts
between individual agency and institutional power that accompanied nineteenth-century industrialism. And modern versions of the
dead hand reflect the forms of corporate agency that emerged and
matured during this period: specifically, in England, the increasingly
felt presence of the economy coined by Adam Smith—the matter of
Chapter 4—and in America, the newly sprung architecture of a
centralized bureaucracy—the matter of Chapter 5.

During the nineteenth century, the figure of the dismembered
hand developed into a small but flourishing genre of narrative
fiction: ghost stories about creepy-crawly hands. Formal innovations in the genre—which produced the distinctive clutching and
reaching hands of Gothic fiction—took place before a backdrop of
intense urbanization and industrial change. Responding to these
changes, the Anglo-European tradition of "beast with five fingers"
stories explores the self-alienating experience of work below stairs
and in the factory. Just as Engels and Marx criticized the work of
the political economists by insisting on the material presence of the
labor behind the "invisible hand" of the market, so these stories literalize the popular synecdoches for labor and the ghostly forces that
possess it. They make the repressions of common euphemisms like
"factory hand" and "field hand" artfully and uncomfortably visible
and suggest in small the epic of alienation compacted in words like
"manufacture." In the process, they reconfigure the earlier dramatic
and anatomical traditions of the dead hand. Works as diverse as
Keats's "This Living Hand" (1919), Sheridan Le Fanu's "Ghost
Stories of the Tiled House" (1861), and W. W. Jacobs's "The
Monkey's Paw" (1902), all reverse the connotations of Aristotle's
grasping hand—turning that commonplace gesture of purpose into
an affront to any kind of autonomous human volition. In this way,
the genre adapts the earlier traditions of manual iconography to
suggest the tenuous hold of individuals on corporate institutions,
from utility companies to the market.

Threats to this tenuous grasp are expressed particularly sharply
in the idiom of *mortmain*: the testamentary clutch of the past on the

present, a concept drawn loosely from the legal term "dead hand" (from medieval Latin *manus mortua*). The ghostly and reaching hands of the Gothic continually pun on this idea of controlling inheritance: now temporally as well as physically dislocated from the will they discharge. The theme of mortmain brings home the challenges of labor Gothic, in this period, turning the paralyzing threat of institutional dispossession on the emergent middle class that seeks to control and distribute its wealth. For the legal term "mortmain" originates in some of the earliest English debates about corporate control of property. Its medieval uses denote the inalienable control of lands by ecclesiastical or other corporations, in their capacity as legal (as opposed to natural) persons. By the nineteenth century, the word refers to the general power of testamentary gifts to control the disposition of property (especially real estate) beyond the life of the testator. But a long history of English contests between the Roman Catholic Church and the Crown over mortmain statutes—and the fact that mortmain law by definition interrupted patrilineal descent of property, causing it to revert to a corporate owner like the church—contributed to the lasting pejorative associations of the term.[22] With its intimations of archaic and Roman Catholic oppression, the notion of mortmain is obviously suited to the furniture of English Gothic. But the quality of creepy perversion it carries is particularly intense in this bourgeois genre because of the institutional threat to individual propriety it implies.

When Mark Twain adapts Gothic conventions to describe the new science of fingerprinting in *Pudd'nhead Wilson* (1894), he suggests the contingency of personal identity, as well as agency, on such institutional dispossessions. Fingerprinting, for Twain, exerts a mortmain-like corporate grasp, one that depends on specifically American alienations of property and legal person. These "sign manuals" signify action that is both intentional and involuntary, and identity that is both essential and institutionally conferred. Celebrated by law-enforcement folklore and cited in early court precedent, Twain's novel illuminates the way the trope of the dead hand has been refracted through state fictions as well as literary ones. It was written during the early growth of American state administration, from the 1870s to the 1920s. (This was roughly the same period in which the modern, bureaucratic sense of the word "agency"—meaning an establishment for the purpose of doing business for another, usually at a distance—emerged.[23]) And the novel contributed to the centralization of one very powerful state agency, the Identification Division of the FBI. Ironically so, since Twain sketches unsettling points of connection between fingerprint detection and race slavery, reflecting with intense concern on the way institutional fictions about identity shape lived experience. Using material he first worked out for lecture in "The Golden Arm" (a ghost story adapted from folk traditions that go back to the story of Grendel), Twain explores the ratifying force of involuntary physical confession in administrative narratives of identity. He perceives such involuntary response to be the heart of forensic fingerprinting and finds it an ambivalent prospect. Fingerprints may be more accurate than other kinds of anthropometry, impervious to voluntary deceptions. But as a bureaucratic instrument, they also reproduce the dispossessive, uncanny effects of the slave economy.

The History of Agency

The concerns mapped out across these different chapters provide a comparatist historical frame to current theoretical debates about agency. The central issues in these debates can be traced in part to the way the word "agent" emerged into English and to the changes that took place in its use during the seventeenth century. To see this development, it is helpful to take a moment to explain the terminology in play. One of the central projects of recent analytic philosophy, as Richard Bernstein points out, has been to clarify the logical grammar and conceptual boundaries of the language of action (n. 237). My understanding of agency relations owes a great deal to this body of writing—in particular, to its precise, formal accounts of the role effectual, intentional action plays in our sense of ourselves as persons. But this sense of self, as early modern scholars have recently shown, is bound to specific historical notions of the agent.[24] And only by placing the language of action in its historical context, as I have begun to do here, can we see the evolution of some of its central dichotomies. Late sixteenth- and early seventeenth-century English usage, derived from medical and legal writing, followed the Latin roots of the word. The *agent* (one who or that which exerts power) is distinguished from the *patient* (that which is acted upon) and the *instrument* (the tool of action). It is useful to think of these terms as part of a set of agency relations that are dynamic. As early modern anatomists recognized, anything might suffer an action as a patient and turn about to perform another, as an agent—the most famous example of this dyad, perhaps, being the soul and senses. Likewise, these relations are layered and complex ones from the start. As A. R. Braunmuller tells us, early English common law defined several degrees of civil responsibility or criminal guilt, distinguishing principal and secondary agents with great care.[25]

The triad of *agent*, *patient*, and *instrument* remain a robust set of terms for discussing agency relations, with the addition of a fourth: what Kenneth Burke calls the *scene*—the background, situation, or context of an act.[26] Burke's own terminology of *act, scene, agent, agency*, and *purpose* might offer an equally handy vocabulary—indeed it makes distinctions similar to the early modern terms—but for his restriction of the word "agency" to mean the "means or instruments" used by an agent. He narrows the range of the word in an uncharacteristically awkward way, dropping its usefully abstract sense, the faculty of action or activity. But paradoxically, this awkward choice proves one of Burke's most important observations about the grammar of action and motive—one that governs my thinking about these terms in their different historical inflections. "What we want is *not terms that avoid ambiguity*, but *terms that clearly reveal the strategic spots at which ambiguities necessarily arise*" (Burke, xii–xiii). In current use, the terms "agent" and "agency" spot precisely such strategic ambiguities. As Perry Anderson and others have noted, the word "agent" ordinarily means opposite things: "at once active initiator and passive instrument."[27] The contradictory senses of passivity and activity, primacy and secondariness comprised by these terms make the idea of agency both fuzzy and capacious—

whether it is understood as a faculty that pertains to history, the economy, the unconscious, or the subject.[28]

Indeed, the way this ambiguity is handled distinguishes the two sides of a debate that has emerged as the defining paradigm in contemporary Marxist accounts of agency. Anderson usefully summarizes this debate, crystallized in E. P. Thompson's critique of Louis Althusser in *The Poverty of Theory*. Its central issue is the role of "conscious human choice, value, action in history," or more simply, whether the pervasive belief that we act sometimes with purpose and real effect is accurate. For Thompson, passionate in his defense of effectual human action, men and women remain the "ever-baffled and ever resurgent agents of an unmastered history"; for Althusser, absolute in his rejection of any form of volition in the shaping of social order, "history is *a process without a subject*."[29] E. P. Thompson's failing, Anderson finds, is his careless use of the ambiguities that define agency; while Althusser's failing is his radical reduction of them. Because Thompson amalgamates the two versions of agency, he reproduces the paradoxes of Marx and Engel's theory of historical action. Because Althusser restricts purposeful human action to a secondary effect of relentless structural necessity, he cannot offer "any materialist account of [the function of] physical sensations or practices" in the production of social order (P. Anderson, 57–58). Neither theorist, in Anderson's view, gets very far in tracing the "actual, variable roles of different types of deliberate venture, personal or collective, in history" (P. Anderson, 21).

The philological history of the word "agent" acts as a kind of conceptual entail on this debate, and it creates the strategic ambiguity Anderson describes. Action for another precedes action for the self chronologically and conceptually. The earliest definitions of the word "agent" recorded in the OED (from the 1570s to 1590s) describe persons or things equally as "the material cause or instrumentality whereby effects are produced," the "doer" rather than the instigator of an act. And they indicate a separate employer or contriver, as when Proteus reads Julia's love letter (in *The Two Gentlemen of Verona*)—"Here is her hand, the agent of her heart" (1.3.46).[30] Agents are first, in Hotspur's angry words, "base second means" for another's action (*Henry IV*, Part I, 1.3.165), and only later agents for themselves. But the concept of agency for another is always inscribed in later uses of the word. And this priority partly accounts for the repeated rediscovery of complex models of agency (layered, multiple, competing) over simple, unified, and individual ones in modern theories of action. By the middle of the seventeenth century, the word "agent" comes to denote an autonomous moral subject. But—as with Locke's definition of the individual as a proprietor of himself—this change internalizes rather than replaces the notion of agency for another. Thus, when Samuel Bolton declares in *The Arraignment of Errour* (1646), "Nor are we to be meer instruments moved by the will of those in authority . . . but are morall Agents" (295), he substitutes an internal moral law for an external, political one, in familiar nonconformist fashion. But autonomous moral agency is still perceived in terms of obedience to a separate authority that is not precisely coincident with the self. Later, when Robinson Crusoe admits, Augustine-like, that he "was still to be the willful Agent of all [his] own miseries" the paradox of such internal self-division is more explicit.[31]

Anderson's point that Althusser and Thompson equally neglect material *practices* suggests his interest in an ethical and political account of action, reflected in the echo of Aristotelian *praxis*: activity performed in the polis, the goal of which is to do it well. Throughout its history, the trope of the dead hand expresses a similar interest. But as in the writings of Perry Anderson (and Marx before him) or Elaine Scarry, the dead hands suggest that *praxis* cannot be separated from what Aristotle defines as *poesis*: making or producing things, such as writing a poem or preparing a meal.[32] As I have suggested, they draw attention to socially significant *activities* of the hand, as well as to their iconographic history. The practices of dissecting, clasping hands, exchanging gifts, taking fingerprints, and even simple domestic tasks become as symbolically important to this trope as the accessories the hand carries or the visual conventions it evokes. Together, these comprise the context or scene that frames relations between the principal and secondary in an action, and the doer and the one who suffers it.

Thinking of action in terms of such ongoing and repeated practices has two important consequences. First, it calls into question any analysis of agency restricted to discrete and intentional events, like the signal to turn right. Bernstein closes his survey of the three generations of contemporary analytic philosophy by pointing in a different direction, inviting precisely the kind of analysis of action dead hand stories typically offer: "We cannot even begin to make sense of what we mean by action unless we consider how specific instances of actions are embodied in the social practices and institutions that shape our lives."[33] Anthony Giddens makes a related point when he summarizes the most significant issues a rigorous social theory of agency should address: the unacknowledged conditions of action, its unexpected consequences, and its continuous and often repetitive nature. This is the contribution social theory can make to analytic philosophy, he suggests: by offering a theory of institutions, by taking into account the temporality of day-to-day conduct, and by addressing the way power shapes social practices.[34] The trope of the dead hand directs us to these wide and interesting margins of the discrete, intentional act. Thus, *Titus Andronicus* discovers the unacknowledged basis of Roman political authority in disability rather than prowess. *The Duchess of Malfi* dramatizes the unexpected consequences of agreements by contract, emphasizing the uncertain connection between intentions and outcomes. "Beast with five fingers" stories describe the oppressive mortmain of events extended over time—and they also meditate on the alienating effect repetitive daily activity has on attention and moral reflection. And Twain's writings illuminate the principles of involuntary confession that provide a foundation both for race slavery and forensic fingerprinting.

Second, by bringing together the social practices and institutions that frame specific actions or gestures, dead hands call attention to the ways we arrive at our sense of intention. Giddens points out that " 'intentions,' like 'reasons' only form discrete accounts in the context of queries, whether initiated by others, or as elements of a process of self-examination by the actor."[35] We feel purposeful or aimless, know our intentions or doubt them, when our attention is called to our performance. The central task of dead hand stories is to launch such queries, and in this respect they tend to engage contemporary legal and scientific discourses that also seek to define or calculate intentional states. Thus, for example, John Webster draws on early modern witchcraft law to explain the uncertain status of intentions in shifting service relations, while Twain draws on contemporary forensic and neurological theory to investigate the physical and social debilities that threaten to become a national condition.

There is a paradox in stories that require the moral interpretation of actions that are nonvolitional. How can we determine the claim, responsibility, or guilt an actor holds for actions that are coerced, determined by social institutions, unconscious, fated, mechanical, or a matter of luck? For, as Bernard Williams pithily phrases it, moral philosophy traditionally holds that "Anything which is the product of happy or unhappy contingency is no proper object of moral assessment, and no proper determinant of it, either."[36] Each work considered in this study addresses some version of this problem. Many are famous for the discomfiting, paradoxical positions in which they put their audience on this account. Indeed, the challenge to moral assessment is part of what keeps the trope of the dead hand disproportionately lively, even in its most abbreviated and popular forms. Dead hands reach out of the world of events and things that are deeply accidental, nonvoluntary, or external, and compel us to see that these have a claim on our compunctions.[37] The notion of agency they subscribe to and the problems they raise can be framed by another passage from Williams: "One's history as an agent is a web in which anything that is the product of the will is surrounded and held up and partly formed by things that are not" (B. Williams, 29). There are only two thoughtful responses to this, Williams goes on to say. Either we conclude "that responsible agency is a fairly superficial concept, which has a limited use in harmonizing what happens, or else that it is not a superficial concept, but that it cannot ultimately be purified." (29). We will continue to struggle with the implications of such impure action, and we should. To paraphrase the conclusion of this passage, if what we have done and what we are responsible for is important to us, many events make a claim on our belief that we are moral actors simply because they happen close to us and because they are real (30). The figure of the severed hand amuses, disturbs, or compels us because it points directly to those things that define this belief even while they remain out of our control.

Chapter One

Divine Complicity: "God's Handy Worke" and the Anatomist's Touch

So the soul is as the hand; for the hand is an instrument with respect to instruments, the intellect is a form with respect to forms,
and sense-perception a form with respect to things perceived.

—Aristotle, *De anima*

Reason, is the hand of the understanding, Speech the hand of
Reason, and the hand it selfe, is the hand of Speech. The hand ex-
ecuteth those things which are commanded, our commandments
are subiect and obedient to reason, and reason it selfe, is the
power, force and efficacie of the understanding.

—Helkiah Crooke, *Microcosmographia*

Early modern writers used the figure of the hand to indicate
the source and conditions of powerful action—corporate or individual, authorized or illicit. The instrumentality of the hand and its
capacity to grasp are the central imaginative vehicles of this figure.
Whether it is used incidentally or elaborately, the hand is defined as
a material sign by its functional properties: its ability to touch, grip,
and gesture. These are the shared formal underpinnings of a broad
range of manual rituals in this period: handclasps indicate consent in
the marriage ceremony of the Church of England, confirm feudal
obedience, signify formal reconciliation after conflict, or ratify a
compact or treaty; the raised right hand signifies political suffrage
and affirms obedience to civil or royal authority, as in the English
National Covenant of 1640. Similar motions animate visual images,
like the pointing hands from the margins of medieval codexes and

from fourteenth-century Italian painting; these organize each work, call attention to significant passages or images, and direct individual readers to a common narrative.[1]

The idiom of manual activity that represents different kinds of agency across such disparate spheres has its own internal logic and formal conventions. These can be charted by looking more carefully at a larger fiction that often frames the literary use of the hand: the allegory of the body politic. The early and influential example of the *Policraticus* condenses this logic particularly clearly. In its formal strategies, John of Salisbury's famous meditation on administrative performance and moral culpability epitomizes the role of the hand in early modern theories of natural obligation. It demonstrates the complicated explanatory power of bodily metaphor, particularly for representations of civil and personal action—and it illustrates the close association between the component trope of the hand and the impulse to examine the logic of bodily metaphor itself. In a famous passage of the *Policraticus*, John of Salisbury defines the natural allegiance of officers, magistrates, and ministers:

> And so the hand of the republic is either armed or unarmed. The armed hand is of course that which is occupied with marching and the blood-letting of warfare; the unarmed hand is that which expedites justice and attends to the warfare of legal right, distanced from arms. . . .
>
> And so the armed hand is exercised strictly against enemies, but the unarmed is extended also against the citizen. In addition, discipline is necessary for both because both are notoriously accustomed to being wicked. The use of the hand testifies to the qualities of the head itself because, as Wisdom asserts, the iniquitous king has entirely impious ministers. . . . For the continence of governors is laudable when they restrain their hands and hold back the hands of others from exactions and injuries.
>
> Still, the hand of both sorts of soldiers, namely, armed and unarmed, is the hand of the prince; and unless he constrains both, he is not very continent. And surely the unarmed hand is to be curbed more closely because while the armed hand is commanded to abstain from exactions and rapine, the unarmed hand is also prohibited presents.[2]

The metaphor of the body politic is often read as if it expressed Menenius's strategy of mob control, but although it can be used to justify political hierarchies by analogy to organic structures, John of Salisbury's allegory of the hand proposes a more complex set of problems. As in *Titus Andronicus* and other, later tragedies of dismemberment, the passage evaluates the explanatory power of this allegory by putting some strain on its component figures. Here the concrete possibilities of manual action (hands are grasping and aggressive) undo the organic metaphor just at the moment when the continuity of moral action appears most important to his argument. As John explains the moral import of his figure, its tenor and vehicle mix: the continent prince must use his actual hand to restrain his figurative hand—whose multiplying officers are prone to seizure and graft. The limbs that stand here for deputation and ministry thus emphasize the problematic nature of these substitutions and the moral complications they produce. Far from naturalizing the notion of a single, neatly described person of the state, they signify the mixed and sometimes dangerously contaminated agencies that warrant John's ongoing meditation and analysis.[3] In its emphasis on the mobility of hands and their ability to grasp (weapons or someone else's property) and its play on their simultaneously figurative and functional nature, the *Policraticus* encapsulates the principal strategies that characterize early modern uses of the hand as a figure for human action.

By the late sixteenth century, when political fictions make use of the hand in this way, they tend to emphasize the punning byplay on grasping princes and deceitful officers that runs through this passage of the *Policraticus*. In doing so, they draw not only on a loose and ubiquitous family of metaphors associated with the hand, but also on specific traditions concerned with the nature of action and performance.[4] The words "agent" and "agency" come into general English use during this period, adapted from their technical contexts in legal and medical writing.[5] Of these two, medical texts—particularly medical anatomies—offer the most sustained analysis of the conditions and mechanics of physical action in this period. They complicate our easy assumptions about the essentialist logic that sustains metaphors like the body politic and offer a remarkably complex and self-conscious account of bodily action, one that is both practical and theoretical.

In the context of medical anatomies, the commonplace of the able, grasping hand has a specific technical charge. For early modern anatomists, following Aristotle by way of Galen, the analysis of bodily action finds its most vivid vehicle in the dissection of the hand. Anatomists explore intention and action as bodily functions: tracing the mechanics of motion and grasp and describing the perceptual faculties of touch. In this way, they offer insight into the anatomical logic that informs concepts like self-evident guilt (in its earliest legal forms known as *hand-habbende* and "red-hand"), attestation, or intention. They seek to explain the mechanism that allows a physician like John Bulwer to assert that "What we put our hand unto we are infallibly understood to *will* and *intend*" (50). Early modern anatomies describe such functions in mechanical terms that seem familiar to us from the roughly contemporary discourse of Descartes, detailing the process by which internal spiritual motions impel bodily instruments and delineating the different roles in sensual action. And they offer a full and orderly vocabulary, defining the conditions of *principal* (moral or spirtual authority, motive force), *agent* (the actor or body manifesting that authority), *instrument* (the tool or means of action, not itself invested with authority), and *patient* (that which suffers an action).[6]

Yet, as an organic ground for legal and political metaphor, anatomical discussions of agency are, paradoxically, equally layered and complex. The boundaries between principal, agent, instrument, and patient in bodily action, as they are carefully recorded, often shift and collapse. Thus, for example, the word "agent" characterizes that part or organ that mechanically performs the commands of a motive spirit, and that part—especially in the case of the hand—in which that spirit is sometimes immanent. In keeping with these mixed definitions, anatomists writing as late as the seventeenth century return to medieval analogies of the body as microcosm, in ways that seem incompatible with their increasingly mechanical descriptions. This rhetorical strategy recuperates bodiliness as a locus of virtue in a way that is insistently antidualist. By linking analogical and functional analysis to mechanical description, medical anatomies conjure the body as a locus of self and agency, not merely the instrument of a noncorporeal essence.

In subtle ways, early modern anatomists continue the Aristotelian and Galenic tradition by modeling their theory of anatomy (as Galen recommended in his opening book of *De usu partium*) on the anatomy of the hand.[7] As both instrument and object of dissection—and thus of the epistemological illumination this brings—this part becomes the prominent vehicle for integrating sacred mystery with corporeal mechanism. From Galen to the seventeenth century, the dissection of the hand persists as one of the central moral topos of anatomy demonstrations: celebrated for its difficulty and beauty, it reveals God's intentions as no other part can. In this way, its mechanics are invested with the creative force most important to the form of the body, at once incorporating and illustrating God's agency and design. Most importantly, anatomies construe the *demonstratio* of divine intentions as both a symbolic and a functional property of the hand. To take in hand the rational work of dissection, they imply, is to do what the surgeon John Banister calls "God's handy worke": to reveal and perform God's will in the flesh.[8] This argument emerges in both text and image. Manual puns and allusions shape the textual exposition of the hand in medical anatomies and keep the actions of the dissecting hand in close focus. Anatomical illustration, drawing on traditional visual representations of God's hand, also returns repeatedly to the image of two clasping hands, suggesting the interlaced and mutual nature of divine and human agency embodied in this part.

The body revealed by sixteenth- and seventeenth-century anatomies can look very different from what I am beginning to describe here. Recent scholarship has emphasized the emergence of the anatomized interior as a separate space: chaotic, confused, and dark. The anatomist navigates this confusion, strategically eliding the violence of his practice and its complicity with forms of state control such as execution.[9] This account depends on a clear split between the body as a locus of passivity and the agencies (here cultural and political) that work on it from the outside. The body imagined in relation to its hand, however, takes on the qualities of rationality, manufacture, and action particular to the hand. In this way it appears less Foucauldian: more nimble and mobile than the horizontal poses of dissected corpses imply; more animate, finally, even when dismembered and anatomized. Indeed, it is precisely the clear split between body and the forces that move it that the dissection of the hand—with its emphasis on function and organic connection—struggles with and attempts to suspend. By drawing analogies between the internal structures that facilitate grasp (the flexor-muscles), the scene of instruments and demonstration immediately surrounding the hand of the anatomist (touching, cutting, and displaying), and the spiritual authority that inhabits both (God's hand), this dissection complicates any easy alignment of interiority and intention.

Thus, to take seriously the notion—common to much historical criticism today—that the interior of the body is not separable from the practices that make it visible, it is necessary to retain a sense of the discursive complexity of these practices. The rhetorical strategies associated with the dissection of the hand offer one of the most complex instances of such practices—and one that is self-consciously examined. Helkiah Crooke's *Microcosmographia, A Description of the Body of Man*, for example, demonstrates the profoundly varied responses the opened, dissected body can generate in this period. Anatomical investigation moves Crooke to delight, as his frequent use of adjectives like "exquisite" attests. Rational exposition of parts is modulated in a variety of ways: by long clauses that emphasize the contiguity of tissues; by celebratory digression; by reference to ancient and folk authority; by punning allusion to the mucky work of dissection that plays up rather than evades the anatomist's intimate contact with viscera. *Microcosmographia* looks back to medieval visions of the body and forward to Harveian mechanics and attempts a difficult but compelling synthesis of mechanical analysis and the mystical homologies of the body-as-microcosm.[10] In it, Crooke explores the nature of agency in the body within the same complex, mixed registers—concrete and figurative, corporeal and social—used in political and legal philosophy. How can the relations between parts and wholes be made stable? Where can the boundaries of person and the limits of action be identified? Its underlying physiological puzzle—how do incorporeal motions of the soul move corporeal organs and instruments?—intensifies the contradictions apparent in an attempt to integrate mechanical and analogical modes of analysis. These questions surface throughout Crooke's work, but especially in two related sections: his introduction to anatomy as a discipline and the anatomy of the muscles that move the fingers. Here, the text proposes a kind of corporeal metonymy; its focus on the physical contiguity of parts, the property of touch, and the manual activities of dissection anchors this mixed mode of analysis. Crooke's close attention to the habits and functions of the hand in these sections constitutes an early modern theory and practice of touch, which amply illustrates the mixed complicities exemplified by the hand in early modern literature, exploring in concrete terms an imaginative territory that—as in John of Salisbury's analysis—is both figurative and corporeal, both singular and corporate, partly in and partly of the world of objects. Offering a theory of a specific kind of manual practice, Crooke's anatomy illuminates a part defined by and constituted in material qualities that are habits, motions, and functions.

"A Diligent and Curious Section"

Dissections in the sixteenth and seventeenth century began with the parts that decompose soonest: the abdomen, torso, and head. In general, the limbs were dissected last.[11] In the case of the arm, the exposition proceeds from the shoulder to the fingers. In this sequence, what begins as a necessary response to bodily decay emerges as an implicit argument about the relatedness of parts. These trajectories reinforce one of the central narratives of anatomy: the contiguity of "joynte" and body, part and whole maintains continuity of action. Crooke raises two important historical exceptions to this order, both pertaining to the hand proper. He notes that for both Galen and Columbus the location of the hand in the anatomy reflects its preeminence as a part: Galen famously begins *De usu partium* with the hand, Crooke reminds us, because it is the ideal and exemplar of all the other parts. "Indeed," according to Galen, "if we train ourselves thoroughly by discussing this part, whose action is perfectly clear, we shall the more easily learn the method to be used in discussing other parts later on."[12] Columbus treats the hand last, Crooke tells us, for a related reason: "Because (saiyth he) the wonderfull and miraculous frame thereof might remaine infixed in our memories" (Crooke, 784). Crooke likes Columbus's intimation that the uniquely memorable quality of this dissection constitutes a kind of coherence in itself, reinforcing our sense of the body's perfection as a conceptual unity.[13] The coherence of impression and memory we get from the hand is reinforced by the condition of the tissues themselves during anatomy. Since the tissues of the hand "the longest endure uncorrupted," this dissection, coming last, mitigates the palpable disintegration of the body as a whole.[14]

Whether it is dissected early or late, the analogical character of the hand, following Aristotle's seminal definition, makes it a mediator between the ancient and sacred homologies of the body as microcosm and a rational inquiry into physical mechanics. Crooke follows the order of dissection in his own account of the parts, yet conceptually he follows Galen and Aristotle in emphasizing the ideational primacy of the hand. The hand incorporates an ideal correspondence between parts and wholes and guides us in understanding their mechanical interactions. The pattern of unity in division it offers is expressed in both its structure and function, as Crooke's meditation on the mechanics of grasp demonstrates:

> The true office of the Hand is to apprehend or to holde, and his proper action is apprehension (for *Hand* and *Hold* are Conjugates as we term them in Schooles). . . .
>
> The Figure is long and divided into many parts that it might comprehend in one all kinde of Figures, the round or Spherick, the right and the hollow, for all figures are made of three lines, a crooked, an hollow, and a straight. Beside, this figure doth equally apprehend both greater bodies and lesse; for small things it holdeth with the ends of two fingers, the great finger or the thumbe and the fore-finger. . . .
>
> Now, if the hand had been made of one continuall peece, it would onely have apprehended a body of one magnitude. Neither was it sufficient that the Hand should be divided into fingers, unlesse the same fingers had beene placed in a divers order and not in the same right line, so as one was to be set or opposed to the other foure, which being bowed with a small flection might meete and agree with the action of the other foure opposite unto it. (730)

This description resonates with allusions to the medieval microcosm of the body, whose perfection can square the circle. For Crooke, the

divided parts and united action of the hand typify the Baconian
ideal of anatomy as an epistemological endeavor: "a diligent and curious Section, undertaken to get knowledge or skill by" (26).
Anatomy consists of a fruitful correspondence between cutting,
"the action which is done with the Hand," and the rational "habite
of the mind, that is, the most perfect action of the Intellect" (26).

> The first is called Practicall Anatomie, the latter Theoricall or
> Contemplative: the first is gained by experience, the second by rea-
> son and discourse: The first we attaine onely by Section and
> Inspection, the second by the living voice of a Teacher, or by their
> learned writings: The first we call Historical Anatomy, the second
> Scientificall: the first is altogether necessarie for the practise of
> anatomy, the second is onely profitable; but yet this profite is often-
> times more beneficiall then the use it self of Anatomy: the first
> looketh into the structure of the partes, the second into the causes of
> the structure, and the actions and uses there-from proceeding. (26)

As he continues his carefully balanced oppositions, Crooke takes
pains to distinguish practical anatomy, "Artificiall section," from the
accidental investigations of warfare. The first is an orderly history—
or telling, as in the French *histoire*—that preserves the integrity of
parts as wholes. The second is a Spenserian meander, "rash and at
adventure," that obscures the delicate distinctions of the first and
threatens violence:

> For often-times in great wounds we observe the Figure, Situation,
> Magnitude, and Structure of the outward and inward Parts; but that
> observation is but confused, for we cannot distinctly perceive the
> branchings of the Nerves, the Serpentine and writhen Meanders of
> the Veines, nor the infinite divarications of the Arteries. Now that a
> Dissection may be made artificially, it is first requisite that the parts be
> so separated one from another, that they may all be preserved whole,
> not rent and torne asunder. Next, that those which grow not to-
> gether, be gently divided. Thirdly, that those which do grow together,
> be carefully separated. Fourthly, that we mistake not many parts
> joyned together for one, nor yet make many parts of one. (26)

In either its order or confusion, the interior of the body can only be
understood in relation to the style of investigation. Crooke's phrase,

"the action which is done with the hande," is thus not a casual one. It hearkens back to the classical source of anatomical descriptions of the hand: "So the soul is as the hand; for the hand is an instrument with respect to instruments, the intellect is a form with respect to forms."[15] Aristotle's enduring analogies provide anatomy with a marvelous, recursive logic. The hand that actually cuts and orders embodies the rational design it produces: unity in division. Supporting this conceit is the central aesthetic of *Microcosmographia*: a vision of unity and divine providence extrapolated from the marvelous design of the hand. As William Schupbach has shown in his seminal analysis of Rembrandt's *Anatomy of Dr. Nicholas Tulp*, the renowned beauty of the anatomy of the hand developed its own visual and textual tradition. Schupbach summarizes its two central themes. First, the flexor-muscles of the hand, which specifically control apprehension, link divine intentions and the work of civilization. In his chapter "Of the Excellency of the Hands," Crooke extols: "By the help of the hand Lawes are written, Temples built for the service of our Maker, ships, houses, instruments, and all kind of weapons are formed. I list not to stand upon the nice skill of painting, drawing, carving and such like right noble Artes." (729). Second, the celebrated beauty and sophistication of this anatomy proves the Argument from Design as no other evidence could.[16] In his 1578 *Historie of Man*, John Banister expands it this way: "Thus if we wel perpend the construction, and composition of the partes, and bones of the hand, our senses shall soone conceive the maner of the action, with no lesse admiration, in beholdyng the handy worke of the incomprehensible Creator" (Banister, fol. 31r).

In emphasizing "the action which is done with the hande," Crooke's definition of practical anatomy adds a specific historical charge to the Argument from Design. In the sixteenth century, when Vesalius began to practice anatomy demonstrations, barbers or surgeons generally wielded the knife, while the higher-ranking physicians lectured from the text. Vesalius condemns the "very capricious division of an art into separate specialties" in his preface to the *Fabrica*. He speaks acidly and at length of the decay in contemporary medical fashions, "miserably distorted," by the avoidance of "treatment made by the hands" and manual "investigation of nature":[17]

> We see learned physicians abstain from the use of the hands as from a plague lest the rabbins of medicine decry them before the ignorant mass as barbers and they acquire less wealth and honor than those scarcely half-physicians. . . . Indeed, it is especially this detestable, vulgar opinion that prevents us, even in our age, from taking up the art of treatment as a whole, limiting us to the treatment of only internal diseases, to the great harm of mankind, and—if I may speak frankly— we strive to be physicians only in part. (O'Malley, 319)

Genuine and accurate revelation, he insists, can be gained only through dedicated application of the hand. That "pleasure in the employment of his hands" and zealous use "handed down to posterity" by Galen makes both physician and his practice whole (318).

Delicately suggesting this complex of themes, Crooke defines anatomy as a "diligent" and "careful" discipline. He displaces its potential for violence onto an opportunistic, rending and tearing anatomy of wounds. Treating the interior mechanism of the body through dissection obviously requires touching it, placing the hands inside it, lifting successive layers of tissue to reveal their points of origin and arrival. In other contexts, this activity would produce the pain and physical outrage behind words like "rent and torne asunder." Given these charged associations, it would seem remarkable that Crooke should keep "the action which is done with the hande" in the foreground of his text. Yet he does, in an ongoing series of puns that play on the commonplace of "handlygne" and "touching" a topic. Typically, these passing puns introduce and close the separate chapters of *Microcosmographia*. Sometimes they are gleefully integrated into the exposition. Without the sense of touch, Crooke warns us at one point, physicians "must of necessity grope uncertainly in darke and palpable ignorance" (648).

In certain respects, "handlynge" puns draw on the same sources that inform the graphic hands that appear in anatomy portraits, as in the portrait of Vesalius facing the first page of the *Fabrica* (Figure 1). Both invoke a visual tradition of didactic hands to maintain their decorum—even while the pointing fingers of the physician appear

FIGURE 1. Portrait of Vesalius. Appended to the front of the *Fabrica* (Basel, 1543). Courtesy of Yale University, Harvey Cushing/John Hay Whitney Medical Library.

entwined in entrails or sinews. Read thus, "handlynge" puns continually remind readers and listeners of the indexical, "textual" nature of the hands that dissect. They confirm that the anatomist performs a *demonstratio* when he handles the body. To an audience in a dissection theater, the puns might accordingly evoke a moral context, supporting Crooke's assertion that the hand that sections and inspects is a teacherly hand, like a *manicula*, a hand of "learned writing." To the readers of an anatomy text, the puns evoke the vivid scene of dissection in a way that complicates this moral decorum. From either vantage, the puns test the organic wholeness of hand and body, and the sense of control didactic gestures imply, against the more questionable activities hands can be imagined doing. If Crooke gropes "uncertainly in darke and palpable ignorance" should it make our guts tighten a little? Wouldn't decorum be more successfully controlled by restraining such play?

To ask this is to raise the corollary question of intention: whose is expressed in these puns, and to what end? These questions direct us to the polemic and narrative aims of *Microcosmographia*. The history of Crooke's relation to the Royal College of Physicians of London is well traveled but worth summarizing again for the complex relation between professional status and anatomical labor it reveals.[18] Discomfort is one of the responses that Crooke knows he is getting from one part of his audience, the Fellows of the Royal College; violating certain kinds of professional decorum is a central part of his project. *Microcosmographia* appeared in English, with a preface addressed to the company of Barber Surgeons: at the time, barbers and surgeons were still the general practitioners of dissection in England and few spoke or read Latin. Thus, when Crooke puns in English part of the point—and annoyance—may be that the surgeons will grasp his wit. The College strenuously objected to Crooke's translation, attempting to delay and emend it. They contended that the general circulation of an English language anatomy was unethical (it would lead to the unscrupulous practice of physic) and improper. During the period when the first three editions of *Microcosmographia* were published, Crooke attempted unsuccessfully to be admitted a Fellow of the Royal College. In response, as O'Malley observes, he belittles their objections in his prefaces. He implies that their sense of decorum is intellectually obstructive, points out that all of his material had been covered already in public dissection, and stresses its medical necessity. Surgeons must understand anatomical theory; physicians should be versed in anatomical practice.

In this context, it's not surprising that Crooke's first-person pronouns reveal an odd betwixt-and-betweenness of address. He uses "we" in his preface to associate himself both with the adept surgeons he formally addresses and the physicians who are his hoped-for professional peers, his source of authority and his antagonists. In addition, Crooke struggles to define professional boundaries that justify the circulation of medical knowledge while confirming his own ethical, authoritative status. Surgeons and physicians should share manual skills but remain separate in practice, he says: physicians in particular should know how to dissect, but choose not to. Thus, his puns negotiate the charged and mixed allegiances suggested by the definition of anatomy as a "gentle" manual discipline. At the same time they redirect accusations of impropriety by attributing them to weak-minded distaste. With Vesalian acerbity he describes a physician whose hands are not practiced in anatomy—the physician whose touch (not the anatomist's) discomfits by groping in palpable ignorance. If the prospect of such groping discomfits anyone, it is presumably the same physicians— too squeamish to perform dissections—who are left uneasy.

These puns also work at a second, very different register of literary effect, one that suspends the question of intention in order symbolically to integrate the anatomist's gestures with the formal structures they reveal. The puns idealize and internalize the action of the anatomist's hand in the body itself: the body is permeable, Crooke implies repeatedly, in its ideal state and optimum functions. Thus the groping pun that plays on the sense of touch is part of a larger theory of that sense:

> But we in the meane time admiring this majestie & certaintie of the Senses, will make entrance into so faire and pleasant a Field of Discourse, and handle everie one of them in particular, beginning with the Sense of Touching, which as it is more common than the rest, so without doubt deserves the first place: For this is the ground of all the rest . . . hence it was that Aristotle (and with him all other Philosophers) . . . [call it] *The Sense*; as if they should have said, the onely Sense of all Senses." (647)

"O healthfull and saving Touch! O searching Sense!" he continues, suggesting a moral structure for anatomical inquiry that builds on the physician's healing touch: healthful, saving, searching (649). "But we holde our handes," he finishes, "both Time and the Matter requires that we prosecute the remaining Senses in as few words as we can" (649). Touch is the "innermost" sense, yet its organ—skin—is "neerer to the occursation or confluence of outward objects; because it is the limit and border as it were of all the parts" (86). Its mediating and delimiting role makes the sense of touch "exquisite" and helps make the audience comfortable with the movement of the anatomist's hand in and out of the corpse.

While touch is the common sense, distributed throughout the body, the hand is its rational and controlling agent: a "Judge and discerner of the Touch" (730) that directs and analyzes it: "For albeit this touching vertue or tactive quality be diffused through the whole body both within and without, as being the foundation of the *Animall Being*, which may be called *Animality*, yet we doe more curiously and exquisitely feele and discerne both the first and second qualities which strike the Sense in the Hand then in other parts" (730). The rational and dignified connotations of "Judge and discerner of the Touch" combined in this phrase help sustain the notion of a "gentle" and "careful" handling of innermost parts. Yet the term "discerner" implicitly insists on the primacy of such handling as the means of judgment. To *discern of*, in its legal contexts, is synonymous with judging: to have cognizance of and to interpret judiciously; the verb *to discern* also held the sense it retains now, to perceive distinctions and differences. In the sixteenth and seventeenth centuries, however, it also maintained a transitive sense: to separate as distinct, to distinguish and divide. Thus, in the epithet "Judge and discerner of the Touch" the perceptual and ethical attributes of touch—the discrimination of moral, logical, and spiritual differences between things—are identified with the manual practices of anatomy.

Most importantly, then, "handlynge" puns alert us that the motion of the anatomist's hand itself is a symbolically necessary part of anatomical exposition, as well as a practical requirement. In mechanical terms, the motion of the hand—and thus its seamless expression of intention and volition—is a function of its contiguity to the body. In this respect, the anatomist's hand performs what the sectioned parts display. The dependency of motion on contiguity thus becomes a central theme of the dissection of the arm, as a closer look shows us: first in the textual exposition and then the illustration of this anatomy.

The practice of "diligent" and "curious" dissection maintains a careful distinction between parts while preserving their right connections. Even more, it defines relations and traces continuities *through* rational separation. By way of introducing the parts of the hand proper, Crooke reminds us that anatomically, the word "hand" denotes the whole limb from shoulder to fingertip:

> There are therefore two kinds of Joynts, the upper and the lower; the upper joynts are called by the common name of the *Hand,* for the Ancients accounted the whole member from the shoulder to the fingers ends to be all the *Hand. . . .* The whole Hand *Hippocrates* and *Galen* doe devide into three parts in *Brachium, Cubitum* and *Summam* or *extremam manum,* that is, the Arme, the Cubit and the Hand as we use to call it. (728)

Similarly, the illustrations that accompany this section show the whole arm, shoulder muscles fanned out to the clavicle and blade. The exposition of the working parts of the hand emphasizes contiguity and continuity as well. Crooke describes the progress of the flexor-muscles across the ulna (Ell) and radius (Wand) as follows:

> The first Bender ariseth with a round beginning and large, mixed of a fleshy and Nervous substance, from the internall proturberation of the arme under the heads of the Palme-muscle and those two which bend the Wrist, Afterward becomming broader, it passeth thorough the middle and anterior parts of the Ell and the Wand, and becommeth fleshy and round, yet before it attaine unto the roote of the Wriste, his Venter or Belly is angustated or straightned, and divided into foure fleshy parts, all which doe determine into tendons exquisitely nervous and transparant: and being together involved in one common, thin and mucous membrane; for their more safe progression doe passe along under the annular or round Ligament which is seated overthwart the wrist; & at the second bone of the forefingers nere the middest of the Joynt are divided with a long Section or slit through which the tendons of the next muscle to bee described

(which lyeth under them) which were to reach unto the third Joynt,
are transmitted. There they become broader that they might moove
more easily and apprehend or take holde the better, and a little after
the division or section they are inserted into the second bones of the
foure Fingers. (787)

The long prepositional clauses of this passage seem to emulate the
path of the muscles across the two bones of the forearm. Its layered
and extended syntax maintains the sense of continuous connection
from upper insertion to lower, from muscle to tendon, from single
tissue to four-part division.

In Galen's *De usu partium*, it is important to recall, the hand
serves as the ideal and type of part-whole relationships. When this
dissection arrives at its celebrated goal, the finger-insertions of the
flexor-muscles, its harmony of action facilitated by division moves
the anatomist to wonder: "And truly this progresse and insertion of
these muscles is an admirable and strange worke of Nature: for they
are so severed, that the fingers in their motion might orderly follow
one another, and each of them alone bend inward" (Crooke, 787).
Crooke's illustrations, likewise, emphasize continuity in division:
they tend to expose or detach the lower rather than the upper in-
sertions of these muscles, as if to imply the continued integrity of
the body above the dissection.

Later illustrations, with their greater interest in morphology,
still maintain this emphasis. A 1685 engraving for Govaert Bidloo's
Anatomia humani corporis shows the striking tension and balance between the teleology of this dissection and its interest in contiguity
of tissues (Figure 2). Here, the muscles above the flexor-tendons are
detached and pulled back at the fingers in order to show their complicated stratification and interpenetration. Still, the dissected tissues
are pulled tautly against the heavy arm in a way that emphasizes
how well anchored they remain. The one detached muscle, the top
of the *flexor digitorum superficialis* (labeled "A" in the engraving),
even points stiffly back up to the shoulder, almost blending into the
shadow of the upper arm. It points against the pull of gravity as if it
still maintained its upper attachment. Like its earlier, textual versions, the Bidloo engraving illustrates the dependency of motion

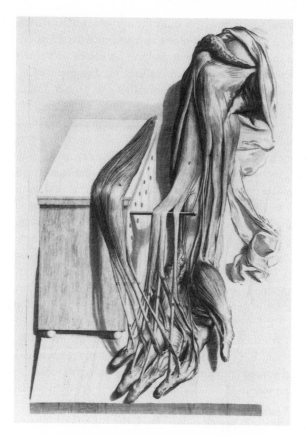

FIGURE 2. Engraving of the flexor-muscles and tendons of the forearm. Govaert Bidloo, *Anatomia humani corporis* (Amsterdam, 1685), table 67. Courtesy of Yale University, Harvey Cushing/ John Hay Whitney Medical Library.

and attachment. In these ways, both the rhetorical and visual vectors of this dissection emphasize the contiguity of tissues, reminding us to look backward to a whole body, even as its tissues are gradually sectioned and exposed.

The continuities symbolized by the muscles that grasp remain implicit and sustaining characteristics of the hand in early modern

political and social rituals, as now. From rhetorical treatises to political theory, the hand symbolizes an apparently seamless continuity
between the instrumental part and the person or power that it acts
for. Anatomical form seems to confirm this, by explicating the organs of volition: "Seeing therefore that the proper action of the
Hand is Apprehension, and Apprehension a Motion depending
upon our will, it was also necessary that the hand should have muscles which are the instruments of voluntary motion whereby it
might bee mooved altogether and every finger apart" (Crooke, 785).

Yet, to show the physical connections that sustain this logic,
they must be severed—a practical necessity that would seem to disrupt the mechanical certainties that make "Apprehension a Motion
depending upon our will." The visual strategies medical anatomies
deploy to manage this paradox work self-reflexively, like their cor-
rollary "handlynge" puns, to pair the motions of a dissecting hand
with the hand dissected. As William Schupbach has shown, the
flexor-muscle dissection develops into a coherent motif, used emblematically in early seventeenth-century title pages and anatomy
portraits. Although the muscles displayed are those of a dead and
severed part, they remain symbolically inseparable from the process
of dissection. The action of the anatomist's hand dissecting the forearm is absorbed into the emblem and the Aristotelian system of
ideas it represents. Thus, for example, an engraving in Heironymus
Fabricus Aquapendente's *De visione voci auditu* (Venice, 1600) includes Anatomia herself pulling back the superficial flexor-muscles
of a dissected arm.[19] As in the Vesalius portrait, emblems of the
flexor-muscle dissection make the hand agent, instrument, and patient of the *demonstratio*. In this way, cut tissue and cutting hand become a symbolic unit, signifying effective, voluntary action and the
unity of parts.

Ownerless Arms

Anatomy illustrations draw on contemporary visual art in a
number of additional ways that emphasize the actions of the hand.
Muscle-men and skeletons hold out the specific props of dissection

(knives to flay, ropes to suspend) or present the generic ones familiar from emblem books (hourglasses, apples, spades, mirrors, and skulls). These pictures offer the double aesthetic that has become a commonplace of critical commentary. Like saints pointing at props that symbolize their martyrdom, these figures carry their symbolic attributes—*vanitas* and *memento mori* motifs—while they helpfully display the anatomy under examination. Elsewhere, full-figure illustrations gesture toward their anatomized parts or an explanatory table, using the body concretely to illustrate the dissection and as a pointer. Increasingly in the seventeenth century, such figures handle themselves: écorchés brandish flayed skins and sharp knives, anatomized torsos pull back their abdominal skin, as in the infamous detail from Valverde's *Historia de la composicion del cuerpo humano* (Figure 3). Remarkably, these figures rarely make cautionary or protective gestures. Far from warding off investigation, the hands in anatomy illustrations seem to invite and offer it. Unlike the powerful grips of the emblem tradition, their fingers often appear slightly spread, the palm open to view, the arm slanting down—as one might welcome a guest into a house (Figure 3). In later anatomical drawings this open-handed pose is ubiquitous, whether the hand is drawn alone or as part of a body, and it is worth noting that this is not an effect of death. Immediate rigor mortis contracts the fingers more tightly, and the relaxation that follows does not flex them flat again. In his portrait, Vesalius holds the corpse's hand and arm in this classical anatomical position, signaling his formal intervention. Yet contemporary theory of gesture gives this pose a specific valence that shifts its emphasis. In his compendious study, *Chirologia, or the Natural Language of the Hand*, John Bulwer interprets this kind of open-handed posture as the habit and sign of liberality: "To put forth the right hand spread is the habit of bounty, liberality and a free heart; thus we reward and friendly bestow our gifts. Hence, 'to open the hand' in the Hebrew phrase implies to be free-hearted, munificent, and liberal. For the Hebrews when they would express a profuse munificence, they say *jad pethucha*, that is, [an open hand]" (55–56).[20] Illustrations of the dissected arm show similar postures: palms open, fingers spread, as though freely

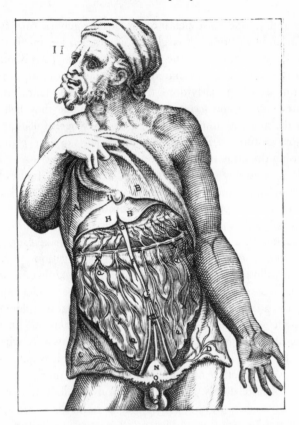

FIGURE 3. Detail from abdominal illustration. Valverde, *Historia de la composicion del cuerpo humano* (Rome, 1556), table 1, book 3. Courtesy of Yale University, Harvey Cushing/John Hay Whitney Medical Library.

offering. These arms tend to emphasize the mortal weight of gravity, slanting down as if partly relaxed, yet some, as in Figure 2, surprise us with their invitational force.

These mixed modes of representation, naturalistic and emblematic, have drawn much critical commentary, especially attentive to the apparent complicity of the corpse in the process of dissection.

As Jonathan Sawday has argued, the helpful postures of anatomy illustrations seem to internalize the didactic and surgical work of the anatomist's hand in the body dissected. Their liberal gestures suggest a body inviting its own dissection and actively engaged in the *demonstratio*: signaling the multiple agencies and shifting authority of the dissection theater.[21] At a formal level, as Glenn Harcourt has shown, illustrations of dissection adopt *demonstratio* as a general aesthetic.[22] Their mixed mode addresses a contemporary problem of representation: the difficulty of painting intention. As Leonardo Da Vinci famously framed it, "The good painter has to paint two principal things, that is to say, man and the intention of his mind. The first is easy and the second difficult, because the latter has to be represented through gestures and movements of the limbs."[23] The engraving of the flexor-muscles for Bidloo's anatomy (Figure 2) undertakes just such a complex representation: although its didactic interests initially seem very far from aesthetic problems, it is striking precisely for the intentional force of its implied invitation. To the extent that it seems to gesture, such an illustration displays the faculty of agency (understood as the animation of the muscles by the motions of the soul) as an essential feature of the hand, a structural quality like shape and position of the muscles. As Luke Wilson has put it, describing Harvey's dissection of the eye, the process of dissection "restores [the] soul as an intentional structure," implicitly connecting "anatomical procedure and the notion of the body as agent."[24]

For Wilson, this observation leads to deeper recognition of the transactions between anatomist and cadaver, each both agent and patient, produced by mutual agency; the intimate, supportive gesture and entwined fingers of the Vesalius portrait suggest this clearly (Wilson, 68–69, 88). Crooke describes this kind of gesture explicitly as a mutual compact, reprising the symbolic tradition of the handclasp as a sign of reconciliation and truce: "*Numa Pompilius* consecrated the Hands to *Faith*, & therefore all Compacts, Covenants, Truces and enter-courses whatsoever are held inviolably ratified by the very touch of the Hand" (Crooke, 730). However, anatomies summon a third agent to this covenant, maintaining that

the "action which is done" by the anatomist's hand is Godly hand-
craft. Read in this light, Crooke's insistent return to microcosmic
analogies emerges as part of a larger rhetorical strategy. Like his
"handlynge" puns and like his theory of touch, these supply a moral
framework for dissection that inheres both in the structure of the
body and in anatomical procedure. In a defining instance,
Microcosmographia opens with an analogy frequently found in
anatomy texts: the story of Noah's Ark, which implicitly compares
the practice of dissection with Noah's carpentry. The story of the
Ark eases the strains of professional decorum that emerge in
Crooke's preface, by uniting a covenant with the elect and a divine
directive to manual labor. Furthermore, the story associates arti-
sanry, measure, and manufacture with dissection through the etymology of the bones of the arm: brachium, cubit, and ell (the
ulna).[25]

> Now the . . . due proportion, composition, or correspondencie of the
> parts of mans body, with respect each to other, and of them all to the
> whole, is admirable. This alone (for a patterne) doe all work-men and
> Arts-masters set before them: to this, as to *Polycletus* rule, doe the
> Surveighers, Master Carpenters and Masons, referre all their plotts
> and projects; they builde Temples, Houses, Engines, Shipping, Forts,
> yea and the Arke of *Noah* (as it is recorded), was three hundred cu-
> bites, the bredth fifty, in heighth thirtie. (6)

The traditional measurement of the Ark in human proportions goes
back to Augustine and Origen, to be reprised in early modern treatises on architecture and painting: the trope is a kind of architectural
commonplace of the mystical unities expressed by the proportions
of the human body.[26] Names of the bones and units of measure are
mutually derived from the practice of linear measurement (as the
contemporary etymology for cubit and ell has it). Thus for anatomy,
as for architectural practice, the Noah story implies that ideal qualities of the instrument inhere in procedure and performance as well
as form. Anatomical handiwork, like Noah's, emerges as a creative,
constructive, and restorative labor: an undertaking in service to and
imitation of God.

     If the anatomist's hand does God's work, the hand he dissects is also, by extension, God's. Medical illustrations of the hand draw on several other conventions from the emblem and *imprese* tradition in ways that suggest God's hand as a pattern for anatomical exposition. Illustrations of the arm, as for example, from Berengario's *Commentaria* (1521), often draw on an old motif in religious art. God's hand emerges from the clouds, sometimes surrounded by a nimbus, often swathed in cloth. The clouds or classical sweep of fabric that circle the shoulder where the limb ends mark the point past which God's actions must not and cannot be traced. The evidence of God's work on earth (denoted by the reaching hand) is visible, but God's person and intentions remain inscrutable. Discussing this tradition in the context of emblem books, Bernard Scholz points out that secular and religious readings of such "ownerless arms" sometimes work together, often to suggest human action in accordance with God's will.[27] Contemporary representations of the physician's hand do just this; typically they integrate the actions of God's hand and the human hand in the same inscription. A glance at the Grant of Arms of the Royal College of Physicians, for example, reminds us of the mixed nature of the physician's hand (Figure 4). At first reading, the upper hand looks like the hand of God: it emerges from a cloudy nimbus at the top of the shield and grasps a wrist that stretches from the side—the middle space of human activity. Because it wears an aristocratic ruff and takes a pulse, however, it is also clearly a physician's hand. The commonplace of the regal and divine healing touch inscribes God's faculties in this human hand. In the context of dissection, however, the challenge to anatomists is to assimilate a touch that looks like wounding—the surgeon's touch—into the physician's divine ministry.

In order to do this, illustrations of the dissected hand must refigure the incision itself, and metonymically, the practice of "section," as a process that makes as well as signifies contiguity of action. In his compelling analysis of emblem aesthetics, Scholz is very clear about how the boundary of an apparently severed arm should be interpreted. The apparent dismemberment of "ownerless arms" must remain semantically invisible if the arms are to be read as icons of powerful agency. In this way, the circling clouds and classical swags

FIGURE 4. Armorial Bearings granted by Christopher Barker, Garter King of Arms, to the Royal College of Physicians (1546). Reproduced by kind permission of the Royal College of Physicians of London. The Grant of Arms describes them as "Sables, a border with demy fflouredeluces golde, in the chefe an arme charnois oute of a clowde argent and azure, with the Rase of the son golde, with a cuffe ermin, the hand ffelenge the powllse of an arm in fesse charnois, in point a powme grannatt golde."

that serve as "theologically motivated metonym[ies]" in religious emblems function in secular ones "to prevent the semantic interpretation 'cut off' in conjunction with the inscriptions of the other constituent characters . . . which cannot have been too far-fetched in an age of man-to-man combat" (Scholz, 258–59, 264).[28] When spiritual inscription converts to secular, he argues, the metonymy is retained as a sign of powerful agency in and of itself. By extension, then, an ownerless arm in a secular context cannot be read as force-ful, if it is read as dismembered. However, the conventions of med-ical anatomy in this period do not bear this out. For the anatomist, as Crooke's definition makes clear, the difference between dissec-tion and combat is certainly an important and delicate one. Yet in-stead of directing our attention away from the boundary between cut and uncut tissue, representations of the dissected arm rework it. In doing so, they seem less concerned with the implicit violence of anatomy than with expanding the possibilities of this visual metonymy—in particular, its spiritual and epistemological inscrip-tions—and with making dismemberment symbolically as well as vi-sually legible.

Illustrations of the dissected arm borrow their encircling fabric borders from the earlier visual tradition, reworking them either as cloths and bandages (as in Figure 2) or incorporating them into the body itself. In Vesalius's portrait, for example (Figure 1), the skin of the corpse's upper arm curves smoothly around it like a sleeve. Unlike their emblem cousins, these border motifs imply scrutibility, rather than inscrutability. They insist that the boundary of the anat-omized limb—either skin or cloth—can be read as a metonymy for coherent connections, epistemological as well as physical. When anatomy illustrations naturalize the cloth boundary, for example, making it part of the corpse, they translate a perceptual and episte-mological limit into a mechanical coupling that can be described fully. Anatomists learn to trace the action of Creation and demon-strate its marvelous ingenuity; the dissection of the human hand makes visible the trace of God's molding hand in a kind of *imitatio Dei*. As Crooke reminds us: "Because the Hand was the most noble and perfect organ or instrument of the body: God the Creator moulded it up of divers particles, all which for our better under-standing we will referre unto 4 kinds" (Crooke, 731). A subtle and beautiful revision of the cloth border motif makes this point differently in the engraving of the forearm dissection for Govaert Bidloo (Figure 2). Here a loosened bandage trails the arm, visually balancing the stretched flexor-muscles. The cloth that would oth-

erwise wrap and border the shoulder curls along the forearm, as if
to propose that what used to be an imaginative constraint on the
demonstratio of God's omnipotence is now gracefully loosened,
part of the field of scrutiny. Its symmetrical path beside the flexor-
muscles suggests that this dissection of the hand somehow surpasses
that profound limit of perception and knowledge.

To trace continuous connections across distinct parts is to
know the local actions of the hand that manifest the motions of the
soul. As the Galenic panegyric to the hand insists, it is also to know
the perfection of the body as a manifestation of God's creation. In
the dissection of the hand, the mechanics of apprehension stand in
for what we could neither apprehend nor experience: divine creation in process. The hand of the anatomist, emulating God's hand
as it composes the flexor-muscles for display, supplies this missing
link. As it looses the metonymic constraints to knowledge, however,
the anatomist's hand aligns itself only uneasily with God's. The multiple agencies represented in the recursive scene of hand dissecting
hand register a subtle discordance: the potential competition implicit in any *imitatio*.

The paradoxical condition of the hand in this dissection—as
object, instrument, and metonymy for moral authority—offers an
anatomical conundrum to which later fictions return. Writers in
the late sixteenth and early seventeenth century, in particular, draw
on the charged metonymies of touch and grasp represented in medical anatomies to explain the roles of principal, agent, instrument,
and patient. However, they do so more for the fraught relations embodied in the hand than for the technical vocabulary that promises
to order these relations. In this respect, the dissection of the hand is
typical of the way manual dismemberment develops in the period
as a visual and textual trope. The *demonstratio* of this dissection establishes four central patterns for the severed or disembodied hands
in later fiction: first, the complex conversion of dismemberment
into a sign of powerful, authoritative action; second, an emphasis on
the performative as well as symbolic properties of the hand; third, a
mixed mode of argument, both mechanical and analogical. Finally,
the incipient competition among the multiple agencies articulated

in this dissection lends itself to other, more sinister conflicts of agency and moral authority.

To understand the progress of this trope is to see the many graphic dismemberments on the late Elizabethan and early Jacobean stage, in particular, as something other than audience-grabbing shockers. Or rather, it is to read the significance of sensational performance differently, as one component of a sustained examination of agency relations. Shakespeare's *Titus Andronicus*, a play notorious for its collection of bloody parts, should be read in this way: as a profoundly disturbing analysis of the conditions of political action defined by military, marital, and filial convention. The graphic display of severed hands on Shakespeare's stage illuminates the connections between contemporary anatomical theory and legal discussions of criminal guilt and civil liability in this period. The play explores the mechanical capacities and limitations of an acting body, drawing on a different set of visual conventions for manual dismemberment: the martial and marital hands of emblem and *imprese* books. These images share a common strategy with the anatomical tradition, however: they foreground the visual breaks between the body parts they display, yet make those breaks conventional metonymies for political and moral authority. Using them, Shakespeare anatomizes contemporary social fictions that depend on this conventional translation of dismemberment into the sign of powerful action. The dramatic analysis of this translation and the aesthetic and interpretive challenges it presents to modern audiences are the subject of the next chapter.

Chapter Two

"Effectless Use": Dismembering and Forgetting in Titus Andronicus

> Ah, wherefore dost thou urge the name of hands
> To bid Aeneas tell the tale twice o'er
> How Troy was burnt and he made miserable?
> O, handle not the theme, to talk of hands,
> Lest we remember still that we have none.
>
> —*Titus Andronicus*

How should the dismembered body parts of Shakespeare's *Titus Andronicus* be understood? As part of the world of stage properties or of character? Read as grotesque and abstract, aesthetically engaging and distancing, dramatically pivotal and superfluous, the severed hands, heads, and tongue have always had a profoundly equivocal status in the critical and theatrical reception of the play. A flurry of intense theatrical and scholarly interest in the drama has marked the two decades since Albert Tricomi's essay "The Aesthetics of Mutilation in *Titus Andronicus*" established a coherent aesthetic in the discomfort produced by its scenes of dismemberment. More recently, the explosive violence of the play has called for psychoanalytic readings.[1] In this light, dismemberment becomes legible as a conventional figure of castration. Yet to read the play's severed parts as exclusively phallic risks missing their specific range of reference as hands, tongue, and heads. It is not that castration is bowdlerized or displaced from its proper place on the stage of *Titus Andronicus*; on the contrary, human sacrifice, rape, mutilation, and cannibalism are among its stock events. Yet, while psychoanalysis provides an important translation of the figure of dismemberment into the language of individual psychology, the centrality of the hand calls for careful reading as an instance of dismemberment particular in itself: connected to the complex visual imagery of the Renaissance body politic. The action of the play unfolds through a series of emblematic tableaux of clasped hands, or "hands in hands," which figure the affiliative relations between persons and between individuals and the sovereign state. These tableaux profoundly disrupt modern expectations about the necessary connection between interior subjectivity and powerful personal effect in the world.

These tableaux frame the problem of dismembered parts within the discursive and iconographic traditions invoked by the martial, marital, and genealogical plots of the play. How should the return of Titus's hand to the stage—as a property passed from one player to another—be understood? What is lost when Lavinia and her father lose their hands? The lopped, wandering hands of *Titus Andronicus* function within a Renaissance tradition of manual semiotics that draws on the early anatomies discussed in the previous chapter. That tradition is elaborated and modified in sixteenth-century emblem books, heraldry, and genealogical charts, and in contemporary marriage ritual. Read in these diverse contexts, the severed hands of *Titus Andronicus* display the sufficiencies and insufficiencies of the metaphor of the political body as a means of constituting political community. The play offers two possibilities for political action defined by two kinds of hands: one "effectless," the other "victorious." The lopped hands of Lavinia and Titus, converted into props, emerge as icons of these alternatives.

When Shakespeare's semiotics of manual action are read in this iconographic context, the trope of manual dismemberment reveals a kind of false physiological synecdoche: the hand appears to be an essential, continuous part of the body, but as a sign of agency it exists only in contingent relation to it. The contingencies of this relation seem profoundly odd, often grotesque, and they generate some of the uncomfortable paradoxes modern audiences find in this play.

Moral authority emerges as a radically portable commodity, shifting from one violent actor to another, and a subject's capacity for effective action seems to have no necessary connection to interiority. To illuminate the conceptual differences that make these constructions of agency feel so peculiar, it is useful to begin by comparing them to the model of agency canonized in Thomas Hobbes's *Leviathan*. We inherit from Hobbes's work a tradition of "person" that sees the capacity to act as an essential faculty of the body. Yet, the tropes of dismemberment dramatized in *Titus Andronicus* are at odds with this notion of "acting person." They imply that the capacity for effective action inheres not in persons, but in the objects and instruments of an action. This kind of effectual instrumentality is particularly clear in the case of Lavinia's dismemberment but also particularly counter intuitive for modern audiences. Lavinia's dramatic loss of expressive autonomy contradicts some of the central qualities we have come to associate, since Freud, with powerful personal agency. By comparing the kind of instrumentality Lavinia dramatizes with the psychoanalytic model that seems closest to it (Freud's theory of the fetish), we can see the wider range of symbolic reference—beyond trauma—evoked by manual dismemberment on the Renaissance stage.

Parts *"Taken Severally"*

Theories of agency always depend on assumptions about the essential faculties of the body: its continuity, wholeness, and motion. In the early modern period, these concepts were central both to the imaginative constitution of political community (as in the *Policraticus*) and of persons. Hobbes's famous definition of "natural" and "artificial" persons encapsulates what we have come to accept as intuitive connection between physical experience and the political conditions it ratifies. Hobbes begins by making a distinction between "actor" and "author" that uses political and social relationships to explain the instrumentality of the agent:

> A *person*, is the same that an *actor* is, both on the stage and in common conversation; and to *personate*, is to *act*, or *represent* himself, or another;

and he that acteth another, is said to bear his person or act in his name; . . . and is called in divers occasions, diversely; as a *representer*, or *representative*, a *lieutenant*, a *vicar*, an *attorney*, a *deputy*, a *procurator*, an *actor*, and the like. . . . . Of persons artificial, some have their words and actions owned by those whom they represent. And then the person is the *actor*, and he that owneth his words and actions, is the AUTHOR: in which case the actor acteth by authority.[2]

The differentiation of actor and author on the basis of ownership becomes the heart of the modern tradition of possessive individualism, a notion of person grounded in self-ownership. But the familiarity of this passage obscures certain assumptions about power and physiology explicit in Hobbes's distinction between the acting agent and the author. Earlier in *Leviathan*, Hobbes introduces an argument about civil authority and consent by means of a definition of power:

> The power *of a man*, to take it universally, is his present means, to obtain some future apparent good; and is either *original* or *instrumental*.
>
> *Natural power*, is the eminence of the faculties of body, or mind: as extraordinary strength, form, prudence, arts, eloquence, liberality, nobility. *Instrumental* are those powers, which acquired by these, or by fortune, are means and instruments to acquire more: as riches, reputation, friends, and the secret working of God, which men call good luck.
>
> The greatest of human powers, is that which is compounded of the powers of most men, united by consent, in one person, natural or civil, that has the use of all their powers depending on his will; such as is the power of a commonwealth: or depending on the wills of each particular; such as is the power of a faction or of divers factions leagued. Therefore to have servants, is power; to have friends, is power; for they are strengths united. (Hobbes, 72)

Emphasizing the difference between instrumental and natural forms of action, Hobbes lays out a notion of agency grounded in physical facts: the "faculties of body or mind." He understands agency as an uncomplicated relation between intention and action that works in slightly more complicated terms when distributed among actors, but which assumes the capacity for action to inhere in the fact of embodiment.

This is a reflex naturalized in later political theory, but an example closer to the period of Shakespeare's play suggests it is central to early modern writings on action across a variety of discourses. Earlier legal discussions of agency—concerned with the relations between principal and accessory, master and servant, lord and steward—often resort to bodily metaphor to explain guilt or liability.[3] Edmund Plowden's attempt to untangle principal and agent in criminal cases is a good example. In one particularly difficult scenario, several malevolent persons are present at a murder but only one strikes a blow:

> And notwithstanding there is but one Wound given by one only, yet it shall be adjudged in Law the Wound of every one, that is, it shall be looked upon as given by him who gave it, by himself, and given by the rest by him as their Minister and Instrument. And it is as much the Deed of the others, as if they had all jointly holden with their Hands the Club or other Instrument with which the Wound was given, and as if they had all together struck the Person that was killed.[4]

Plowden's fiction of an instrument "jointly holden," like Hobbes's vision of "strengths united," covers up a seam between "natural" and "instrumental" characteristics of persons that *Titus Andronicus* dramatically rips apart. Making dismemberment central to an examination of just action and political dynasty, the play deconstructs this familiar bodily metaphor.

Plowden's conventional use of the hand in legal metaphor depends on the anatomical commonplaces discussed in the previous chapter, which established the hand as the exemplar of physical agency. Looking back at Galen's influential analysis, however, it's clear that the hand makes a good model for the body as a whole because it internalizes the several actions of parts that work individually. Trying to explain the instrumentality of all body parts and using this "most important part" as his archetype, Galen quotes Hippocrates's description of cooperative action in the hand:

> Thus [describing the ideal hand] Hippocrates says, "A good shape for the fingers, a wide space between, and the thumb opposite the forefinger," and if you ask again why this is so, the answer he has writ-

ten is at hand: "Taken as a whole, all the parts in sympathy, but taken
severally, the parts in each part cooperate for its work." (Galen, 79)

Accordingly, Galen goes on to argue, as the fingers are to the hand,
so the hands are to the other parts of the body. What motivates
Galen to quote Hippocrates—and what he goes on to worry over
throughout the work—is *how* the cooperation of separate parts is
achieved. Indeed, what is the true order of the body? Which parts
should be considered properly separate, subordinate instruments,
and which should be "taken as a whole"? The commonplace
metaphors for action that hands supply Galen—like the anatomical
order they model—internalize these persistent concerns about par-
tition, multiple instruments, and multiple sources of motion. The
ostensive force of the image of the hand, however, is such that it
implies an authorizing, intending principal even when separate or
severed.

When writers call attention to this ostensive, naturalizing function, it tends to turn back on itself—emphasizing craft, rather than
nature, as its governing principle. For example, the persistent ten-
dency to pun on hand imagery calls attention to the multiple registers in which hands can be interpreted. Thus, for Galen, hands are
demonstrative figures as well as models and objects of analysis:
hence what looks like a pun about Hippocrates's answer being "at
hand." This kind of humorous self-awareness is not typical of
Galen's generally serious tone; it is, however, almost conventional in
descriptions and definitions of the hand.[5] As with John of Salisbury's
political puns, it emphasizes the internal conflicts and self-divisions
figured in the hand. The contemporary case of John Stubbs is
particularly telling in this respect. In 1579 Stubbs published *The
Discovery of a Gaping Gulf Wherinto England Is Like to Be Swallowed
by Another French Marriage if the Lord Forbid Not the Banns by Letting
Her Majesty See the Sin and Punishment Thereof*. A few months later—
along with William Page, his publisher—he lost his hand for what
Queen Elizabeth judged to be the seditious publication of this treatise against the Alençon marriage. The event is most famous for the
eyewitness account that Camden recorded: "Stubbs, having his
right hand cut off, put off his hat with his left and said with a loud

voice, 'God save the Queen,' " before apparently fainting.[6] More to the point, however, is the gruesome pun that slipped into Stubbs's final comments on the scaffold: "The hand ready on the block to be stricken off, he said often to the people, 'Pray for me, now my calamity is at hand.' And so, with three blows, it was smitten off" (Berry, xxxvi). In Camden's description of the scene, idiomatic and nominative uses of the word "hand" overlap in an odd way (was Stubbs's calamity smitten off along with his hand?). Overshadowed by the brutal event, this colloquial grammar makes a perfectly conventional, pious request seem like a shocking breach of decorum— in much the same way, in fact, that Titus's and Marcus's astonishing puns on Lavinia's missing limbs have struck so many critics and playgoers.[7] Like those speeches, the Stubbs anecdote emphasizes in the strongest way how the early modern display of hands always seems to obtrude its self-referential and figurative qualities, disrupting the fundamental assumptions about continuity of person and action hands traditionally represent. They do this even—perhaps especially—when least appropriate.

Victorious and Effectless Use

For Galen, considering the relation between volition and action in functional terms, the physiological identity between the two faculties is a truism embodied by the hand: the motions of the hand "are of course voluntary."[8] For Shakespeare, in contrast, the figurative and physical connections between intention and act embodied in the hand are material for dramatic play: to be stretched and exposed rather than assumed. A familiar example of this kind of play is the ghostly dagger that seems to offer its handle to Macbeth's hand at the moment he decides to act on his ambitions. The dagger promises to give material form to his immaterial fantasy: "Is this a dagger which I see before me, / The handle toward my hand? Come, let me clutch thee, / I have thee not, and yet I see thee still" (2.1.33–35). From the moment Macbeth clutches at it, fails to grasp it, and draws his own dagger in its place, the weapon seems to signify an identity between his intention to murder and the bloody

act. Yet whose intentions his hand performs with this instrument—
whether his own, Lady Macbeth's, or the Witches'—remains the
subject of vexed analysis throughout the play.

The attenuated link between handle and hand alluded to in
Macbeth is the object of intense interest in *Titus Andronicus*. Not, as
in *Macbeth*, as a vehicle for exploring the psychological consequences of acting on phantasmal ambitions, but instead a means of
testing the metaphors that connect actions with intentions. Titus's
dead hand and Lavinia's lost ones—along with the various tools that
take their places—play the metonymic connection between hand
and tool in both directions. Whereas Macbeth's dagger becomes a
kind of extension—a fantastic or literal substitute for his hand—
hands in this earlier play become severed objects, assimilated into
the world of manual tools. To have a hand in *Titus Andronicus* is to
possess the sign and instrument of agency only tenuously and temporarily. If for Galen a "dead hand or one made of stone" represents
the antithesis of agency (of effective action, of grasp), for Shakespeare it represents something more complex. In its vulnerability to
loss and theft, its mobility on the stage, the severed hand in Shakespeare's play paradoxically exemplifies the supplemental and contingent nature of purposeful action.

Consider a series of allusions invoked in the opening scene of
the play: the image of Titus's martial hand, the emblem tradition it
alludes to, and the symbolic gestures of handclasp it encodes. The
first scene is one of internal political contest, framed by contest with
an external enemy. Titus enters from the war with the Goths, his
sword unsheathed, to be offered election in place of the contend-
ing imperial heirs, Bassianus and Saturninus. His daughter Lavinia
greets him with words that suggestively combine the imagery of
political consensus and martial prowess: "O, bless me here with thy
victorious hand, / Whose fortunes Rome's best citizens applaud"
(1.1.163–64).[9] As the play unfolds, this "victorious hand" becomes
the touchstone of the uncertain Andronici right to the state and of
their ability to act for and as its principal. The hand that symbolizes
Titus's martial prowess and the Roman hands that "applaud" his
election seem a neatly paired set of manual metonymies. They are

recalled when the citizens elect Lucius emperor at the close of the play instead of letting him "hand in hand all headlong hurl" himself with Marcus into "a mutual closure of our house" (5.3.131–34). From the moment the first scene opens, however, the symbolic and functional power invested in these victorious hands is put in question. To begin with, Titus immediately gives up the martial prowess that seemed their essential virtue.

Refusing the candidacy that the citizens applaud and metaphorically refusing to restore the dismembered body politic by setting "a head on headless Rome," Titus asks to exchange the symbols of office for those of retirement: "Give me a staff of honor for mine age, / But not a sceptre to control the world" (1.1.198–200). The swords, staff, and scepter of this scene are part of a technical iconography of kingly instruments often associated with the medieval doctrine of the body politic. (These are the same props that Richard II, for example, famously releases as he divests his Royal person: "Now mark me how I will undo myself. / I give this heavy weight from off my head, / And this unwieldy sceptre from my hand" [*Richard II*, 4.1.193–95].) Titus declines to take up the scepter of Empire on the grounds of natural propriety: having been the sword-arm of the state, later described as the "true hand that fought Rome's quarrel out" (5.3.102), he argues that he cannot properly embody the principal "member." As the "Agent," "Instrument," and "Member" of the "glorious body" of sovereign Rome (1.1.187), he sees himself as the proverbial "Soldier Arm" familiar from Menenius's famous parable of the Belly.[10] As with Galen, the instrumentality of the tool and the instrumentality of the hand that holds it coincide in this allusion to the body politic.

The sword and scepter that Titus wields in imagination here also invoke a related iconographic tradition: the convention of severed, sword-bearing arms depicted in emblem and heraldic *imprese* books. Especially popular in the sixteenth century, these collections are like visual dictionaries: codifying a set of conventions and tropes as they are borrowed, reprinted, glossed, and translated from one collection to another. Like dictionaries, emblem books standardize iconographic conventions, but also record the accumulation and

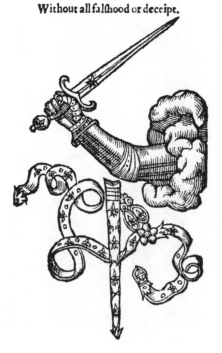

FIGURE 5. "Without all falshood or deceit." Claude Paradin, *Devises Heroïques* (1557), 111. By permission of the Folger Shakespeare Library.

variation of meaning within a single motif, over time. The complex display of martial and severed hands in this play draws directly on the rich visual vocabulary of this genre. A typical example of the heraldic trope of the severed arm can be seen in a traditional military device in Paradin's *Devises Heroïques* (see Figure 5); this collection was translated into English in 1591 but widely circulated in Europe well before that date.[11] Heraldic severed arms, which hold

DEVISES.
Non sine causa.
Not without cauſe.

FIGURE 6. "Non sine causa." Paradin, *Devises Heroïques*, 27. By
permission of the Folger Shakespeare Library.

a variety of symbolic objects, are explicit icons of power. Like
Galen's hand, they are distinguished primarily by their capacity to
grasp.[12] Emerging from puffy clouds at the side or upper corner of
the scene, they draw on the medieval convention of God's provi-
dent hand. Yet unlike both of these sources, they foreground the
trope of dismemberment explicitly, emphasizing the figurative nature of the image. A striking device from Paradin illustrates this
characteristic emphasis. *Non sine causa*, an emblem for just rule, de-
picts a hand holding a sword-like scepter, which is topped with the

To Kings, *both* Sword *and* Mace *pertaine ;*
And, *thefe they doe not beare in* vaine.

FIGURE 7. "Non sine causa." George Wither, *Collection of Emblemes, Ancient and Moderne: Quickened with Metricall Illustrations, both Moral and Divine* (1635), 137. By permission of the Folger Shakespeare Library.

figure of a hand holding a sword. (See Figure 6, and also Wither's later elaboration of the same emblem, Figure 7.) The recursive character of this image emphasizes the always severed and symbolic nature of the connection between the hand and the weapon it grasps. The small sword-in-hand that tops the scepter seems to reverse the metonymic link that makes the sword a kind of material extension of the hand-as-weapon: it makes the hand, itself disembodied, a kind of objectified extension of the tool. Furthermore, this inversion makes the emblem's claim to illustrate "just cause" ambiguous; it seems to pun on the word "cause" itself and to raise questions about the not-so-simple figure of causality that the sword-scepter represents. Where, along the sequence of a hand brandishing a scepter topped by a hand holding a sword should a reader locate the origin of an action? Recognizably figures of political power, emblems of the martial hand thus depend on a conventional dismemberment that complicates the attribution of authority and cause.

Titus's "victorious hand" is a version of these complex and ambiguous martial hands. Throughout his opening exchanges with his brother Marcus and with Saturninus, Titus imagines himself in a heroic relation of fealty to the emperor and state of Rome—a relation symbolized by the "victorious hand" that fought in their service and "warded [his Majesty] from a thousand dangers." His language, and that of both Bassianus and Saturninus, is marked by the rhetoric of gift exchange that traditionally composes martial community.[13] Having chosen Saturninus as emperor, Titus consecrates his spoils of war in tribute to their mutual duties as vassal and lord:

> And here in the sight of Rome to Saturnine,
> King and commander of our commonweal,
> The wide world's emperor, do I consecrate
> My sword, my chariot, and my prisoners—
> Presents well worthy Rome's imperious lord.
> Receive them, then, the tribute that I owe,
> Mine honour's ensigns humbled at thy feet.
> (1.1.246–52)

Once elected, Saturninus appears graciously to requite this service and thanks Titus in similar terms of exchange and mutual duty:

> Thanks, noble Titus, father of my life.
> How proud I am of thee and of thy gifts
> Rome shall record, and when I do forget
> The least of these unspeakable deserts,
> Romans, forget your fealty to me.
> (1.1.253–57)

Saturninus's fulsome and insincere speech intimates his enmity fairly clearly, however. With this preview, it is not surprising to find a few lines later that the politics of fealty are fundamentally ineffective in Rome. All along Saturninus has read his exchange with Titus in terms of the antonyms of gift giving and tribute: theft and begging. When Titus first offers to choose between the brothers, Saturninus threatens him: "Andronicus, would thou were shipped to hell / Rather than rob me of the people's hearts!" (1.1.206–7). Later, after Bassianus's abduction of Lavinia (whom the new emperor had chosen to marry), Saturninus scorns Titus: "Full well, Andronicus, / Agree these deeds with that proud brag of thine / That saidst I begged the empire at thy hands" (1.1.302–4).

Ironically, and most significantly, the only effective service Titus's hand can offer as the play unfolds is to excise the sign of *effect*—or capability—from his body:

> Give me a sword, I'll chop off my hands too,
> For they have fought for Rome, and all in vain;
> And they have nursed this woe in feeding life;
> In bootless prayer have they been held up,
> And they have served me to effectless use.
> Now all the service I require of them
> Is that the one will help to cut the other.
> 'Tis well, Lavinia, that thou hast no hands,
> For hands to do Rome service is but vain.
> (3.1.72–80)

In accordance with the dramatic logic of revenge tragedy, Aaron enters on cue to supply Titus the opportunity he looks for and to help cut off his hand. If Titus sends Saturninus his hand, Aaron suggests, the emperor will spare the life of his sons, accused of murdering Bassianus. The scene that follows grotesquely parodies the ritual gesture of handclasping that often accompanies gift exchange in the heroic tradition; and in doing so, it confirms the failure of Titus's "victorious hand" to secure his soldierly bond with the emperor. Shakespeare sets up here and then radically disrupts a conventional tableau of a *hand-in-hand*: the figure of joined hands, which represents faithful contract in emblems of friendship and service (see Figure 8, "Concordia," from Geffrey Whitney's *A Choice of Emblemes* [1586], as well as Figure 9, "En Dextra Fides Que," George Wither's later version). Determined to give up his own hand and to prevent Lucius or Marcus from sacrificing theirs, Titus tricks them into leaving him alone with Aaron:

> *Tit.* Come hither, Aaron. I'll deceive them both.
> Lend me thy hand, and I will give thee mine.

FIGURE 8. "Concordia." Geffrey Whitney, *A Choice of Emblemes*
(1586), 76. By permission of the Folger Shakespeare Library.

> *Aar.* [*Aside*] If that be called deceit, I will be honest
> And never whilst I live deceive men so.
>   (3.1.185–88)

Undaunted by the cold shoulder Saturninus offered his gifts in the
opening scene, Titus imagines his dismemberment as a second gift
exchange, but, as it becomes clear from its literal deconstruction,
the language of lending and giving lacks political force in Rome.
Punctuated by Aaron's sardonic aside, the tableau dramatizes not
only the actual severance of political contract, but the fact that
Titus's "victorious hand" was never able to effect it in the first place.
Of course, Saturninus's offer that Titus ransom his sons with his
hand is no more genuine than his earlier promises were. That this
offer comes through Aaron—the Vice who describes his own hand

My Hand and Heart, in one agree,
What can you more defire of mee?

FIGURE 9. "En Dextra Fides Que." Wither, *Collection of Emblemes*, 230. By permission of the Folger Shakespeare Library.

in the stock vocabulary of revenge—makes it clear that such a handshake will never produce concord: Aaron declaims, "Vengeance is in my heart, death in my hand, / Blood and revenge are hammering in my head" (2.3.38–39).

Hoping to trade his hand for his sons' lives, Titus addresses Aaron in terms that evoke a second tradition of manual iconography: the image of two hands clasped in marriage. "With all my heart I'll send the Emperor my hand" (3.1.160), he asserts before asking Aaron to "Lend me thy hand, and I will give thee mine" (3.1.186). In an excellent survey of marital imagery, Dale Randall has connected such conventional symbolism of heart and hand to the tradition of betrothal rings. Common practice dictated that such rings—characteristically showing two clasped hands—should be

worn on the third finger of the left hand, thought to be connected
to the heart by a vein or nerve.[14] A late example of this pervasive
imagery is Wither's emblem "*En Dextra Fides Que*," which illustrates
this trope as a hand-in-hand holding a heart (Figure 9). In Wither's
emblem, the special physiological connection that Randall describes allows the heart to stand for will and intention and the hand
for the action or "deed" proceeding directly from it. However, in
attempting to explain the agreement between intention and deed,
Wither glosses the emblem oddly: warning of the dangers implied
by his synecdochic logic:

> When thou dost reach thy hand unto thy friend,
> Take order, that thy *heart* the same intend:
> For, otherwise in *Hand*, or *Heart*, thou lyest,
> And, cuttest off a Member, e'er thou dyest.[15]

Wither goes on to invoke the loving "gift" of hearts by hands as a
positive analogy, but he argues by so many negative examples that
deceit turns out to be the topos of the hand-in-hand:

> Yea, some can very cunningly expresse,
> In outward shew, a winning heartinesse,
> And, steale the deare *affections* they have sought,
> From those, to whom they meant, nor promis'd ought.
> Then, will they, if *advantage* come thereby,
> Make all their *Deeds*, for want of *Words*, a ly.
> > Among Dissemblers, in things temporall,
> > These *Raskalls* are the ver'est *Knaves* of all.
> > > (Wither, 230)

As in Wither's emblem, so in *Titus Andronicus* marital bonds
seem always to hint at their own severance. This helps to explain
the significance of the bloody ring that glows on the finger of
Bassianus's corpse. Like Lavinia's "lopp'd" hands, the ring on the
dead finger (presumably a betrothal ring) symbolizes the violation
of their marriage, and like Wither's hand-in-hand, the dead, ringed
finger stands for a bond distinguished by discord and dissemblance.
(The marriage began with Bassianus seizing Lavinia, and Titus pre-
cipitately murdering his own son, who defended the match.) Here,
the disruptive betrothal of Bassianus and Lavinia can be read as a

milder version of the marriage between Tamora and Saturninus: in both cases, betrothal initiates violence and political deceit, driving the machinery of revenge.

Thus, in both the martial and marital senses of the hand-in-hand, the parts that appear to be easy synecdoches for acting persons disarm the conventions of political dynasty—fealty and marriage—that they are supposed to represent and implement. In this context, when Titus plights his troth with Aaron, the play appears dramatically to deconstruct the possibility of his body—or any body—holding or signifying political agency at all. In a sense, hands in *Titus Andronicus* mean the same thing attached or severed. Or to put it differently, their dramatic dismemberment confirms what is an already precarious and temporary attachment of the powers they symbolize.

Lavinia's Pattern

To construct a politically powerful and dynastically ensured identity—the kind so much at risk in Titus's Rome—one has first to lay claim to the capacity to construct. Titus's ravished and injured daughter, Lavinia, paradoxically becomes the operative instrument in ratifying such a claim. If Galen's "dead hand or hand of stone" has no motion and cannot signify agency, Lavinia's mutilation constitutes a much more complicated case, made legible in the light of the emblematic conventions discussed above. Her dismemberment elicits a complex set of responses in the play: dramatic "readings" of her stumps and mouth that in turn provide crucial insights into the disturbing scene in which she carries Titus's dead hand offstage in her teeth.

Lavinia enters the stage after her rape, with Chiron and Demetrius, *"her hands cut off and her tongue cut out, and ravished"* (as the stage direction for 2.4 indicates). The brothers add insult to her injury in terms that graphically emphasize her loss of the basic capacity to act on her own behalf:

> *Dem.* So, now go tell, an if thy tongue can speak,
> Who 'twas that cut thy tongue and ravish'd thee.

> *Chi.* Write down thy mind, bewray thy meaning so,
> An if thy stumps will let thee play the scribe.
> *Dem.* See how with signs and tokens she can scrawl.
> *Chi.* Go home, call for sweet water, wash thy hands.
> *Dem.* She hath no tongue to call nor hands to wash,
> And so let's leave her to her silent walks.
> *Chi.* An 'twere my cause, I should go hang myself.
> *Dem.* If thou hadst hands to help thee knit the cord.
>   (2.4.1–10)

If Titus's "effectless hand" can at least contribute to its own dismemberment, Lavinia seems to undergo a more radical loss of the
signs and instruments of agency. In losing her hands, Lavinia appears
to lose the ability to *do* for herself: to wash, to express thirst, or even
to hang herself. Loss of these means represents a contingent loss of
self-representation, of the capacity to "bewray" her own meaning.
When Marcus first encounters her after her rape, he compares her
state with Philomela's in a way that neatly puns on this double loss
of means and meaning: Philomela might seek revenge by figuring
her own story in a sampler, "But, lovely niece," he says, "that mean
is cut from thee" (2.4.40).

   Signifying her own lack of expressive agency, Lavinia thus con-
veniently represents to her onstage audience only their own experience. Accordingly, Marcus's initial gesture of recognition culmi-
nates in a fantasy of *his* own release into tears and anger: "Shall I
speak for thee? Shall I say 'tis so? / O that I knew thy heart, and
knew the beast, / That I might rail at him to ease my mind!"
(2.4.33–35). Likewise Titus's initial greeting translates her dismemberment into his own experience of it: "Speak, Lavinia, what
accursed hand / Hath made thee handless in thy father's sight?"
(3.1.66–67). His protestations that he can "wrest an alphabet" from
Lavinia's gestures, tears, and "martyr'd signs," resolve into a fantasy
of perfect visual understanding—a Lear-like scene of mutual narcis-
sism. In this passage, a few lines later, the "fountain" of Lavinia's
bloody mouth becomes a mirror for her male relatives to gaze into:

> Shall thy good uncle, and thy brother Lucius,
> And thou, and I, sit round about some fountain,

> Looking all downwards to behold our cheeks
> How they are stained like meadows yet not dry,
> With miry slime left on them by a flood?
> And in the fountain shall we gaze so long
> Till the fresh taste be taken from that clearness,
> And made a brine-pit with our bitter tears?
> Or shall we cut away our hands like thine?
> (3.1.122–30)

Her relatives see Lavinia as a mirror and through a mirror. The flood of masculine tears replaces the flood of Lavinia's blood, while the objects of their gaze—the bloody stains on her cheeks—become the tearful stains on their own. Thus, while these tears appear to signify empathy and shared experience, they in fact become the material for understanding her loss only as a reflection of their own.

Titus's and Marcus's tearful gaze converts Lavinia—as a fountain—into a briny echo of the "abhorred pit" of her own ravishment. To her "readers," she becomes a continual reinscription of her own helplessness and their own uncontested interpretive skills. So at the moment when she writes in the sandy plot, it comes as no surprise that the signs "writ without the help of any hand at all" express what Marcus concluded at the first moment he saw her, the story of Philomela. Like the pointing figures of fourteenth-century Italian painting that direct the viewer's eyes along an index finger to an image outside the plane of the gesturing figure, Lavinia's stumps seem continually to point elsewhere: indices to the powerful ability of someone else's hand.[16] "Handless in her father's sight," she silently attests to the agency of the "accursed hand" that made her so. Fittingly, Titus's repeated claim that he can perfectly "[wrest] an alphabet" from her "signs and tokens" continues to confirm what Marcus had already established, Ovid's master-plot of rape.

The Ovidian gloss on Lavinia's condition is repeated, but obviously not so that the audience can discover the mystery of her dismemberment. Nor, given the infamous stage direction, does it seem as if the play must labor to uncover an internal violation that has no external analog. Instead, what for the audience appears to be a superfluous revelation of Ovidian rape serves Lavinia's family as an

HEROICAL
Fiducia concors,
We truſt or hope all one thing.

FIGURE 10. "Fiducia concors." Paradin, *Devises Heroïques*, 75. By permission of the Folger Shakespeare Library.

enabling display of political precedent. Like Titus's returned dead hand, Lavinia becomes an icon that justifies and excuses filial revenge, ratifying the family's retribution and eventual reclamation of Rome. Accordingly, when she carries Titus's hand offstage in her mouth, she symbolizes her instrumentality as the vehicle and emblem of his efficacious action. As final proof of his radical interpretive prowess, her death at "his own right hand" in the closing scene reinvests him with "mighty, strong, and *effectual*" agency (5.3.43, my emphasis). Serving this function, Lavinia appears in act 5 as an embodied emblem of Titus's claim to justice: a human version of the scepter topped by the Roman *main de justice* (see Figure 10).[17]

When Lavinia exits with Titus's hand in her mouth, the expressive conversion of her disability into Titus's renewed ability is at once shocking and ambiguous. Like the scene in which Lavinia takes a stick in her mouth to write "Stuprum—Chiron—Demetrius," this earlier scene seems to reinscribe her absence from the world of direct articulation and action.[18] It seems the only thing that can be read from her signs and "scrowls" is what her readers already know. For modern audiences, our morally outraged response dramatically collapses this stage dismemberment into "real" mutilation and "real" rape and makes it hard to read Lavinia as anything but a representation of the sexually violent erasure of female subjectivity. Yet to read her this way is to understand her dismembered parts in exclusively genital terms and to miss their complex range of reference as hands. As with the visual indices of quattrocento painting, the gestures that seem to direct the audience's interpretive eyes away from Lavinia's central figure also emphasize their own powerfully directive force. Lavinia functions in *Titus Andronicus* as a space where the political distribution of the signs of agency is worked out. She blurs the boundaries between instrument and principal, actor and prop in disturbing but compelling ways. In this respect, her loss is representative rather than exceptional. She exemplifies the general condition of action in the play: "pattern, president and lively warrant" of Titus's performance, and not his passive opposite. In understanding Lavinia's exemplary function, Sigmund Freud's analysis of the psychosocial syndrome of fetishism provides an illuminating counterpoint. In "Fetishism," Freud theorizes a similar conceptual instability between persons and things, and a similar enabling instrumentality symbolized by dismembered parts. Like *Titus Andronicus*, "Fetishism" describes the conversion of helplessness into a sign of agency, by means of a strategic displacement. But the differences between Freud's model and what happens in this play, as much as the similarities, explain the interpretive challenges modern audiences find in the figure of the severed, instrumental hand.

"Remember Still That We Have None":
"Fetishism" and Rome

One of the most compelling features of Freud's essay is that it explains a paradox of essentialist thinking: that the use of bodily experience to ratify rhetorical, political, or emotional truth is a strategic response to the disabling experience of being in a body. This is precisely the kind of experience that Lavinia—testifying to an apparently essential, female vulnerability—seems to represent. Demetrius sums her up: "She is a woman, therefore may be wooed, / She is a woman, therefore may be won, / She is Lavinia, therefore must be loved" (2.1.83–85). His syllogisms devolve to perverse Petrarchisms, which reduce her even further to the ever-fleeing, ever-pursued object of desire: "What, hast thou not full often strook a doe?" (2.1.93). These Petrarchan clichés then quickly arrive at the most reductive version of their underlying logic, "rape and villainy" (2.1.116).

In Freud's work, the type and emblem of such essential, feminized vulnerability is castration. In "Fetishism," he describes the pathological masculine defense against such a prospect, conjuring a scene in which a little boy looks up a woman's skirt to discover she apparently has no penis. The child's horror of her apparent lack leads him to substitute a proximate object (shoes, skirt, hair) for the memory of this event: for "the horror of castration [sets up] a memorial to itself in the creation of this substitute."[19] Characteristically, Freud goes on to generalize from the apparent loss of a penis to the general experience of vulnerability. The essay describes a kind of material tautology based on synecdoche: if my body can be cut into parts, I shall establish being-in-parts as the sign of wholeness and use my parts to deny my helplessness. The logic of fetishism, broadly put, displaces the experience of disability onto a material symbol of that experience, the fetish object. Therefore, that object retains its significance and emotional power only in relation to the fantasy of the dismembered body it holds off. What makes Freud's essay useful in reading Shakespeare's play is that it theorizes dismemberment, explaining it as a kind of strategic displacement of forgotten experience in a *material* referent or location.

What makes *Titus Andronicus* useful in reading Freud is that it connects this strategic displacement to a scene of political action. In different but related ways, both fables of dismemberment understand agency as the interaction of memorial investment with material things. What's forgotten, and memorialized, in the signs and props of powerful action is the insistent experience of inefficacy.

For Freud, the importance of the fetish as a material memorial is that objects come so easily to hand. He describes the fetish explicitly in terms of control and almost admiringly: what is "withheld" from other men, "can be had by the fetishist with no trouble at all" (154). However, the converted experience—from psychic helplessness to social mastery—that fetishes symbolize has one important qualification: the arbitrary or contingent nature of the fetish itself, selected for its accidental and proximate relation to the object of trauma. Instinct, rather than will, governs the compensatory substitution that invests the fetish with all the emotional energy of the child's traumatic vision. For Freud, the contingent nature of this substitution constitutes a secondary trauma, one that helps keep the pathology of fetishism unresolved. For a fetishist, his erotic object represents both his consummate, interpretive, and appropriative skills and the double threat of memory deferred—both the memory of trauma itself and the involuntary and thus uncertain way in which it is held off. Thus fetishism is characterized by intense perseveration: suspending the double trauma, keeping it always unforgettable and always unrecalled. Moreover, the fetish insistently calls attention to this perseveration. It memorializes deeply disabling experience with the kind of fixed scotoma of attention described in Titus's "handle-not-the-theme" speech:

> O, handle not the theme, to talk of hands,
> Lest we remember still that we have none.
> Fie, fie, how franticly I square my talk,
> As if we should forget we had no hands
> If Marcus did not name the word of hands!
> (3.2.29–33)

For Freud, the stakes of this perseverating economy are obliquely political and social, as well as psychic. Explaining the equivocating function of memory in fetishism, he uses the example of a young patient who had forgotten the death of his father. His "divided" *memento mori patris* yokes together, in opposition, a crisis of action and a question of inheritance: "The patient oscillated in every situation in life between two assumptions: the one, that his father was still alive and was hindering his activities; the other, opposite one, that he was entitled to regard himself as his father's successor" (156). In Freud's anecdote the ghostly reminder of the father's control both explains an experience of helplessness and repossesses the tokens of self-possession to the child. Like the Messenger moved to "remembrance of [his] father's death" by Titus's severed hand (3.1.240), this patient makes a fetish out of his father's memory: turning the uncanny mortmain of inheritance into tangible evidence of self-possession and "title"—strategically converting disabling experience into evidence of succession. So is the will of a dead father converted to the will of a living child.

Looking back at Shakespeare's play, it is easy to read Titus's obsession with hands present and absent as a fetishizing process of sorts. To produce a "true" and victorious hand out of the "effectless" one, at the end of the play, requires a memorial displacement of disability—recasting the severed hand within the conventions of martial emblems, to remake it as a figure of authority and title. Dismemberment, in this sense permits the displacement and circulation of the hand as symbolic instrument, which can then be displayed as the sign of just revenge. Yet, in this performance economy Shakespeare's version of the fetish differs markedly from Freud's. First, display rather than concealment or hoarding is its operative function. By contrast, if Freud's fetish circulates or is publicly displayed as a significant object, it cannot by definition serve as a fetish. Second, libidinal investment in the fetish is regulated by instinct and accident; whereas in *Titus Andronicus*, the compensatory dramatic investment in severed hands as props is regulated by iconographic and social convention. The secondary trauma of the play's theatrical substitutions is not the fact of substitution as such, but the radically available and manipulable nature of the conventions of authority and right. Certainly one of the central dramatic projects of the play is to fix dangerously unfixed persons and roles: like those of emperor and empress, too easily filled by disastrous substitutes as the play opens. Likewise, Titus's aim in the peculiar masque in act 5, scene 2—in which Tamora dresses as Revenge while her sons disguise themselves as Murder and Rape—is to fix these labels legally and publicly to the persons who play them as roles.[20] In these scenes, the concerns about theatrical substitution that preoccupy contemporary antitheatrical treatises—for example, the construction of persons like the monarch as roles playable by any subject, but wholly persuasive nevertheless—are disturbingly dramatized, and their disastrous consequences fulfilled. The play goes further, however, to assert that the signs that identify and ratify political authority, are likewise essentially unattached to that authority—though no less persuasive for it. This makes it possible, for example, for the Andronici to manipulate the available visual vocabulary for moral authority and political right and reinstate themselves in Rome. Such authority and right is not something they can claim before Lavinia's injuries, however. Indeed, Titus's actions in the opening scene make him as dangerous and unfit as Saturninus; when his family does succeed to govern, they do so by leaguing with the Goths—a threat the protectionist state has been anxious to hold off throughout the play. Such a conclusion cannot be comfortable for an audience facing the uncertain prospects of international alliances late in Elizabeth's reign.

The dramatic substitutions and symbolic investments of severed hands in this play differ in another important respect from the compensatory cathexis described by Freud—and that is the evidence of autonomous interiority that the fetish provides. By contrast, the material signs of effectual action in Shakespeare's play neither depend on nor always illuminate such interiority. The peculiar conundrum Lavinia poses makes this disturbingly, vividly clear. "Lopp'd" of "means and meaning," a representation of her own helplessness, Lavinia continually embodies her "readers" uncontested interpretive skills. As such, she appears to exemplify the permanently "castrated" woman of Freud's fetish-world. As if to confirm this, the disturbing display of Titus's hand in her mouth presents Lavinia's disability as a condition of Titus's ability: the hand of the violated father returns as a successful and oppressive mortmain, evidence of Titus's "mighty, strong and effectual" revenge. Certainly, selective remembering of this kind in act 5 allows Lucius ceremonially to recall Titus's "true," martial and potent hand and to cancel the memory of his "effectless" one. Thus, dismembering as forgetting enables the fantasy of a body reknit—the Roman state like the Freudian child—out of the "broken limbs" of bodily experience.[21]

There is compelling truth to this kind of a reading, but it looks past Lavinia's active participation in the plot of revenge. The problem the play poses is one of acute interpretive ambivalence over how to read Lavinia: is she a character that functions as a prop, or, like a fetish, a kind of prop that presses to be read in characterological terms? We are led into this problem, obliquely, by internalizing the gendered codes of dismemberment inherited from Freud's essay: reading Lavinia's dismemberment in exclusively genital terms, understanding the set piece of hand-in-mouth as a confirmation of her loss of the powers represented by castration and fetishizing substitution. Yet this scene illuminates an important difference between the symbolic fields of manual and genital imagery. The penis does not grasp, nor does it symbolize this faculty in particular; the hand, however, does. To read it otherwise is to be anachronistic in a specific sense: to ignore the charged associations with grasp that hand imagery carries in the sixteenth century. Thus, when Lavinia carries Titus's hand off stage, and earlier when she writes with a stick, she redefines her mouth as a grasping part in a way that complicates its earlier identification with the passive bubbling fountain and the "Cocytus's mouth" of the scene of her rape. Taking up the severed hand as a supplement to her lost tongue, Lavinia converts herself from a figure of dismemberment into a figure of agency in the tradition of the emblems discussed above. It's worth noting here the commonplace attribution of "speaking gestures" to the hand, in contemporary rhetorical theory. John Bulwer, for one, makes it a better tongue, and he in turn follows the anatomists, who assert the same: "The servant and minister of this reason and wisedome is the hand: they are the Vicars or Substitutes and Suffraganes of the speech, the interpreters of the secret Language of our silent conceits."[22]

In part, the problem of reading Lavinia is that the play offers only glimpses of her when she is not dismembered and silenced; despite Titus's claims, her hands give the audience little access to her "silent conceits." Instead, she seems to dramatize conventions recognizable from Petrarchan blazon, acting out the oppressive experience of an anatomized lady in "lively body" (3.1.105). Certainly, the stage "readings" of Lavinia emphasize their Petrarchan model, with numerous references to hunting and deer. This rhetoric is so bound up in the politics of revenge that it becomes hard to read Lavinia as anything but a figure for what it might be like to *feel* the erasure of female subjectivity in service of patriarchal institutions. This is an interpretation that the play invites, but it is only half of the story. For the play continually explodes the conventions of sentimental understanding that entice us into reading this way. We are frequently reminded not to interpret Lavinia as Titus does, in a "sympathy of woe" (3.1.148). This charge is forcefully conveyed by Titus's failure to share Lavinia's experience when he gazes, Lear-like, into her face, and it is reinforced by the bathetic passion with which he protests Marcus's killing of a fly. Indeed, this scene parodies any humanist appeal to sympathetic understanding, with grotesque protests: "How if that fly had a father, and a brother? / How would he hang his slender gilded wings / And buzz lamenting dirges in the air!" (3.2.60–62). Sentimental understanding of subjectivity as *interior* experience is precisely not the project of this play. Instead, the play's violent events, like Chiron and Demetrius's taunts, hover painfully on the verge of identifying this absence in Lavinia as an ethical problem.

Nevertheless, if we imagine that signs of agency can be articulated separately from interiority, as they perversely are in *Titus Andronicus*, we can read Lavinia as an intending agent who deploys manual icons to powerful effect. In taking up Titus's hand, Lavinia assumes the iconography of agency to herself. Significantly, this exit is an original Andronicus invention, not scripted by Ovid or

Petrarch, but evoking the kind of ritual iconographic display popularized in heraldic emblems. Expanding the range of reference the
play brings to dismemberment, beyond trauma, Lavinia deploys
these visual conventions less as a kind of walking *main de justice* than
as a *non sine causa*. In doing so, she reintroduces herself into the sequence of revenges that eventually leads to the Andronici takeover
of Rome.

The Politics of Forgetting

The surreal re-membering of substitute parts in this scene suggests a final reading of the "hand-in-hand" tableau and of the play's
closing gestures. What is at stake in the last scene of *Titus Andronicus*
is the literal inclusion of the Andronici into Roman history. Like
Alarbus's limbs, Lavinia's "lopp'd" hands disrupt the dynastic codes
of Renaissance genealogy. The resonant term "lopp'd" recalls a related passage in *Cymbeline* that describes the king's missing sons as
the "lopp'd branches" of the tree of state: "The lofty cedar, royal
Cymbeline, / Personates thee, and thy lopped branches point / Thy
two sons forth" (5.5.452–54).

The family tree whose limbs are filial bonds is a proverbial
metaphor for succession and generation in the Renaissance. John
Speed's remarkable "Genealogies of the Holy Scriptures," inserted
before Genesis in the *Authorized Version of the English Bible* (1611), illuminates its constituent conventions. Thirty-four pages of illustrations trace the lineage of Christ through the circles that indicate each
ancestor. The "rundles" indicating married partners are frequently
linked by what the introduction calls the "sculpture of an hand in
hand": clasped pairs of right hands (or left hands, in the case of Lot
and his daughters) (Figure 11). Taken as a whole, this tree of clasped
hands represents both generational connections and marital ones. It
subtly revises the narrative teleology implicit in the more conventional genealogical emblem of the Jesse Tree. The latter imagines a
single and central causal sequence: sap rises directly from Jesse's
"root" to flower in the topmost figure (Christ, Mary, or Mary holding the Christ child). Intermediate figures in the genealogy are clas-

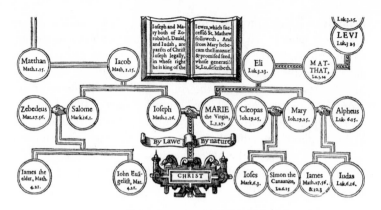

FIGURE 11. Detail from the "Genealogies of the Holy Scriptures" (1611). King James Bible. By permission of the Folger Shakespeare Library.

sically pictured as offshoots, blooming incidentally along the rising trunk. Speed's genealogy highlights a central bloodline ("knowne by a Chaine-like traile") but it descends from the linked hands between rundles. Here, as in the lateral branches of biblical descent, each hand-in-hand maintains and represents dynastic continuity.

Dynastic anxiety about the failure of filial bonds inflects the play's tableaux of hand-in-hands throughout. For example, it is a filial handclasp that pulls Martius and Quintus helplessly into Aaron's plot and symbolically to their death:

> *Quin.* Reach me thy hand, that I may help thee out,
> Or, wanting strength to do thee so much good,
> I may be plucked into the swallowing womb
> Of this deep pit, poor Bassianus' grave.
> I have no strength to pluck thee to the brink.
> *Mart.* Nor I no strength to climb without thy help.
> *Quin.* Thy hand once more, I will not loose again
> Till thou art here aloft or I below.
> Thou canst not come to me; I come to thee.
> (2.3.237–45)

Later engravings of this scene connect it to the tradition of Lazarus raised, popular in contemporary illustration. Yet the redemptive teleology promised by the story of Lazarus and figured in Christ's helping touch is inverted as Quintus tumbles into the pit, to be framed for the murder of Bassianus and put to death. The anxieties of this scene return in Marcus's closing threat that he will hurl the "poor remainder of the Andronici" "hand in hand" into a more figurative dynastic fall, the "mutual closure of [their] house." The prospect he hazards here—of not being remembered, like Old Hamlet's ghost, into the closing stories of the state—is tenuously held off at the end of the play, when Lucius promises to retell the tale of the play, thus displacing the interminable cycles of revenge into narrative repetition:

> Come hither, boy, come, come, and learn of us
> To melt in showers; thy grandsire loved thee well.
> Many a time he danced thee on his knee,
> Sung thee asleep, his loving brest thy pillow.
> Many a story hath he told to thee,
> And bid thee bear his pretty tales in mind,
> And talk of them when he was dead and gone.
>   (5.3.159–65)

Surprisingly, Lucius's story consists of a nostalgic reiteration of the events that occurred before the action of the play and that seem largely foreign to it: a time of generational intimacy and benign paternal authority. In this respect, Lucius's story differs from the play-closing tales of other revenge tragedies, which tend to reiterate "carnal, bloody, and unnatural acts" as a warning and purifying process. Horatio repeats the typical formula to protect the new Denmark at the end of *Hamlet*:

> Of that I shall have also cause to speak,
> And from his mouth whose voice will draw on more.
> But let this same be presently perform'd
> Even while men's minds are wild, lest more mischance
> On plots and errors happen.
>   (5.2.391–94)

Lucius's turn away from the events of the play, by contrast, emphasizes the fears that drive Rome's explosive violence. In revealing the breakdown of the affiliations forged in the manual bonds of fealty, marriage, and generation, the severed hands in *Titus Andronicus* symbolize the horror of a lost fiction of continuous, redemptive history. Like the cooperative function of the fingers of the hand in Galen's model, these hands themselves stand for the affiliative wholeness of the community. Unlike Fortinbras's entrance into Denmark, then, the entrance of the Andronici into Roman history depends explicitly on forgetting. Lucius's final words ward off the events of the play fetishistically: nostalgically recalling a time before the signs of political agency revealed their tenuous relation to the acting subject, but with a nostalgia so defensive and improbable it calls attention to itself. For the audience registering such defensive notes, the ending of the play offers a modulated, examined nostalgia for a time when the fictions that sustain political authority—communal agreement, mutual fealty, dynastic continuity—were less revealing of their crafted and manipulable nature: more like the simple heraldic devices of Paradin than *Non sine causa*.

The dismemberments of Lavinia and Titus test the seamlessness of physical metaphor—questioning the "natural" associative logic that grounds the faculty of action in the fact of being in a body and having a hand. If dismemberment encodes loss of effect on the world and loss of the capacity to represent effect, the instrumentality of the dismembered part can powerfully recoup this trauma. Effective political action, in *Titus Andronicus*, requires a strategic displacement and display of the signs of disability; in this play, as in *Non sine causa*, it is that strategic performance that is the focus of attention and concern. This emblem inside an emblem suggests that the figures of agency that embody authority and effect are fashioned from a fragmented, already fictive physical body—but a body whose fragmentation draws on a wider range of meanings than Petrarchan (or Freudian) trauma. Reading from the point of view of a culture that has profoundly absorbed the legacy of seventeenth-century English political theory, a notion of human agency that depends on performance, instrumentality, and display rather than propriety seems paradoxical. The normative conditions for agency defined by this legacy are possession of our proper bodies and the consequent possession of their actions. Moral and legal responsibility derives from such principles of propriety, and our notions of subjectivity likewise presume it—or the prospect that a character like Lavinia might be defined as a powerful agent would not seem so peculiar. For Lavinia's body will not ratify her own internal states—like intention and consent—though her vengeful, injured performances ensure the political claims of her family.

The question of what internal states the body will substantiate became especially important to English writers and thinkers in the seventeenth century, who used bodily metaphor to define contractual relations between persons. For early social contractarians like Hobbes and Locke, the evidence of the body was essential to secure political contract: as, for example, when Hobbes famously argues that "by plurality of voices" men "confer all their power and strength upon one man, or upon one assembly of men, that may reduce all their wills . . . unto one will" in a commonwealth (Hobbes, 132). However, the conceptual work of defining will, consent, and the boundaries of action in terms of contract began much earlier in the century. The role of the body in ratifying such definitions was tested intensively during the early decades of the century, and one of the most important testing grounds for this work was the Jacobean theater. The works of Webster, Jonson, Middleton, and their contemporaries abound with scenes of formal contract, which dramatize the changing foundations of dependency, deputation, and substitution in this period. John Webster, in particular, was preoccupied by scenes of formal agreement: vows of marriage and divorce, arrangements for service and intelligence, occult compacts and preparations. The ritual handclasps that typically center these scenes suggest the range of vocabularies Webster brings to bear on relations of substitution and deputation—for they call up discourses as diverse as Protestant marriage sermons and witchcraft law. In doing so, they illuminate the conflicts that preoccupy early explorations of contract in this period: conflicts between rational self-interest and affectionate faith and between voluntary agreement and moral duty. The striking emergence of witchcraft imagery in these set pieces registers a profound shift in the way the subordinate action of servants and dependents is imagined: from the late Tudor drama—with its traditions of morally centered, disobedient courtiers—to the early Stuart period that projected obedience and waywardness as equally dangerous and occult performances.[23] In keeping with this shift, the severed hands displayed on the Stuart stage, drawn from exotic and occult contexts, develop an aesthetic that's profoundly creepier than the earlier, emblematic vision of *Titus Andronicus*.

Chapter Three

"That Curious Engine":
Action at a Distance in The Duchess of Malfi

The question of whether human agency is something that can be located, fixed, and attributed properly to individual actors pervades the plays of the early seventeenth century. Metaphors of bodily shape and physiology that served well to ground earlier political allegories unravel the social and political fictions that define persons in these plays. Thus, to the alternate discomfort and thrill of generations of critics, Jacobean tragedy unseams the body in unseemly ways—staging dismemberments, rapes, virginity tests, poisoned kisses, and tortures that surpass the earlier Senecan dramas like *Titus Andronicus* in their frequency and vivid display. Recent scholarship has interpreted these spectacles in both aesthetic and political terms. For example, Peter Stallybrass's adaptation of Bakhtin's paradigm of classical and grotesque bodies makes it clear that Jacobean bodily aesthetics undermine any confidence in an "enclosed individuality that does not merge with other bodies and the world."[1] Feminist scholars like Theodora Jankowski and Kathleen McLuskie have illuminated the gender politics of this aesthetic by concentrating on the challenges to patriarchal order posed by the female grotesque in these plays.[2]

The emphasis of such scholarship needs to be shifted from the display of bodies "that are open to the outside world," in Bakhtin's words—"the open mouth, the genital organs, the breasts, the phallus, the potbelly, the nose"—to grotesqueries of action and performance.[3] Jacobean tragedy dramatizes the permeable boundaries between acting subjects, staging an intellectual problem: what does it mean to make one person the bearer of another's deeds, the instrument of another's intentions? The graphic play of hands in this drama provides an important vocabulary for addressing such concerns, adapting the commonplace motifs of political theory—where hands stand for relations of office, deputation, substitution, or other mediating service—to the stage. Equally important is the related tradition of vicious servants, which translated these motifs into dramatic character during the mid- to late sixteenth century. Ambidexter, the Vice character of Elizabethan drama who "plays with both hands," exemplifies this convention. His plot is probably most familiar from the moral-chronicle play *Cambises*, where he undermines the authority of every master he serves, playing each against the other and eventually bringing down the state. The history of his name clarifies the conceptual problems Ambidexter embodies. As early as the fourteenth century, Lollard polemics against Simoniac clerics (who bought and sold ecclesiastical preferment) labeled "such men of double estate" ambidexters.[4] Later, the epithet was extended to judges or advocates who profited from their cases. And eventually, it came to include the general order of deceptive intermediaries: those who serve two masters or perform the letter of a command for their own profit. In this way, debates about delegation and proxy in early ecclesiastical and legal writings provided a ready vocabulary for representing similar conflicts as they developed in financial, political, and amorous relations.

The Machiavellian servants, duplicitous officers, and intelligencers that proliferated on the Jacobean stage inherited Ambidexter's plot and made it newly urgent. The principles that sustained social obligations in England underwent gradual but profound shifts at the beginning of the seventeenth century, which Henry Sumner Maine first identified as the movement from a status to a contract society.[5] These changes are reflected both in the emergence of the notion of the agent as a conceptual category, and in the shifting terms of deputation and substitution the label comprises. The traditional obligations of social position that first define an agent simply as a "doer" expand in this period to include the self-interest of the "doer or meddler in a thing."[6] And the renovated Ambidexters of contemporary drama focus our attention on the problems of performance such meddling entails. Repeatedly, they pose questions raised by the possibility of conflicting self-interest in contracts for service: if actions by deputy or proxy are a matter of voluntary agreement by both parties rather than of traditional duties, how can their outcomes be secured?

These concerns are staged most vividly in a scene that recurs across many of the plays in this period: when two characters, usually master and servant, take hands in compact or agreement—only to have that handclasp ironized or interrupted. The creepily erotic pledge between Iago and Othello, punctuated by Iago's ironic asides, is a familiar instance. Middleton and Rowley's *The Changeling* offers a later, more extended and more graphic example. Early in the play, the villain DeFlores murders a man betrothed to the woman he lusts for and cuts off the dead man's ring finger. Beatrice had asked for his help in murdering the man, for their betrothal was based on political interests and not her own choice. The severed finger that DeFlores returns with testifies to that broken troth, and it also symbolizes the new coercive compact that replaces it: the bargain between Beatrice and her henchman. In the ensuing action the finger haunts Beatrice as DeFlores does, a talisman of the permanent hold his service has over her and the sexual blackmail it permits. Loathing DeFlores, Beatrice had not meant to agree either to a continuing or a sexual relationship with him. But the contract for murder returns more than she contracted for. In the most famous line of the play, she becomes "the deed's creature" (3.4.138): the subordinate agent of an action in which she had imagined herself a distant and superior principal.

The central problems in Beatrice's perverse contract with DeFlores—the tenuous relation between intentions and outcomes, the equivocal nature of consent, and the role reversals of agent and principal, servant and master—are framed in the language of marriage and court service. Recent scholarship has illuminated the important role marital metaphors played in early explorations of contract, across the discourses of law, political theory, and literature. Feminist historians have emphasized the unequal distribution of rights and obligations naturalized—and sometimes critiqued—by marriage metaphors in early contract theory.[7] Less attention has been paid to the related idiom of service in the period: despite the challenges a surplus of educated professionals posed to traditional systems of courtiership and patronage; despite important changes taking place in the common law that governed dealers, deputies, factors, and other agents; and despite the call of such resonant literary figures as DeFlores's verdict, "y'are the deed's creature."[8]

The connections between the discourses of marriage and service that give rise to such complex relations between agent, principal, and act are particularly clear in the four scenes of formal agreement that punctuate John Webster's *The Duchess of Malfi* (1612). These scenes illuminate a third, equally important discourse brought to bear on these relations in this period: the discourse of witchcraft. The language of witchcraft permeates *The Duchess of Malfi*—with its familiars, invisible devils, mandrake roots, and digging up of the dead. These practices are associated throughout with problems of contract. Occult relations shadow most of the ritual handclasps that punctuate the action of the play, but they appear most explicitly in the last of these tableaux. In the first act, the Duchess secretly gives her hand in marriage to her steward Antonio; next her brother Ferdinand take hands with his Machiavellian servant, Bosola, as he hires Bosola to spy on her. Bosola pledges his service to the Duchess in a similar scene, even as he machinates to discover her secrets. And in the final, most infamous of these scenes, Ferdinand hands the Duchess a "dead man's hand" in revenge for her wayward choice. When he dramatically raises the lights, the Duchess responds in shock, "Oh, horrible! . . . What witchcraft doth he practise that he hath left a dead man's hand here?"[9] Critics have long recognized the way Ferdinand's trick perversely evokes the rituals of marriage, but the Duchess's query tends to languish in footnotes that cite folk tradition and go no further. Yet the dead man's hand, or Hand of Glory, raises specific jurisprudential issues pertinent to understanding Webster's analysis of agency relations elsewhere in the play. The common law pertaining to its use in the practice of witchcraft defined the key problem of actions over distance: what kinds of evidence will help us trace the connections between intent and the consequences of a deed? The manual imagery that marks these scenes thus supplies a common vocabulary, linking shared concerns with self-interest, authority, and performance across disparate spheres. In this way, the discourses of marriage, service, and occult practice intersect in the figure of the dead man's hand, illuminating the epistemological challenges raised by changing notions of obligation in the early seventeenth century.

"That First Good Deed . . . The Sacrament of Marriage"

From at least as early as Chaucer's "Wife of Bathe's Tale," medieval and early modern literature deploys the language of obligation in two registers: the Pauline rhetoric of mutual debt and affection owed by husband and wife, a debt that is often imagined as generative, returning more than it exacts; and the mercantile language of exchange and economic value, which seems to promise due equivalence for property or service. By the early seventeenth century, the difference between kinds of debt began to be negotiated as a difference between modes of affiliation or promise: parties to an agreement would be bound either by status and condition (which carried their own moral obligations) or by voluntarily committing themselves to a contract. As scholars like Don Wayne and Luke Wilson have shown, the rise of the common-law action of assumpsit (legal "promise"), reflected what Wayne calls "an unmistakable tension between, on the one hand, the traditional moral doctrine of social obligation according to status, and on the other, the more modern principles of rational self-interest and voluntary contractual obligation."[10] Marital contracts remained an important vehicle for exploring this tension, for traditionally, they unified the notions of obligation based on status and voluntary contract. However, promises to marry came increasingly to be tried under the common law of assumpsit, as Wayne notes. This shift emphasized less the legal fiction of one person—and *cou-*

verture—that marriage created, and more the voluntary—and thus paradoxical—nature of the agreement required to sustain that fiction. The conflict between the voluntary nature of marital consent and legal absence of female will in marriage became an important idiom for the conflict between kinds of contract: motivated either by self-interest or affectionate duty, based either on voluntary agreement or on status.

This is a dramatic trope that Webster returns to over and over again in his plays, as if it offers a particularly fruitful or intractable intellectual puzzle. For example, *The Devil's Law Case* opens with a forced betrothal, explicitly setting the claims of voluntary agreement against those of subordinate status, when the merchant Romelio gives his sister Jolenta away in marriage against her will. The play goes on to rehearse a variety of conditions that might obviate her consent, some legitimate, others not: duress, madness, bewitchment, the prior claims of filial duty, and the youth of the parties involved. Similarly, Webster's *The White Devil* explores the variety of ways consent might be suborned: by deception, lust, and surprisingly, loyalty. When the Duke Brachiano divorces his wife Isabella, for example, Webster stages a vow that paradoxically dissolves itself. "I will make / Myself the author of your cursed vow," Isabella says, loyally initiating a divorce that she does not wish, while emphasizing the self-division her loving submission entails.[11]

Thus, when Webster's Duchess woos her steward, Antonio, by dictating her will, her language negotiates familiar territory. The scene replays the gesture of handfasting in several registers, enacting their mutual consent. Early modern audiences would have understood the traditional logic of this gesture implicitly; as the physician John Bulwer later summarizes it: "What we put our hand unto we are infallibly understood to *will* and *intend*, and with *counsel* and *advice* to *undertake*, and *promise our concurrence*."[12] First, the Duchess puts her ring on Antonio's finger as he kneels and then urges him to stand up, metaphorically raising him to her rank by means of the ritual gesture: "Raise yourself, / Or, if you please, my hand to help you: so" (1.1.408–9). Continuing this verbal play, Antonio responds that he was not fishing ambitiously for advancement of this kind: "Conceive not I am so stupid, but I aim / Wherto your favours tend; but he's a fool / That, being a-cold, would thrust his hands i' th' fire / To warm them" (1.1.415–17). Finally, she closes the scene by asking him to take her hand again: "I would have you lead your fortune by the hand, / Unto your marriage bed / . . . O, let me shroud my blushes in your bosom, / Since 'tis the treasury of all my secrets" (1.1.485–86, 492–93).

As this last line suggests, their language crosses the different registers of debt, combining amorous and economic rhetorics in a way that is both erotic and logically vexed. The Duchess flirtatiously offers to submit her will, voluntarily, to the legal person of her husband:

DUCH: O, you are an upright treasurer, but you mistook,
For when I said I meant to make inquiry
What's laid up for tomorrow, I did mean
What's laid up yonder for me.

ANT: Where?

DUCH: In heaven.
I am making my will, as 'tis fit princes should
In perfect memory, and I pray, sir, tell me
Were not one better make it smiling, thus,
Than in deep groans, and terrible ghastly looks,
As if the gifts we parted with procured
That violent distraction?

ANT: O, much better.

DUCH: If I had a husband now, this care were quit;
But I intend to make you overseer;
What good deed shall we first remember? Say.

ANT: Begin with that first good deed begun i'th'world
After man's creation, the sacrament of marriage;
I'd have you first provide for a good husband,
Give him all.

DUCH: All?

ANT: Yes, your excellent self.

         (1.1.363–79)

Yet the fiction of making a will maintains their separation by rank—duchess and steward—and hence the separate executive status of her voluntary agreement.

DUCH: I thank you gentle love,
       And, cause you shall not come to me in debt,
       Being now my steward, here upon your lips
       I sign your Quietus est.
          (1.1.451–54)

Here Webster plays on the contradictory positions the hierarchies of marriage and courtly service offer the Duchess and Antonio. But less obviously, he also dramatizes the tension between affiliations by moral obligation and by mutual agreement that Wayne describes. The Duchess invokes the fiction that promises of the heart will be fulfilled here and that such promises morally quit their differences in rank and value. Yet in the next lines, she complains that her rank forces her to woo by equivocal metaphors, "as a tyrant doubles with his words" (1.1.433). And the dangers inherent in court service, rampant elsewhere in the play, lurk in this courtship as well. She might all too easily become a corrupt and ungrateful ruler like her brothers, dispensing largesse and preferment according to her whim rather than his desserts; like other agents, he might act with dangerous autonomy, according to his own self-interest rather than the duties defined by his station.

The dangers of such service rapidly overtake the principles of mutual obligation and affectionate duty that make the Duchess and Antonio equals in marriage. For when her brothers separate husband and wife, they are forced to play the roles of tyrannical prince and vicious retainer. The Duchess banishes Antonio with the fiction that he defrauded her estate and punningly conceals their marriage by calling his work bad stewardship. Antonio fakes a corresponding complaint, using language that sounds conventional but soon becomes urgent: "O the inconstant / And rotten ground of service!" (3.2.199). After Antonio departs, Bosola pretends to defend him, in a similar vein. He rehearses the terrible uncertainty of reward in the current court climate:

   I would sooner swim to the Bermudes on
   Two politicians' rotten bladders, tied
   Together with an intelligencer's heart-string,
   Than depend on so changeable a prince's favour.
      (3.2.268–71)

This is Bosola's refrain, begun in the opening scene and repeated throughout the play: the principles of court service have fallen from the heroic model of feudal duty and affection; we cannot count on largesse or advancement in return for faithful service to our princes. Instead, as his vivid comparisons suggest, the obligations of prince and steward, lord and servant are Machiavellian—founded on self-interest rather than the pull of the heart. This thin basis for obligation defines the role of the intelligencer as such.

Bosola's complaint, in turn, initiates a plot shift that plays out the threats implicit in the Duchess's equivocal wooing. When Bosola takes Antonio's part, the Duchess immediately reveals her marriage and chooses him as her new "executor," echoing her words to Antonio: "Sir, your direction / Shall lead me by the hand" (3.2.313–14). In Antonio's mouth, the charge of quixotic ingratitude is a fake one, prompted by the need for subterfuge and defense. But it animates Bosola's character entirely, and as the Duchess offers him her hand she chooses her undoing. For Bosola takes Antonio's part in a second sense, playing out the consequences of a Machiavellian contract. The doubling of plots in this scene is suggestive: to the extent that the Duchess's marriage to her steward assimilates their court relationship to a nonhierarchical, consensual one, the new, mixed bond becomes vulnerable to the wayward interest of both parties.

The intrusion of self-interest into established forms of duty—not just incidentally, but as a new basis for obligation—is figured in the severed hand that Ferdinand offers the Duchess. The prop evokes the widespread allegory of the body marital, common in contemporary marriage discourse as a way of describing the subordination of a wife to her husband. It literalizes the gift of hands and hearts that she and Antonio rehearse in the wooing scene. But its prosthetic, disembodied form challenges the fiction of marital *couverture*, or single person, that that symbolic gift is meant to sustain. A contemporary analogue, from Thomas Gataker's 1623 Protestant marriage sermon "A Wife In Deed," clarifies Webster's logic in this scene. Gataker defines marriage in terms of the conflict between the female volition required to execute male intention and its extreme forms—wayward and continuing willfulness. Playing on his title, "A Wife In Deed," he punningly defines subordinate office (subordination "in deed") as the true and natural role of a wife:

> But the Woman that beareth the Name, and standeth in the roome of a Wife, but doth not the office and dutie of a Wife, is but as an eye of glass, or a silver nose, or an ivorie tooth, or an iron hand, or a wood-den leg, that occupieth the place indeed, and beareth the Name of a limbe or a member, but is not truly or properly any part of that bodie whereunto it is fastened; it is but equivocally so called.[13]

Gataker's insistence that a wife internalize her subordinate status, consenting to the loss of her separate will, typifies the self-alienation Webster is at pains to illuminate whenever he raises the paradox of marital consent on stage. As a limb of the marital body, the wife executes the husband's will; but she also *ratifies* their mutual rights and obligations by doing so. Or, as in Gataker's example, she fails to ratify them. The looseness of a wife not well fastened to her husband clarifies the symbolic exchange of the dead man's hand: the severed part marks the eruption of wayward volition into relations of office and duty—suggesting the potentially disastrous results for other kinds of social arrangements, like political or financial contracts, ratified by similar voluntary gestures of consent.

Gataker's misogyny echoes in the rants of Bosola and Ferdinand, who are prone to explode about the sexual waywardness of women, exemplified by the Duchess—"a sister damned; she's loose i'th'hilts, / Grown a notorious strumpet" (2.5.3–4). The play as a whole, however, has a more complicated agenda than Ferdinand does in offering this hand. Webster is interested not so much in female willfulness alone, but in the larger mechanism of volition loosed from the traditional obligations of degree and place that female willfulness types. Like Gataker, he locates this looseness not just beneath the skin but in action or deed: as the cryptic phrase "loose i'th'hilts" implies, suggesting an unwieldy instrument. In this way, the Duchess's own hand comes to exemplify the paradoxes of the dead man's hand. It is redescribed as an instrument that may not perform its proper office or submit to the will of its employer. Just after he tricks her into revealing her marriage, Bosola praises the Duchess with a grim double entendre. He describes her hand in words that recall the testamentary language she used to woo Antonio:

> . . . the neglected poets of your time,
> In honour of this trophy of a man,
> Raised by that curious engine, your white hand,
> Shall thank you, in your grave, for't; and make that
> More reverend than all the cabinets
> Of living princes.
> (3.2.293)

Several sixteenth-century senses of the word "engine" operate here to suggest the self-alienation brought about by her marriage and figured in her hand. First, the notion of engine as a snare, as skill in contriving, or trickery—reinforced by Webster's only other use of the word, early on in the play. When her two brothers confront the Duchess, they moralize, "Hypocrisy is woven of a fine small thread, / Subtler than Vulcan's engine" (1.1.304–5). The parable of Vulcan underwrites Bosola's use of "engine" with a plot of lust discovered that the play acts out—as if the Duchess's handfasting carries in it its own inevitable urge to publish. Her very capacity to choose, Bosola implies, will catch her up; and her subsequent choice of Bosola confirms this prediction. This is one version of what it might be to be the deed's creature.

Bosola develops a second reading of "engine" as stage machinery: describing the marriage as a tragic action that will unfold, will she nil she, to remake the Duchess into her own monument. Here he echoes the rhetoric of the wooing scene, with its language of wills, death, winding-sheets, and shroud. He suggests that the Duchess has given herself away by a kind of mortmain or testamentary "dead hand." The echo scene, late in the play, certainly confirms the reach of her will beyond the grave. But this is not the posterity she contracted for in choosing Antonio. Indeed, she says the opposite when she tells him to kiss her: "This is flesh and blood, sir; / 'Tis not the figure cut in alabaster / Kneels at my husband's tomb" (1.1.443–45). Thus, the plot initiated by this "curious engine" directly reverses her intentions, and in this way, it anticipates a third sense of "engine": the modern notion of a mechanism that drives itself, *sui generis*, like the automata of Hobbes's famous opening to Leviathan.[14] In Bosola's description, the Duchess's hand operates partly under its own power, against the interests of its owner. And it behaves this way precisely by undermining the contract it should ratify.

Thus, just as Lavinia's hand becomes a type of the disabilities that pervade Rome, so the Duchess's hand exemplifies the concerns that plague voluntary contracts in this play. These are several: the paradox of willingly subjecting one's will to another, with the uncanny alienations that entails; the conflict between self-interest and affectionate duty; and the difficulty of controlling the outcomes of actions performed through a deputy or proxy. Pairing the Duchess's "curious engine" with the dead man's hand, Webster expands on this third problem. He invokes the discourse of witchcraft to explore the nature of the ties that bind intention to act and the ways these ties attenuate in relations of service.

The Hand of Glory

By the time Ferdinand offers to "seal his peace" with the Duchess—or take hands in confirmation of renewed accord—this gesture has been established as a contradictory sign, binding intelligencers as well as lovers, signifying parting as well as agreement. When Ferdinand berates the Duchess for dishonoring herself (and him), his parable of the traveling companions Reputation, Love, and Death, reminds us of the separations as well as conjunctions figured by clasped hands:

> "Stay," quoth Reputation,
> "Do not forsake me; for it is my nature,
> If once I part from any man I meet,
> I am never found again." And so, for you:
> You have shook hands with Reputation,
> And made him invisible. (3.2.131–36)

When Ferdinand offers a dead man's hand in place of his own, the travesty undoes the social bonds that such rituals are meant to cement. His language maliciously parodies the affectionate obligations symbolized by the marital handclasp:[15]

FERD: I come to seal my peace with you: here's a hand,
          Gives her a dead man's hand [with a ring]
DUCH: I affectionately kiss it.
FERD: Pray do: and bury the print of it in your heart.
          I will leave this ring with you for a love-token;
          And the hand, as sure as the ring; and do not doubt
          But you shall have the heart too. When you need a friend
          Send it to him that owed it: you shall see
          Whether he can aid you.
DUCH: You are very cold.
          I fear you are not well after your travel.
          [*Bosola brings up lights*]
          Ha! Lights! O horrible!
FERD: Let her have lights enough.
          Exit [Ferdinand]
DUCH: What witchcraft doth he practise that he hath left
          A dead man's hand here? (4.1.43−55)

Critics tend to interpret this exchange emblematically, as a kind of *memento mori* or as a symbolic displacement of Ferdinand's incestuous desires. It is surely both. Yet the Duchess's shocked reaction suggests connections to the language of witchcraft elsewhere in the play and directs us to read the prop in that context as well. Folk tales of the Hand of Glory and contemporary common law governing the use of dead bodies register a specific horror in the dead man's hand: the prospect of losing the part of the body that connects intention and effect (the part "infallibly understood to will and intend" in John Bulwer's words) and finding it subject to the designs of someone else. Ferdinand's offer demonstrates, dismayingly, how easily a hand clasp can be converted to an emblem of its own undoing, or a hand can be made to represent the disability of its holder, as perversely destructive as the "curious engine" of the Duchess's hand.

The Hand of Glory or "Main-de-Gloire" has a fairly extended history in early European witchcraft lore and practice.[16] The famous demonologist Francesco Maria Guazzo's description of the charm in his *Compendium Maleficarum* (1608), includes a recipe for its use and preparation that was well established. Guazzo's primary source is the 1595 *Demonolatreiae* by Nicholas Remy, a notorious French demonologist and judge of witchcraft trials.[17] Remy in turn describes a practice well codified in folk tradition.

To make such a charm, the witch cuts the hand off an exhumed body and prepares it magically: the severed hand is "pickled with various salts, dried in strong sunlight or an oven until . . . quite hard."[18] When employed in witchcraft, the fingers are anointed with devilish oils and either burned or used as a candle-holder (Guazzo, 84–85, 90). As long as the Hand of Glory burns, it causes all those around except the witch to sleep, to be immobilized, or it allows the witch to act invisibly. Later demonologists borrow accounts of this charm, often word for word, from these earlier ones. And by the eighteenth and nineteenth centuries, folk anecdotes, horror stories, and even contemporary incidents involving the Hand of Glory were in lively circulation, presumably deriving renewed popularity from the 1722 publication of the grimoire *Secrets Merveilleux de la Magie Naturelle et Cabalistique de Petit Albert.* According to the *Dictionary of American Regional English*, the colloquial use of the term "hand" for a charm or talisman continues in occasional use in the southern and south-midland United States, where the terms "hand," "lucky-hand," and "hand-giver" denote one who casts a spell on another.

What the charm is used for, and how it is disabled are as much a matter of tradition as its preparation. Demonologists and folklorists alike substantiate their explanations of the charm with "real life" accounts of thieves who were caught using a Hand of Glory during a theft. Typically, the stories concern a relatively recent event in some nearby province. This is the way Guazzo begins his own account of how the Hand of Glory works: "In the Diocese of Liege, relates Caesarius of Heisterbach, in a town which some call Hugo and others Dinant, there came one night to an inn two men" (85). Guazzo describes how the two thieves use the Hand of Glory to witch their victims into a deep sleep, and then recounts their frustration by a perspicacious maidservant, who douses the burning charm. The folklorist Christina Hole offers a more recent anecdote, from *The Observer*, 16 January 1831; it tells of an attempted robbery on 3 January at Loughcrew, Co. Meath in which thieves using a

Hand of Glory were similarly foiled (179). Hole immediately follows this brief reference with a more detailed story from the last decade of the eighteenth century, equally charged with verisimilitude: this account was "originally collected by Charles Wastell from Bella Parkin, the daughter of the maidservant concerned." Like the other versions of the tale, this one tells of an attempted theft at the "Old Spital Inn, near Stainmore," foiled by the alert maidservant who witnesses the use of the Hand and puts it out (180).

The burglary plot becomes a standard feature of the Hand of Glory, remarkably consistent in its particular details across several centuries.[19] The motif of theft suggests the problems caused by the mobile and appropriable nature of physical signs of agency. And it emphasizes the tenuousness of property as a vehicle for effective human action. The detachable, instrumental nature of the Hand of Glory is what makes it a powerful tool and what facilitates supernatural activities. Yet its very status as a thing that can be taken up by another and turned to unwonted uses reveals a profound weakness in—and threat to—each person who employs it—for the thief or witch is always foiled.

For Webster, drawing on these traditions, the dead man's hand also suggests the tenuousness of bodily metaphors as evidence for any theory about effectual human action. The specific form these problems take in *The Duchess of Malfi* is the task of explaining actions performed at a distance, by proxy, or through intermediation, where the evidence that proves the connection between intention and effect is not clear. This is the central problem *maleficia* or evil acts posed in early seventeenth-century common law. Like the leg that Ferdinand is later discovered to have "digged up" as a sign of his mad witchery, the Hand of Glory falls under the criminal category of "digging up the dead," a new offense added to James I's 1604 Statute. The 1604 Statute defines the offense as follows:

> [Taking] up any dead man, woman, or child out of his, her, or their grave, or any other place where the dead body resteth, or the skin, bone, or any other part of any dead person, to be employed or used in any manner of witchcraft, sorcery, charm, or enchantment. (R. Robbins, 280)

Other revisions in the 1604 Statute emphasized contract with the devil or evil spirits, spelling out the variety of pacts that might be engaged in: "consult, covenant with, entertain, employ, feed, or reward" (280). Digging up the dead was one of a set of practices that could provide evidence of such covenants; thus the statute specifies it as a felony punishable by death without benefit of clergy and sanctuary if convicted. Recorded use of dead bodies for witchcraft in England appears sporadic; in his analysis of the Essex Assizes between 1560 to 1680, for example, Alan Macfarlane cites only one indictment for the use of dead bodies.[20] Russell Hope Robbins, on the other hand, records the use of the Hand of Glory as evidence in continental witchcraft prosecutions, citing a case Guazzo borrows from Remy that took place in Guermingen in 1588 (241). Webster's use of the charm with minimal glossing ("What witchcraft doth he practise") suggests that such practices were known widely by reputation, if not by trial. One larger English context for the new provisions in the 1604 legislation was of course James I's increasing persecution of Recusants. The statute might well have been used to demonize Catholic worship of relics by assimilating them to occult practice. Certainly, Bosola's threat that the Duchess's own hand and person will become a site of pilgrimage resonates with the horrifying rather than redeeming potential of such reverence. The Hand of Glory itself conjures the worst potential of contemporary relics. With its elaborate preparation and diabolical use, it evokes the manufacture of false relics and the corrupted interests they serve. It also realizes a profound dissolution of body and person, for this talisman perverts the actual synecdoche, *pars pro toto*, inherent in a true relic, as the body part that should incorporate the whole person is converted to another person's instrument.[21]

What is most important to this brief account of the tradition of the Hand of Glory is less its actual employment—recipes in grimoires and demonologies are certainly of questionable provenance—than its legal status as the sign and tool of *maleficia*, or evil acts. According to the 1604 Statute's rules about exhumation and the felonious use of corpses, a person who used a Hand of Glory would by definition be a witch. Furthermore, as a "known practice of witchcraft," possession of the charm would constitute the "just and sufficient proof" required for conviction in William Perkins's 1608 guide to justices (R. Robbins, 174). Like the use of wax figures and the employment of familiars, the charm offered a particularly powerful kind of evidence for the presumption of *maleficia*—in contrast with the more dubiously grounded presumptions of contract with the devil. Witchcraft trials in the sixteenth and seventeenth centuries often linked malevolent motive and injurious effect in the absence of the kind of direct evidence of causality that other kinds of criminal action required. This was a fact much noted and worried over by contemporary jurists and often the source of skepticism. In a detailed discussion of this problem, Alan Macfarlane cites Gifford's *Dialogue* as an influential critical account of the difficulty of proving such causal links. He argues, "It was only possible to testify to motives and effects, not to witness the actual act of witchcraft or the invisible way in which this force operated" (Macfarlane, 16).[22] Michael Dalton's *Countrey Justice* (1618) is often quoted by modern scholars to illustrate jurisprudential concerns about the attenuation, over time and space, of links between evil effects and the person of the witch who intended them. Dalton's manual bases his guidelines on the *Discovery of Witches*, containing the 1612 arraignments of witches at the Lancaster Assize. He cautions, "Now against these Witches the Justices of peace may not alwaies expect direct evidence, seeing that all their workes are the workes of darknesse, and no witnesses present with them to accuse them."[23] Comparing witchcraft to poisoning, Dalton concludes that "halfe proofes are to be allowed, and are good causes of suspicion" (Dalton, 268).

Trials thus provided a stage on which to adjudicate the differences between evil intentions and their effects, and "natural" or accidental events that occurred by unhappy coincidence. As both explanation and evidence of the peculiar power practiced by witches, the charm provides a missing link that distinguishes these two kinds of events. It is significant that recipes for the Hand of Glory often stipulate that the hand come from the body of a felon, forging an a priori association with criminal action. In this way a clear distinction can be kept between acts of God and felonious ones. The difficulty of maintaining such distinctions is a problem that recurs throughout contemporary debates about the existence of witchcraft and is characteristically couched in the language of manual action. Thomas Ady's work, for example, is full of passages contesting "whose hand is in" an action—God's or witches': "Seldom hath a man the hand of God against him in his estate, or health of body, or any way, but presently he cryeth out of some poor innocent Neighbour, that he, or she hath bewitched him." "And therefore men should look into the Scriptures, and search what sins bring afflictions from Gods hand, and not say presently, what old man or woman was last at my door, that I may hang him or her for a Witch."[24] Much earlier, Reginald Scot argued a similarly skeptical line: "Fewe or none can (nowadaies) with patience indure the hand and correction of God. For if any adversitie, greefe, sicknesse, losse of children, corne, catell, or libertie happen unto them; by & by they exclaim uppon witches."[25]

Amputated from the body whose intentions it should be serving yet generating powerful effects for the one who wields it, the dead man's hand exemplifies the vexed status of testimonial and material evidence in witchcraft prosecutions. It signifies both a compelling forensic connection between intention and act and the urgent need to forge that connection against accepted legal convention. As trial evidence, the Hand of Glory mediates between the person of the witch and distant *maleficia*. And by supplying such evidence, the charm brings the witch under control, for it peculiarly confirms both her temporary power and her ultimate helplessness, as the repeated formula of foiled sorcery confirms. In these contradictory roles, the Hand of Glory remains a "curious engine," working invisibly and inexorably, with an agency attenuated from the body of the acting subject and often against the interests of its possessor.

Evoking this forensic history, Webster stages a punning byplay on the etymology of the term "Hand of Glory," drawing on the continental origins of the name. The phrase "Hand of Glory" translates the French *main de gloire*, a "deformation by 'popular etymology' of the Old French mandegloire": from mandegore, mandragore, or mandrake.[26] Like the dead man's hand, the mandrake plant is associated with felonious acts, supposed by popular tradition to grow under the gallows. In Webster's play, it serves as Ferdinand's explanation of his madness: he has grown mad from digging one up, he says to his brother. "What's the Prodigy?" the cardinal asks. "Read there, a sister damn'ed; she's loose i'th'hilts, / Grown a notorious strumpet" (2.5.1–4). For Ferdinand, as many critics have noted, his sister's sexual willfulness profoundly threatens his own person, much as the loosely fastened wife of Gataker's exemplum threatens her husband—hence, the frequent scholarly diagnosis of incestuous obsession. But the play overlays this erotic subtext with other causes for his madness, leading us through the language of madness back to the relationship between Ferdinand and Bosola.

Occult Contracts

For Webster, the failure of the body to ratify states like intention and consent is epitomized in the dead man's hand: where the part that symbolizes effectual action becomes the grotesque instrument of another's design. As "Main de Gloire," the dead man's hand suggests that the condition for madness is precisely the recognition of will and consent as a property held by another. This is a recognition that both Bosola and Ferdinand come to, in different ways, in the scene in which Bosola claims his reward for killing the Duchess. When Bosola challenges Ferdinand for his reward, Ferdinand denies his role as a principal to the act. His denial is premised on his own madness, the lack of legitimate judicial process, and as a consequence of both, the independent moral authority Bosola has acted with. Bosola contests these claims, reverting over and over to their traditional roles as lord and retainer, which make him an extension of Ferdinand. In this, he reprises the nostalgic imagery with which the play began, with its aphoristic descriptions of the ideal prince as a tree or fountain, from which the character and actions of the court naturally spring.[27] The relationship between Bosola and Ferdinand profoundly undermines these organic models and looks forward, warily, to voluntary and consensual forms of agency. Thus, Webster anatomizes in single relationships the principle of willful subjection to authority that much later writers, like Hobbes and Locke, were to take up in terms of collective consent in a commonwealth.

Just after the Duchess's executioners leave the stage, Ferdinand enters and Bosola confronts him with her body. Ferdinand immediately begins to repent, and as he does so, to imagine Bosola as the agent of justice who might have saved her: the faithful servant of so many conduct manuals, who proves his merit by selective, moral disobedience:[28]

> Let me see her face again.
> Why didst not thou pity her? What an excellent
> Honest man might'st thou have been
> If thou hadst borne her to some sanctuary!
> Or, bold in a good cause, opposed thyself
> With thy advancèd sword above thy head,
> Between her innocence and my revenge!
> I bade thee, when I was distracted of my wits,
> Go kill my dearest friend, and thou hast done't.
> (4.2.264–72)

This is not a specious denial. Ferdinand is mad precisely in the sense that his divided intentions are performed by another and come into conflict when they are executed. In this way, he can imagine Bosola as a rescuer who acts out his internal oppositions. The servant's role imagined here is both more complex and more perverse than traditions of moral disobedience dictate. Bosola acts one part of Ferdinand's intentions, while another reacts to its murderous effects, as if Ferdinand were the audience to a scene he directs:

> For thee (as we observe in tragedies
> That a good actor many times is cursed
> For playing a villain's part), I hate thee for't:
> And for my sake say thou hast done much ill well.
> (4.2.280–83)

Bosola responds by insisting on his role as Ferdinand's servant, implicitly reprising his trademark complaint against ungrateful masters: "Let me quicken your memory; for I perceive / You are falling into ingratitude. I challenge / The reward due to my service" (4.2.284–86). Ferdinand counters by asserting more explicitly that Bosola acted without authority, and when Bosola insists he acted on Ferdinand's authority, Ferdinand objects that it was not legitimate:

> Did any ceremonial form of law
> Doom her to not-being? Did a complete jury
> Deliver her conviction up i'th' court?
> Where shalt thou find this judgement registered
> Unless in hell?
>   (4.2.292–96)

Throughout the rest of this scene, the counterpoint between two notions of service continues: Ferdinand's analysis depends on a service relationship that invests the agent with independent volition and is based on voluntary agreement; Bosola defines obligations according to traditional duties of place and degree. Bosola refuses to leave and again insists on his reward, couching it in terms that emphasize a lord's duties toward his retainers: "I will first receive my *pension*" [my emphasis] (4.2.304). Much more than "reward," the word "pension" connotes regular and periodic payment for allegiance, as well as service, over a long period. Again, Ferdinand disputes such claims by characterizing Bosola as an independently evil actor: "You are a villain." "When your ingratitude / Is judge, I am so" (4.2.305–6), Bosola retorts, calling attention to Ferdinand's sophistic analysis. His master continues nonetheless in the same vein, insisting on Bosola's independent capacity to choose the authority by which he acts, despite his evident failure to have done so: "O horror! / That not the fear of him which binds the devils / Can prescribe man obedience" (4.2.306–8).

Webster closes the scene with a remarkable turn of character, as Bosola—disabused of a fantasy of true service that he had perversely always seemed to acknowledge as illusory—repents. "I stand like one / That long hath ta'en a sweet and golden dream: / I am angry with myself, now that I wake" (4.2.315–17). When Bosola comes to himself, as it were, he comes to accept Ferdinand's redefinition of their relationship: to accept the notion that he might be bound to act as a morally independent agent—and not be bound by duty and loyal affection to his lord:

> I served your tyranny, and rather strove
> To satisfy yourself, than all the world;
> And though I loathed the evil, yet I loved
> You that did counsel it, and rather sought
> To appear a true servant than an honest man.
> (4.2.321–25)

Bosola accepts Ferdinand's mad excuses—"He's much distracted"—and fully internalizes his own moral authority in a newly recognized conscience:

> What would I do, were this to do again?
> I would not change my peace of conscience
> For all the wealth of Europe. She stirs; here's life.
> Return, fair soul, from darkness, and lead mine
> Out of this sensible hell. She's warm, she breathes.
> (4.2.331–35)

The Duchess's revival, however brief, underscores the dramatic significance of this moment of conversion, but the complicated dependency of Bosola's and Ferdinand's intentions elsewhere in the play is suspended rather than resolved here. For Ferdinand has certainly ordered the Duchess's death, and, mad as he is, the play confirms the need for revenge against him. When Bosola proceeds to carry this out, he describes himself in language that seems scripted by Ferdinand's repentant thoughts—as if the roles of moral agent and submissive instrument cannot so clearly be distinguished as his epiphany implied: "The weakest arm is strong enough, that strikes / With the sword of justice" (5.2.339–40). Bosola's service is always preposterous, as Patricia Parker uses the word, coming before explicit command. Thus, when he first meets with Ferdinand to seek service he asks, "Whose throat must I cut?" And Ferdinand answers, "Your inclination to shed blood rides post / Before my occasion to use you" (1.1.240–42).

As a malcontent, Bosola is very far from finding common cause with others, to create a body of men that—as Mark Curtis describes his actual contemporaries—might nourish the beginnings of active parliamentarian discourse.[29] But Webster's interests are more analytical than polemical in this play. He uses the fraught compact between Bosola and Ferdinand to dramatize radical and frightening consequences of voluntary contract, bringing internal states as well as deeds under its sway. When Bosola echoes Ferdinand—as when the heroic Duchess is reduced to the character of Echo in the last act—he comes close to defining intention as an imaginary and social condition: called into being by, expressed by, and even supplied by another.

But Webster finds such mediation occult, illicit, and profoundly self-alienating. It is the state that intelligencers in particular embody, as Bosola's opening line—"I do haunt you still"—promises. When Ferdinand engages Bosola in the first act, they define Bosola's role by comparison to a witch's familiar:

> BOS: It seems you would create me
> One of your familiars.
> FERD: Familiar! what's that?
> BOS: Why, a very quaint invisible devil, in flesh:
> An intelligencer.
> FERD: Such a kind of thriving thing
> I would wish thee, and ere long, thou may'st arrive
> At a higher place by't.
> (1.1.249–54)

Like the Hand of Glory, familiars explain the witch's capacity to act at a distance, in her own absence. Often, as Ferdinand suggests, they were held to be the Devil's agents: low-ranking demons who serve the witch in turn for her own service to the Devil, or sometimes, as Guazzo tells us, the Devil in disguise. In either case, they provide sure proof of a contract with the Devil: both Perkins and Dalton find the presence of a familiar compelling evidence for conviction; R. Robbins summarizes their utility in trials by noting that "as cats and mice were everywhere, it was never difficult to discover and prove a witch" (175). By invoking familiars, Webster suggests the similarly dangerous conditions of agency embodied in the intelligencer: a proxy, representative, or extension of the self who is at once proper and alien. For Webster the threat represented by such substitutes—wife, intelligencer, familiar—is the tenuous hold contract has over them. Of themselves, and not exclusively by dependence or authority, such agents thrive in the world.

If the compact between Bosola and Ferdinand dramatizes the dynamic and uncertain relation between servants and masters bound by contract, the Duchess herself embodies the problem of what it means voluntarily to alienate portions of the self this way. Wooing Antonio, she speaks in her double roles as sovereign and subordinate: one who has a property in herself, as demonstrated by the fact that she may consent to give it away. The language of revenue, expense, and bequest that marks the wooing scene makes this propriety clear. And related terms frame the debate between the Duchess and her brothers, when they challenge it. Facing them off, she brings a remarkably modern interpretation to her economic metaphors: "Diamonds are of most value, / They say, that have passed through most jewellers' hands" (1.1.290–91). Ferdinand retorts in typically nasty, reactionary mode: "Whores, by that rule, are precious": such exchange will profoundly change your status and character. But the market metaphor—supporting a self-determined, self-possessed individual, and sustaining her right selectively to alienate those parts of herself that she chooses—lingers.

English revenge tragedy characteristically literalizes such fictional conversions of the self into property, turning hands and fingers into stage props. These grotesqueries raise uncomfortable questions about the difference between alienable qualities of person—like labor or service—and ostensibly inalienable ones—internal states like virtuous or evil character, purpose, a sense of self. The market logic that begins to surface in the Duchess's self-description emerges with these questions and tends to overshadow them. By the time John Locke makes consensual contract the foundation of political and civil society, the contradictions embodied in the Duchess's ability to give herself away in marriage are naturalized in the notion of a liberal self, whose essential status cannot be changed by contract or exchange. To consent to make oneself a servant to another, Locke says, "by selling him, for a certain time" only the service one undertakes to do, in exchange for wages, "gives the master but a temporary power over [the servant] and no greater than what is contained in the contract between them."[30] Locke's confidence derives in part from the corresponding role labor plays for him in ratifying property rights: what Jean-Christophe Agnew has called the "redeeming discipline of labor."[31] By the late eighteenth century, the grotesque autonomy epitomized by Gataker's prosthetic limbs animates a new genre, which puts such ideals to the test. Writers like Keats, Maupassant, Le Fanu, and Jacobs disrupt the narrow and secure lines of property that define contracts for service in liberal economic theory, and they call into question the redeeming nature of the tasks that ratify such contracts. Their tales of lively, inimical, severed hands address the uncanny dependencies and alienations of domestic service and industrial labor.

Chapter Four

The Beast with Five Fingers: Gothic Labor Relations in Victorian Ghost Stories

There is nothing that man fears more than the touch of the unknown. He wants to *see* what is reaching towards him, and to be able to recognize or at least classify it. Man always tends to avoid physical contact with anything strange. In the dark, the fear of an unexpected touch can mount to panic. Even clothes give insufficient security: it is easy to tear them and pierce through to the naked, smooth, defenseless flesh of the victim.

All the distances which men create round themselves are dictated by this fear. They shut themselves in houses which no-one may enter, and only there feel some measure of security. The fear of burglars is not only the fear of being robbed, but also the fear of a sudden and unexpected clutch out of the darkness.

—Elias Canetti, "The Fear of Being Touched"

Horace Walpole's famous dream of a monstrous, mailed hand—from which, he tells us in his second preface, *The Castle of Otranto* emerged—inaugurated a small but vigorous tradition in the Victorian ghost story. The "beast with five fingers" tale (a label borrowed from William Fryer Harvey's 1920s pastiche of the genre) shapes its narrative around the central device of a wandering, disembodied hand, or its ghostly partner, a hand that reaches unexpectedly from the shadows. These figures are ubiquitous in late Gothic fiction and persist as emblems of the Gothic in contemporary novels and film. They bring together the complex and varied literary traditions discussed in the preceding chapters—religious iconography, anatomical topoi, the folklore of the Hand of Glory, Jacobean theatrical conventions. But their particular resonance depends on the increasing charge of the idiom of the worker's hand during the period of domestic and industrial reform. The evocative synecdoches of Charles Dickens's midcentury *Hard Times* (1854), for example, capture the newly profound constraints on work that turn social interactions into what Dickens calls "fantastic action."[1] When Stephen Blackpool, the factory hand, returns to his loom a "strange old woman" stops him:

> She asked him, when he stopped good-naturedly to shake hands with her before going in, how long he had worked there?
> "A dozen year," he told her.
> "I must kiss the hand," said she, "that has worked in this fine factory for a dozen year!" And she lifted it, though he would have prevented her, and put it to her lips. (Dickens, 80)

Just as Engels and Marx critiqued the work of the political economists by insisting on the material presence of the labor behind the "invisible hand" of the market, so "beast with five fingers" stories literalize that synecdoche in order to probe the uncanny, alienating conditions of labor at home and in the factory. From the latter half of the nineteenth century to the beginning of the twentieth, these stories describe encounters that are cognate with, but much darker than Dickens's peculiar scene.

Writers like Sheridan Le Fanu, Guy de Maupassant, W. W. Jacobs, and William Fryer Harvey use the sudden appearance of a disembodied hand to call attention to what Elias Canetti calls "the distances which men create around themselves." For these writers, Canetti's "distances"—differences of class, condition, and intellect—generate unequal, rather than ubiquitous, experiences of helpless horror. The device of the unexpected clutch thus incorporates both familiar spatial metaphors for social relations—as it reaches across traditional social boundaries like doorways and windows—and a formal narrative strategy—the sudden abruption or collapse of interpersonal distance. Using this device, these stories map the differences between person and thing, servant and master, ape and human onto the narrative distance between speaker and audience.

When the sudden, unexpected clutch collapses that narrative distance, it implicitly or explicitly aligns literary effect with social commentary.

Walpole's influential novel establishes the aesthetic of this effect, though it does not pursue its consequences as the later stories do. The mailed hand that terrifies the servants in *The Castle of Otranto* is one part of a colossal apparition whose coming, part by part, portends the doom of Otranto's tyrant, Manfred. This fantastic literalization of a monarchical body politic confirms the ancient prophecy that haunts Manfred's court: "The castle and lordship of Otranto should pass from the present family, whenever the real owner should be grown too large to inhabit it."[2] The prophecy is fulfilled as the rest of the giant ancestral ghost materializes piece by piece, crushing his son in the process and with him Manfred's dynastic hopes. Manfred reacts to these horrors in the characteristic Gothic mode of speechlessness, fixed gaze, and insensibility (Walpole, 19). But he responds, as Ian Duncan has observed, less to his loss than to the literalization of the prophecy. In this event both he and the reader read "the hollowness of the categories . . . of individual will and subjectivity, figured as the (etymological) reduction of 'character' to the externally inscribed letter of an allegorical scheme."[3] When he tries to pursue an apparition of his grandfather, frantic for an explication of this scheme, an "invisible hand" claps a door in his face, resisting "his utmost efforts" (Walpole, 26). In a later episode, the gigantic mailed hand interrupts Manfred's counterplot, continuing to frustrate his attempts to clarify and control the scheme in which he is written.

The oppressive condition of being "already written," as Duncan goes on to suggest, becomes one of the central themes of Gothic fiction. It is epitomized in the ubiquitous unseen hands that manipulate Gothic protagonists throughout the nineteenth century, and against which, in the Radcliffean tradition, they take their revisionary stands.[4] In *The Castle of Otranto*, Manfred's terrible experience remains, as Duncan points out, "a set of figures," self-reflexively calling attention to its literary and ideological transformations, distant from both author and reader (Duncan, 31). But the sentimental narrative structures that Radcliffe introduces to the Gothic expand such schematic reductions beyond the boundaries of literary character. In ghost stories of the 1860s and later, the trope of ghostly mortmain perpetuates Manfred's oddly detached shock as a textual or reading effect. Writers like Le Fanu, Maupassant, Jacobs, and their imitators extend the experience of helpless, horrified immobility from their characters to their readers, with a perversely mixed interest in sympathetic understanding, moral critique, and illicit, eroticized entertainment.

Mortmain and Surprise

In elaborating the formal strategies behind this effect, it is useful to begin with its *locus romanticus*: John Keats's lyric fragment, "This Living Hand," probably written in 1819. The poem epitomizes the Romantic alienation of the writing subject from the work of his or her hands, repeatedly crossing the uncertain boundaries between past and present, writer and reader, and script and performance in ways that typify the complicated reductions and subjections produced by the unexpected clutch. Like *The Castle of Otranto*, "This Living Hand" is structured around a literalization of commonplace bodily metaphor, in this case the titular pun on "hand" as manuscript, handwriting, handclasp, and grasping organ. The punning gesture the poem inscribes in its deceptively open hand and the affective consequences of this gesture bring together many of the central elements of ghostly hand stories. To read the poem is to take the open hand the speaker seems to offer and to find oneself appallingly shaken by this clasp:

> This living hand, now warm and capable
> Of earnest grasping, would, if it were cold
> And in the icy silence of the tomb,
> So haunt thy days and chill thy dreaming nights
> That thou would wish thine own heart dry of blood,
> So in my veins red life might stream again,
> And thou be conscience-calm'd. See, here it is—
> I hold it towards you.

The poem describes a witty and disturbing dramatic gesture, eerily Websterian in its collocation of shared blood, a silent tomb, and a macabre handclasp—not to mention the mixed complicities and reversals of agency that attend these images. It begins with an oddly passive invitation to the reader or interlocutor: the speaker's hand seems to solicit a handclasp and it is framed in the demonstrative, but it does not complete its gesture. In line 2 the implicit offer is immediately withdrawn, as the speaker reverses from warm to cold welcome. The present moment, "now," in which this offer begins evolves into more complicated deictics with the subjunctive voice of the second line. Here, the phrase "if it were cold" evokes the speaker's death both as a condition inevitably to come and one that is always imaginably present. When the poem breaks out of the subjunctive in the seventh line, beginning its second sentence, the charged sense of death-in-life is carried into the present demonstrative "See, here it is"—now an explicit, demanding offer. In this way, just at the moment that the poem returns to the present tense, from the description of an apparently imminent future, the hand so threateningly offered appears to be returning from the past, as if its imaginary transfusion and revivification had already taken place. Indeed, the macabre thought experiment from which it reemerges has the effect of an actual rather than hypothetical past. The demonstrative "see," followed by a description of the offer—"I hold it towards you"—confirms its tangible, coercive force. Thus the return figured by "here it is" is a return to a self-consciousness constructed in relation to the past, and, willy-nilly, complicit in its reanimation. Once delivered, once read, there is no way to escape the apparently voluntary engagement offered by the speaker's hand.

If we imagine what might follow the gesture of the poem, the two obvious alternatives—that the second person might take the offered hand or that he or she might reject it—are already scripted. But, in the context of lyric temporality, to construct subsequent events like this is somewhat beside the point. Each time the poem is read, it is confirmed as a living voice and gesture, and the reader ritually performs its thought experiment. This is the notion of "dead hand" control, or mortmain, punned on in the title: the oppressive grasp of past relationships, events, and experience on the present—figured in the testamentary qualities of writing as material presence. The phrase "dead hand" is drawn from medieval legal statutes of mortmain, which gave the church and other corporations inalienable rights to lands or tenements. The Church's right to real property by mortmain, in particular, was the subject of extended legal challenge by the Crown beginning in the twelfth century; the modern use of the term retains a sense of improper and inimical seizure that dates from these early legal conflicts. By the seventeenth century, and commonly in the nineteenth, the phrase invoked any attempt by a testator to posthumously control the uses of the property he or she bequeaths.[5] In this vein, Keats's title emphasizes the coercive will of the speaker and the performance he exacts while evoking the general condition of Romantic writing as a posthumous, alienated, and oppressive legacy.

The inverted and recursive temporality illustrated in this poem is one of the hallmarks of Gothic mortmain plots, with their passionate and anxious attachment to the past. The hand that reaches so threateningly into the present figures the dependence of self-consciousness, desire, and action on an oppressive struggle with the tangible structures of the past. In Keats's poem, the specific past events that dominate the present scene remain vague. The force of past experience might be ascribed to any of the lurking family histories (or moral, political, or financial crimes) that drive contemporary Gothic plots. In this respect, Keats is less interested in the nature of determining events than in the anarchic sense of present self that they produce. The second person emerges in the poem at the moment that the speaker's hand makes its first active gesture—to haunt—as if his or her daily existence and desires are contingent on that haunting.

The dependency of present on past is charged with desire as well as with threat, as the long-lived notion that Keats's fragment was a letter to Fanny Brawne suggests. From the nineteenth century on, mortmain tales characteristically follow amorous plots, as in the fifth section of *Middlemarch*, "The Dead Hand," as in Wilkie Collins's short story of the same title, and in Edith Wharton's "The

House of the Dead Hand." In these stories, the grip of the past requites the desire it creates by reassuring us that the past is as obsessed with us as we are with it. In this perverse vein, for instance, we learn from Casaubon's will that he has different feelings toward Dorothea than she supposed. For Eliot, such testamentary control offers the present a consistent and intelligible relation to the past only when resisted (as when Mary and Fred refuse the temptations of Featherstone's will, and Dorothea gives up Casaubon's property to marry Will). Yet Keats's dead hand gives a much darker view of the inexorable dynamics of mortmain. The poem constructs our passion for the absent speaker by inverting a gesture of appeal: the hand that appears "capable of earnest grasping" now, but is not yet clasped, can be welcomed only after its offer is withdrawn. And the heart's death turns out to be the material requirement of requited love.

Furthermore, the expectation of refusal is worked into the scheme of Keats's poem. As with the gargantuan hand that portends Manfred's fall, the reaching hand described here derives its force from a guilty and willful rejection of the larger, fatal scheme that binds the actors. The speaker's bitter tone—if it does not spring from a pure and nasty impulse to harass—implies some previous rebuff or an anxious anticipation of one. Against this rebuff the poem mounts a particularly coercive, accusatory argument. Like a Jacobean revenger, the speaker conjures injuries that will justify retaliation and reorients the moral implications of his own brutality. In this way, it turns out to be the second person (framed by the intimate "thou"), not the speaker, who must calm his or her conscience with self-directed violence. As with a revenge plot, the original injury cannot be traced: it is connoted by absence, silence, and the failed handclasp that might have brought reconciliation. The poem's faint intimations of cause remain unequal to its urgency and anger: its ghosts emerge to signify and stand in for the unreachable motives that can't be fixed neatly within the boundaries of character as "unquiet conscience." There is more to be said about the invisible, unintelligible motives and causes troped by ghostly hands, but for the moment, it is worth concentrating on the dangerous reversibility of touch figured in Keats's poem, which begins with a warm handclasp and ends with something like Canetti's "fearful clutch." When the poem grotesquely literalizes the gift of a heart that comes with the gift of a hand, it draws implicitly on early modern explanations of plighted troth. There, as Dale Randall has shown, the heart and hand are connected by a direct vein: suggesting the mechanism of occult transfusion in lines 5 and 6.[6] What drives that mechanism appears at first to be interior and moral: an anxious Cartesian "conscience" that moves the haunted second person. Yet, as it turns out, this is a conscience constructed by—emerging from—the poem's imaginative mortmain and the embrace it tries to force. The mechanical faculties of touch itself reverse their direction in the dead hand: the poem taken in hand to read and the hand clasped in greeting dominate the spirit that ought to move them.

The translations of agency and guilt that result from such reversals constitute one of the central narrative operations of ghostly hand stories. In this respect, the hands in these tales are closer to the weird, illicit transformations imagined in Keats's poem than to the damaging but eludable grasp of Casaubon's will. In particular, they figure a murky and occult relation between causes and effects, intentions and actions, or past and present events, and they achieve this by means of their peculiar temporality. This is evident in the iconographic and folk traditions that the genre characteristically invokes. Hands that suddenly reach toward the reader or viewer, like the one in "This Living Hand," draw on visual conventions for representing the raising of Lazarus, a scene reflected in contemporary depictions of broken tombs and hands rising from the grave.[7] In exegetical tradition, the story of Lazarus prefigures the raising of the faithful at the Apocalypse and their redemption. Romantic tradition revises the spiritual allegory darkly, challenging its teleological and typological promises. Like the earlier revision of Lazarus rising staged in *Titus Andronicus*, the hand that reaches from below promises to drag its victim into the pit rather than out of it. This macabre version of the Lazarus motif became a favorite signifier of genre for the writers who inherited Walpole's scattered devices, and contemporary practitioners of the form flourish it still: from the decaying hands that burst through windows and doors in George

Romero's zombie hits, to the gargoyle claw that announces the eponymous genre in Ken Russell's *Gothic*, to the parody of a disembodied, white-gloved, paparazzi hand in a Nikon camera ad for the "action touch."[8] To give an example closer to the fiction discussed below, the motif provides the extended, ironic pun that structures the mystery plot of Le Fanu's epistolary novel, *Wylder's Hand*: "Resurgam—I will rise again."[9] At the end of the tale, the absent title character, whose intermittent letters have traced a receding path from England to darkest Italy, finally resurfaces as "a livid hand, rising from the earth." It turns out that the title puns: what appeared to be letters from Wylder were forged by his murderer. This revelation fails, however, to resolve the marriage and inheritance plots suspended by Wylder's absence, and the other central characters depart to a wraithlike existence in Venice, abandoning their English inheritance and property. Here, the figure of Wylder's reaching hand withdraws the progressive promises of the Lazarus motif, dispersing both the narrative and dynastic promises held out in the novel.

In this way, the trope of the unexpected clutch concentrates the formal effects of Gothic recognitions, particularly suspension and interruption. Keats's poem, with its deictic paradoxes, again provides a useful model for the narrative interruptions embodied in this figure. Even in their prose incarnations, these sudden hands have what might be called a lyric temporality and effect: they interrupt, shock, and freeze the scene. In this respect it is not surprising that they should seem available to represent the "captured" moment promoted by a camera or film manufacturer. When they astonish their victims, they compress a complex diachronic narrative, like the dynamic gesture in "This Living Hand," into a synchronic moment of recognition. But the result is a break away from, rather than illumination of, the historical links between cause and effect that lead up to this recognition. Metaphysically, as well as dramatically, these clutching hands come from the dark.

The detailed process of revivification that takes up the middle of Keats's poem frames the Lazarus rising gesture within the folk tradition of the Hand of Glory. As G. L. Kittredge's notes on this tradition attest, Hand of Glory stories were in lively production and circulation well into the early nineteenth century in rural England.[10] As the previous chapter suggests, early accounts of the device, prepared from the severed hand of a felon, give it the property of immobilizing victims at a distance or rendering the user invisible. In the context of this folk tradition, "This Living Hand" might be read as a charm; certainly its coercive effects have a vaguely perverse and occult quality. The textual effect of the grasp inscribed in the poem, as it tells us, is precisely to drain the blood—as if to make of its reader's hand the kind of powerful talisman represented by the Hand of Glory. The recognition that one's own faculties—affective as well as physical—are being used against one intensifies the sense of unease that the poem evokes. And this recognition underlines the constructed, contingent character of emotional response when the poem produces its second person as a haunted subject: "And thou be conscience-calmed"; the reader or interlocutor gains interiority and history, expressed in this sense of guilt, through the thought experiment of lines 2–6. In this way, as the poem demonstrates, affective experience becomes a condition available for strategic manipulation, misappropriation, or theft.

What makes the disembodied-hand stories discussed below particularly interesting is not so much their appalling repetition of such moments of horrified recognition as the uses to which they put them as reading effects. As with Keats's poem, these stories explore the social and intellectual work of Gothic tropes. In the case of "This Living Hand," the speaker's manipulations generate literary-historical as well as textual effects. The disturbing recognition of consciousness as a reading effect plots the speaker's self-consciousness as a poet into his own thought experiment: produced as a text, he remains uncertain of his reception, and ambitious to exert a lasting grasp on his reader. When the poem pulls back its offered hand, withdraws into the tomb, and reframes itself as an allegory of writing, it begins to read like a lyric commentary on the conversion of personal history into a larger Romantic mythology of the self. In this sense, the poem seems to look forward to the role Keats's frailty and early death were to play in the construction of a literary movement: interpreting literary fame as the work of mortmain—and disturbingly dangerous work at that.[11] The speaker's present absence and death-in-life typify the familiar Romantic sense of self-alienation: identity wrested tenuously from or resting precariously in the hands of another; boundaries between the writer and reader, poet and object, obscured. In this context, the subtext of the Hand of Glory suggests an interesting inversion of the literary "anxiety of influence": "Keats's" anxieties about the security of literary glory are directed toward the work of future hands rather than preceding ones. The object of theft and magical coercion in the poem turns out to be the reader and inheritor of the text, and the one who perpetuates such transgressions is the predecessor or testator who leaves a literary legacy.

The revision of personal "experience" in "This Living Hand" in terms of coercive property relations, expressed in these variations of the mortmain theme, illuminates the uses to which writers like Le Fanu, Maupassant, and Jacobs adapt the trope of the severed hand. "Beast with five fingers" stories connect the accusations of bad conscience, fear of appropriation, and demands for restitution signified by mortmain to the commonplace synecdoche of the laboring, producing hand. This connection depends in part on the introduction of the anatomical tropes of the "instrument for instruments" and the grasping hand into the discourse of historical analysis: work that was done explicitly by Friedrich Engels and indirectly by Thomas Carlyle. Notably, though Keats's poem emphasizes the mechanical properties of the hand—capable and grasping—and the material forms of writing—manuscript, letter, and will—it does not anticipate the preoccupation with labor that animates the later stories. The word "grasping," as Keats uses it, lacks its longstanding anatomical associations with human making, manufacture, and construction. As it is modified by "now" and "earnest," in the present moment of the speaker's writing, it seems to remain in a purely emotional field of diction. Yet our sense of the word changes to be haunted by the adjectival, economic sense of "grasping" when the dead hand emerges from its tomb for revenge. By then, the speaker implies, his grasp will be greedy rather than earnest: exceeding his reach, lively, and at work long after the heart that moved it is dead.

The ambivalence of this figure, hovering between independent agency and dependent instrumentality, is what offers Marx and Engels and the political economists of the late eighteenth and nineteenth centuries their powerful tropes for *homo economicus*. Backs, feet, and shoulders labor too, whether in factory, below-stairs, or at a writing table. But the synecdoches they offer do not carry with them the same conventional history of manufacture and invention. More importantly, they do not carry the same charged possibilities of mixed and transgressive agency nor imaginative reversals of authority and dependence. The laboring hand, like the hand that Keats conjures, threatens to take when it should offer, to make other hands complicit in its transactions, and to complicate the simple instrumentality of the worker or servant it represents. Haunting hands suit precisely that uneasy ambiguity of agency that characterizes the relationship between individuals and the economy, from Adam Smith's resonant invention of the "invisible hand" of the market to Engels's essay on human evolution. Is the hand that crawls about an object or a subject? Does the hand that rises suddenly from oblivion represent, in E. P. Thompson's evocative phrase, the actions of the "ever-baffled and ever resurgent agents of an unmastered history" or the effects of that history on them?[12]

"Beast with five fingers" stories raise these questions, but in order to pursue the contingencies of agency on which this dualism, in its simple or complex versions, depends. They capsize the arguments from natural history and anatomy in which contemporary definitions of historical action are so often grounded, questioning the definitions of human consciousness that these arguments develop. They challenge the temporality of progressive history, and they stage local reversals and revenges against the stable boundaries of class experience. Taken together, they offer a kind of labor theory of "experience"—that vague and capacious term of historical theory—tracing the ways in which a sudden consciousness of self in social relations can be produced, commodified, and put on the market.

The Labor Theory of Evolution
and the Beast with Five Fingers

> In genuine storytelling the hand plays a part which supports what
> is expressed in a hundred ways with its gestures trained by work.
>
> —Walter Benjamin, "The Storyteller"

When Friedrich Engels adapts Lamarckian models to a labor theory of history, in his introduction to *Dialectics of Nature* (1875–76), the physical development of the hand and its "productive effects" is his defining instance and central cause:

> Man, too, arises by differentiation. Not only individually, differentiated out of a single egg cell to the most complicated organism that nature produces—no, also historically. When, after thousands of years of struggle, the differentiation of hand from foot, and erect gait, were finally established, man became distinct from the ape and the basis was laid for the development of articulate speech and the mighty development of the brain that has since made the gulf between man and ape unbridgeable. The specialisation of the hand—this implies the *tool*, and the tool implies specifically human activity, the transforming reaction of man on nature, production. Animals in the narrower sense also have tools, but only as limbs of their bodies: the ant, the bee, the beaver; animals also produce, but their productive effect on surrounding nature in relation to the latter amounts to nothing at all. Man alone has succeeded in impressing his stamp on nature, not only by shifting plants and animals from one place to another, but also by so altering the aspect and climate of his dwelling place, and even the plants and animals themselves, that the consequences of his activity can disappear only with the general extinction of the terrestrial globe. And he has accomplished this primarily and essentially by means of the *hand*. Even the steam engine, so far his most powerful tool for the transformation of nature, depends, because it is a tool, in the last resort on the hand. But step by step with the development of the hand went that of the brain; came consciousness, first of all of the conditions for producing separate practically useful results . . . the hand alone would never have achieved the steam engine if the brain of man had not developed correlatively with and alongside of it, and partly owing to it.[13]

Engels defines the hand here in terms that harken back to Aristotle and Galen: as instrument of and for instruments; distinguished from the specialized "tools" of animals by its capacity to make and control other tools; bound by mutual evolutionary debt to the motive force of consciousness.[14] The passage offers a natural philosophy for the images of labor power that dominated contemporary industrial iconography in Germany and in England: the hands with hammers and wrenches that signify an increasingly fraught relationship between those who produce and those who own the means of production.[15] Like these visual counterparts and like the Renaissance tradition of martial emblems they draw on, Engels's specialized hand embodies a problematic ambiguity of agency. Its actions are both individually performed and structurally determined. This ambiguity reflects the broad conflicts within Marx and Engels's definition of historical action. As Engels puts it in a late letter to H. Starkenburg, "Men make their history themselves" but the outcome of their clashing interests is determined by economic necessity.[16] Anthony Giddens traces this paradox to the way a "Hegelian inheritance . . . with its connotation of active consciousness and the coming-to-itself in history, mingles uneasily and in an unresolved way . . . with an allegiance to a deterministic theory in which actors are propelled by historical laws."[17]

But who is uneasy, and when? It is worth emphasizing that by definition, for Marx and Engels, labor shapes those laboring as much as they shape the material world. This mutual determination is not particularly uncanny, except to the degree that it is forgotten. For example, when Engels continues his discussion of hand differentiation in "The Part Played by Labour in the Transition from Ape to Man," he begins by contrasting the manual activities of apes and humans and goes on to describe the decisive consequences of tool use:

> Thus the hand is not only the organ of labour, *it is also the product of labour*. Labour, adaptation to ever new operations, the inheritance of muscles, ligaments, and, over longer periods of time, bones that had undergone special development and the ever-renewed employment of this inherited finesse in new, more and more complicated opera-

tions, have given the human hand the high degree of perfection required to conjure into being the pictures of a Raphael, the statues of a Thorwaldsen, the music of a Paganini.

But the hand did not exist alone, it was only one member of an integral, highly complex organism. And what benefited the hand, benefited also the whole body it served. ("The Part Played by Labour," 359)

Returning to his discussion of anatomical specialization, in the introduction to *Dialectics of Nature*, it is clear that for Engels the form of the hand and the principles of differentiation provide the deterministic structures within which human action can be imagined as both decisive and conscious. Indeed, Engels continues directly from this discussion to his central claim about the distinction between human and animal history, arguing that human history is characterized by the triumph of intentional action over unreasoned and uncontrolled effects:

With man we enter *history*. Animals also have a history, that of their derivation and gradual evolution to their present state. This history, however is made for them. . . . On the other hand, the further human beings become removed from animals in the narrower sense of the word, the more they make their history themselves, consciously, the less becomes the influence of unforeseen effects and uncontrolled forces on this history, and the more accurately does the historical result correspond to the aim laid down in advance. ("The Part Played by Labour," 353)

To come to consciousness of oneself in history is precisely to gain control over, and effectively intervene in its outcome. The alternative condition, as Engels describes it, occurs exactly at the moment at which hands begin to act indirectly, by proxy, and the experience of manual labor is forgotten:

Along with trade and industry, art and science finally appeared. Tribes developed into nations and states. Law and politics arose, and with them that fantastic reflection of human things in the human mind—religion. In the face of all these images, which appeared in the first place to be products of the mind and seemed to dominate human societies, the more modest productions of the working hand retreated into the background, the more so since the mind that planned the labour was able, at a very early stage in the development of society (for example, already in the primitive family), to have the labour that had been planned carried out by other hands than its own. . . . Men became accustomed to explain their actions as arising out of thoughts instead of their needs . . . under this ideological influence they do not recognize the part that has been played therein by labour. ("The Part Played by Labour," 364)

Here, one imagines, is the evolutionary root of the political economy that makes the emergence of a laboring hand out of its forgotten place uncanny. The unease with mixed agency that Giddens identifies arises, Engels might argue, from such postlapsarian perceptions that repress the experience of labor constrained by necessity. Conversely, Engels's comfort derives at least in part from the anatomical topoi he chooses, which import a tradition of mixed agency (divine and human, procedural and personal, practical and spiritual) to his new science of historiography.

In the early development of the English Gothic, as Maurice Lévy argues, the genre offered a vocabulary and architecture for exploring the experience of cataclysmic historical change—the "march of horror" on the Continent—and setting it at a distance.[18] De Sade first draws this connection in his famous assertion that *The Monk* (1796) emerged from the "shocks of revolution that were felt by all of Europe"; and Austen confirms the defensive and exploratory functions of the genre when she spoofs the English fear of lurking secrets in *Northanger Abbey* (1818). This tradition made Gothic motifs particularly available toward the end of the century for exploring the potentially anarchic consequences of enfranchising the industrial classes. It also established Gothicism as, in Jonathan Arac's words, the pervasive "idiom of historical representation."[19] Comparing the language of haunting and the spectral atmosphere in Marx and Engels's writings with similar conventions in Carlyle's, he explains how the third and fourth decades of the nineteenth century democratized this idiom:

The use of such language by Marx and Engels suggests its availability for the most serious purposes and its compatibility with scientific intentions, a commitment to the truth, as best one understands it, about the historical depth of a given social situation. The mysterious correspondences that link character and architecture in Gothic fiction could blend with the new, holistic scientific language of the later eighteenth and early nineteenth centuries to create striking descriptions of the coherence of social process. (Arac, 125)

Yet, later in the nineteenth century, as the stories discussed below make clear, the Gothic conventions of social critique began to challenge the intelligibility and rationality of historical processes as such. The "mysterious correspondences" that hold true for architectural conventions of the Gothic fragment under the pressure of a trope that discloses the wayward mechanics of occult causality. When these ghostly and crawling hands come knocking at the door and invading the house, they undermine the assumptions of knowable cause and explicable effect that are the foundation of the scientific Gothicism of the beginning of the century. As a number of scholars have argued, the Enlightenment principles of rational control and progressive history are called into question by the fragmented and fantastic sequencing of Gothic plots. The oppressive, "invisible agencies" that haunt Gothic protagonists may be recuperated as the benevolent workings of Providence in a world of explicable horrors in Radcliffean tradition; or they may, following Matthew Lewis's lead, remain the work of genuinely diabolical powers. However, as a subset of Gothic fiction, "beast with five fingers" stories, question the knowability and order of experience as such, by framing "experience" in specifically social and economic terms. In the aesthetic of the dead hand, to come to consciousness in the emerging future is to come to a sense of helplessness, rather than historical mastery— to the sense of oppressed dependence figured in Keats's poem.

"Beast with five fingers" stories target the underlying differences between human and beast, person and thing, that Engels's evolutionary history depends on—and through these differences the model of effective coming-to-consciousness in action they sustain. The characteristic way these disembodied hands are described makes this particularly clear. To begin with, hands that creep about are invariably compared with creatures at the lowest end of the evolutionary scale. Guy de Maupassant's famous pair of stories, "La Main d'écorché" (1875) and "La Main" (1883) provide typical and influential examples.[20] They were among the most widely read and translated of the flourishing French tradition of severed hand stories, and they generated a series of Anglo-American imitations, responses, and pastiches: from William Fryer Harvey's "The Beast with Five Fingers" (1928) to Theodore Dreiser's "The Hand" (1929) to Clive Barker's "The Body Politic" (1982). Both stories have been frequently anthologized, and Maupassant's "La Main d'écorché" was widely circulated in the 1940s in an American comic-book version by EC Classic Comics. In France, Maupassant's use of the severed hand reflected a flurry of contemporary interest in the trope, including Fortune Du Boisgobey's *La Main Coupée* (1880), Henry Cauvain's *La Main Sanglante* (1885), and Edouard Montagne's *La Main du Mort* (1885).[21]

Maupassant draws closely on the Hand of Glory folk traditions: borrowing the themes of criminality, dispossession, and witchcraft from these tales. The Gothic hands in his stories are desiccated and decaying, but still palpably fleshy—not so much polished memento mori as something still in the process of dying. When they move, as the narrator of "La Main" tells us, the severed hands crawl about like arachnids:

> One night, three months after the crime, I had a terrible nightmare. I seemed to see the hand, that horrible hand, running like a scorpion or a spider along my curtains and walls. Three times I woke up; three times I fell back asleep; three times I saw the hideous relic galloping around my room, using its fingers for paws.[22]

This galloping hand alludes to Gérard de Nerval's marvelously macabre adaptation of the Hand of Glory folk tradition, "La Main de gloire" (1832), set in 1609.[23] There the hand, ensorcelled by a conjurer, is cut from the hanged body of the young draper's apprentice whose ambition for "gloire" leads him into the conjurer's net. When first enchanted, the apprentice watches his hand swell, stretch, and crack its knuckles, "like a animal awakening"; after this, unable to control it, he is condemned to hang for a variety of "outrages manuels"; "as soon as the drapier's body was perfectly slack and inanimate," Nerval tells us toward the end of the tale, "his arm rose and his hand waved joyfully like the tail of a dog who sees its master."[24] After it is cut from his body, the "possessed" hand leaps away through the crowd, "then, clinging again with its fingers like a crab to the rough spots and cracks in the wall, it climbed up to the embrasure where the bohemian waited" (Nerval, 142). A century later William Fryer Harvey, prolific writer of psychological ghost stories in the early twentieth century, playfully reprises these descriptions in "The Beast with Five Fingers" (1928). His protagonist, a gifted naturalist—"possessed in a special degree the power of systematizing his knowledge" and specializing in heredity and variation—is tormented by a horrible family legacy.[25] The hand of his late beloved uncle, apparently possessed by an inimical ancestral ghost, manages to get itself cut off the corpse and pursues him: "About ten yards in front of him, crawling along the floor, was a man's hand. Eustace stared at it in utter amazement. It was moving quickly in the manner of a geometer caterpillar, the fingers humped up one moment, flattened out the next; the thumb appeared to give a crablike motion to the whole" (Harvey, 28).

The "beast" hides in his library and terrifies the servants, who mistake it for a "half-frozen toad," a rat, and (as Harvey nods to the legacy of the natural philosophers) "a young monkey." When Theodore Dreiser experiments with the genre, he offers a less palpable version of these pursuers that draws on related similes. His ghostly hand, with a host of vile companions, swims in his narrator's hysterical gaze "like wavy, stringy jellyfish."[26]

Comparisons to arachnids, reptiles, crustaceans, and invertebrates ironically disrupt the neat evolutionary divisions that the hand exemplifies in natural philosophy—from Aristotle to Engels's own natural history. Furthermore, the variety of Harvey's list and the implacable way in which the hand pursues and destroys his gifted naturalist effectively deflate the powerful claims of scientific classification and "systemization of knowledge." In the end of Harvey's story, for example, the young naturalist's elderly butler is left pursuing an evolutionary absurdity, looking for a beast with five fingers. "This afternoon, since he has been in the Reptile House, I suppose it will be a reptile with a hand. Next week it will be a monkey with practically no body. The poor chap is a born materialist" (Harvey, 47). Thus, in their most inimical and active forms, disembodied hands confirm the disquieting impotence of human actions in the presence of what Engels calls "unforeseen effects and uncontrolled forces," that can neither be harnessed nor described.

Such deflating comparisons introduce additional problems with the privileged place of human actors in history, when these hands invade the province of culture—specifically, writing and story telling. Though they are distinctly detached from the mind or soul of any person, they embody evident, usually malevolent, design. As if flouting Engels's Aristotelian account of manual differentiation, they show a terrible aptitude with tools, especially pen and paper. They forge signatures, command the servants by letter, and possess the hands of their owners with a kind of automatic writing. And their actions, rather than the actions of those who possess them, tend to drive the plot (as when Nerval's ambitious apprentice is betrayed, by the willful actions of his enchanted hand, into the duel for which he subsequently hangs). Typically, they carry the meaning (or absence thereof) of the story itself: "L'index"—the index finger and the key to the mystery—as Maupassant puns toward the end of "La Main." Significantly, as the narrator tells his dissatisfied audience, "l'index manquait" (226); there is no point to this story. Far from representing a mysterious but beneficent providence, far from offering human agents control of a progressive history, they mock any predictable, systematic account of events.

As Sima Godfrey (who points out this pun) argues, the figure of the severed hand elaborates the anxieties and ambitions associated with the work of writing in the Romantic period, especially the loss of boundaries between reading and writing subject (Godfrey, 74). And indeed, it records an actual and haunting loss of such boundaries. Godfrey traces the immense contemporary appeal of this figure in the French tradition to the mummified hand of Pierre-François Lacenaire, a "poet-assassin" executed in 1835, who became a type of the Romantic antihero (77–78). Lacenaire's hand, on display in a Paris salon, inspired Theophile Gautier's poem "Études de

Mains," and it resonates in Maupassant's own obsession with a similar flayed hand: "celle d'un parricide," as he describes it years later, encountered at the villa of Algernon Swinburne in 1868 (Godfrey, 80). Maupassant bought the hand two years later, after Swinburne's departure, and as Godfrey goes on to show, the complex of artistic authority and criminal transgression embodied in this relic interprets the macabre events that overtake those who possess similar relics in Maupassant's stories. In both "La Main" and "La Main d'écorché" the ghostly owners of the severed hands return for revenge against those who misappropriate them, in a double allegory of psychic repression and of the anxiety of influence. Enchanted by, and stealing posthumously from Swinburne, the younger artist records his own literary guilt, triumph, and yearning for requital in these stories. For Godfrey, these allegories are charged by the theme of parricide; to this one might add the traditional folk associations of the Hand of Glory with theft and coercion (as in Keats's poem), picked up in a new form in the person of Lacenaire.[27]

In reading these stories as complex psychological allegories, Godfrey identifies a theme of repression and displacement that runs through one strain of dead hand stories, from the complex versions she discusses through Sigmund Freud's essay on "The Uncanny" to the more reductive psychodramas of popular film.[28] But the theme of repression is less a dominating device than a version of the problem of automatic action that the genre addresses in broad terms: variously psychic, aesthetic, economic, and social. Disembodied hands are uncanny in the sense that Freud first described, drawing on Wilhelm Hauff's popular tale "The Story of the Cut-Off Hand" (1886). "Dismembered limbs, a severed head, a hand cut off at the wrist [here Freud footnotes Hauff], feet which dance by themselves—all these have something peculiarly uncanny about them, especially when, as in the last instance, they prove able to move of themselves in addition."[29] This group of allusions ties together the separate characteristics of the uncanny for Freud by assimilating the different kinds of severed limb stories into each other. Hauff's tale, for example, is a frame-narrative that binds its embedded stories with a tale of murder, revenge, and restitution, not a story about a hand that moves by itself.[30] Its structures of narrative repetition and revenge suggest the overdetermined mechanisms of repression and return that Freud reads into severed limbs in general. Further, severed limbs as a category invoke the fetishizing character of memory associated with the castration complex, simultaneously fascinating and repulsive. In this way, the emotional translations and displacements symbolized by dismemberment evidence the otherwise invisible but active force of the unconscious. This is among the most significant aspects of uncanny experience in the essay, because it offers aesthetic as well as intellectual evidence for the existence of the unconscious: proof by experience that carries a sting for prospective unbelievers. The stakes are clear when—immediately before he cites the Hauff and Schaeffer stories—Freud offers this aside: "Indeed, I should not be surprised to hear that psycho-analysis, which is concerned with laying bare these hidden forces, has itself become uncanny to many people for that very reason" (397).

The discomfort and potential skepticism of such a response rises apparently from Freud's scientific exposure of psychic processes that were formerly hidden but deeply familiar, reflecting the basic plot of uncanny return. But presumably it also reflects the intellectual dissonance he describes earlier in the essay, for uncanny things "excite in the spectator the feeling that automatic, mechanical processes are at work, concealed beneath the ordinary appearance of animation" (378). This is the added charge carried by disembodied parts that move by themselves—as in Freud's final example of the dancing feet—and it highlights the differences his list of body parts finesses. As with the economic and historical versions of the severed hand, the different degrees of animation in these dismembered parts reflect a tension within the notion of the unconscious between structural and subjective, and automatic and intentional forms of agency. This interest in automatic processes and the discomfort they produce—as much as or more than the theme of repression—preoccupies "beast with five fingers" stories in the late nineteenth and early twentieth centuries. Like Freud's essay, but more explicitly, these stories explore the politics of uncanny experience: as they trace a declination from apparently willful human action to instinctive animal response, to the helpless inertia of inanimate things.

Uncanny Mechanics and the Monkey's Paw

> There is thus a separate destructiveness of the hand, not immediately connected with prey and killing. It is of a purely mechanical nature and mechanical inventions are extensions of it. Precisely because of its innocence it has become particularly dangerous. It knows itself to be without any intention to kill, and thus feels free to embark on anything. What it does appears to be the concern of the hands alone, of their flexibility and skill, their harmless usefulness. It is this mechanical destructiveness of the hands, now grown to a complex system of technology, which, whenever it is linked with a real intention to kill, supplies the automatic element of the resulting process, that empty mindlessness which is so particularly disquieting. No one actually intends anything; it all happens, as it were, of itself.
>
> Privately, and on a small scale, everyone experiences the same process in himself whenever his fingers thoughtlessly break matches or crumple paper.
>
> —Elias Canetti, "Destructiveness in Monkeys and Men"

Monkeys turn up consistently in descriptions of these wandering hands, and their presence clarifies what is at stake in the challenge to Darwinian "systemization" and Aristotelian allusion that marks the uncanny moments of automatic response in these stories. The richest example might be the "ordinary little paw, dried to a mummy" in W. W. Jacobs's immensely popular tale, *The Monkey's Paw* (1902).[31] The story deploys the deterministic aspects of Darwin's evolutionary narrative—suggested by the use of the monkey—against the apparently empowering forms of rational, systematic knowledge—represented by such technological advancements as electricity. The charm was invented, as we learn, specifically to show the tragic consequences of any confidence in human self-determination. "It had a spell put on it by an old fakir," explains the retired officer who brings it back from India, "a very holy man. He wanted to show that fate ruled people's lives, and that those who interfered with it did so to their sorrow" (Jacobs, 33). When his unwary friend, Mr. White, insists on using the paw, making a wish for two hundred pounds to clear his mortgage, the charm delivers. It causes the death of White's son and produces the sum in the form of worker's compensation from the son's employer. A dramatic adaptation produced for *French's Acting Edition* offers a grotesque pun on this particular hand of fate. In this version, the Sergeant-Major tells us the fakir wanted to show "that fate ruled people. That everything was cut and dried from the beginning, as you might say."[32] But the charm does not passively embody an outcome that is cut and dried; it produces it, in its own image. Human action turns out at best to be as instinctive and involuntary as an ape's, at worst, to be the pathetic relic of a past social order.

In the popular stage adaptation of the story, the subtext of industrial labor is developed more explicitly. Here the conflict between human action and the workings of a generalized fate emerges as a conflict between industrial forces and their employees. The fate that rules the characters turns out, as in many of these stories, to be the occulted causality of an industrial economy. Herbert, the son, works for the electric company—evocatively named Maw and Meggins—a technological analog to the mummified paw.[33] Like the charm, Herbert's machines appear to confer fantastic and divine powers on their operator. As his father says, "If Herbert took a nap, and let his what-d'you-call-ums—dynamos, run down, all Fulham would be in darkness. Lord! what a joke!" (Parker, 9–10). "Ah!, you electricians!" exclaims the Sergeant-Major, "Sort o' magicians, you are. Light! says you—and light it is. And, power! says you—and the trams go whizzin'. And, knowledge! says you—and words go 'ummin' to the ends o' the world. It fair beats me—and I've seen a bit in my time, too" (12). Yet, like the monkey's paw, this technology challenges any claims to divine fiat. The vulnerability of the operator to his machine and the social estrangement that comes from this relationship first emerge in Herbert's self-important rejection of a drink. "Oh! 'tisn't for want of being sociable. But my work don't go with it. Not if 'twas ever so little. I've got to keep a cool head, a steady eye, and a still hand. The fly-wheel might gobble me up" (12). As it turns out, the occult powers of the paw and dynamo work in concert. When the family first proposes a wish, Herbert's mother flippantly asks that they transform her into a domestic dynamo of sorts, requesting "four pair o' hands" to speed her house work (17). Instead of this grotesque transformation, they wish for the sum that will cancel the equally oppressive burden of their mortgage debt. The next day, Herbert—flippantly confident in his mastery of the machines—slips. The news is delivered with off-putting economy by a company representative: "He was caught in the machinery" (Jacobs, 38). *French's Acting Edition* elaborates the occult forces in this event and shifts from the passive to active voice—lest we miss the dominating, inimical agency at work. "He was telling his mates a story. Something that had happened here last night. He was laughing, and wasn't noticing and—and—(*hushed*) the machinery caught him" (Parker, 28). What catches Herbert here is a mechanical version of the reversible touch figured so powerfully by Keats.

As Jonathan Arac has shown, the problem of human response to and participation in social change emerged early in the nineteenth century as a problem of mechanics.[34] Glossing Carlyle's famous personification of historical cataclysm in the twitching finger of a man about to fire a pistol, from *The History of the French Revolution*, Arac writes:

> This sense of the moment of crisis, in which the "twitch of a muscle" may totally and permanently transform an individual, haunts the nineteenth century. At the same time that industrial technology was making more and more mechanical power available in response to ever-decreasing human input, and that daily life saw more and more devices activated by a mere flick—the match, the camera, the electric switch—writers brooded on this feared experience of shocking change. (Arac, 45)

When Carlyle labels his age the Mechanical Age in "Signs of the Times" (1829), he characterizes the profound loss of effect and control he finds, paradoxically, in the dominance of mechanical things:

> Nothing is now done directly, or by hand; all is by rule and calculated contrivance. For the simplest operation, some helps and accompaniments, some cunning abbreviating process is in readiness. . . . On every hand, the living artisan is driven from his workshop, to make room for a speedier, inanimate one. The shuttle drops from the fingers of the weaver, and falls into iron fingers that ply it faster.[35]

The transformations of labor are paralleled in all social institutions—from education and charity to politics—and in all intellectual and moral ones: "Not the external and physical alone is now managed by machinery, but the internal and spiritual also. . . . Everything has its cunningly devised implements, its pre-established apparatus, it is not done by hand, but by machinery" (Carlyle, 65). The dominance of mechanical tools and institutions is matched by an intellectual devotion to linear explanations of cause and effect; this devotion, in turn, reverses the relation between mechanical things and the persons who imagine and produce them:

> For the same habit regulates not our modes of action alone, but our modes of thought and feeling. Men are grown mechanical in head and in heart, as well as in hand. They have lost faith in individual endeavor, and in natural force, of any kind. . . . Their whole efforts, attachments, opinions, turn on mechanism, and are of a mechanical character. (Carlyle, 67)

Echoes of Cartesian mechanics sound here in the implicit link between head, heart, and hand, but Carlyle's imaginative contagion reverses Descartes's motive forces, traveling from the practices of the hand back to the head and heart. For Carlyle, this relation typifies a grotesque reversal in the popular recognition of the power of internal, invisible, and wonderful forces—as opposed to external, material, and mechanical—ones. Turning back to Jacobs's story, it is precisely this reversal of effect from external to internal things, and its grotesquely "pre-established" consequences, that the monkey's paw represents. Thus, when Herbert stops paying attention—is caught napping, as it were—he is caught figuratively as well as physically in what Canetti calls the "empty mindlessness" of technological tools.[36] His lapse of mindfulness figures a lapse in the essential relationship between intentions and actions that the natural connection between hand and tool represents for Carlyle, Engels, and the anatomists before them. In contrast to the way Gothic imagery works for Carlyle to challenge the mechanical isolation of cause and effect, however, Jacobs's charm confirms this isolation.[37] The play of hands in machinery raises the haunting prospect of their essential separation from personal intentions and character; and the occult causality of the paw operates not by providential or wondrous means, but by the detached institutional machinery of Maw and Meggins. By extension, the paw, with its cut and dried message, impresses on us the essentially marginal place of human agency in events. Far from plunging all Fulham in darkness, for example, Herbert's death generates only the faintest of enigmatic responses in the story's final image, as his father opens the door to vacancy. "The street lamp flickering opposite shone on a quiet and deserted road" (Jacobs, 42).

Also at stake in the occult mechanics of Herbert's death is the degree of intentionality and therefore moral culpability in those who employ his labor. Are they to him as he is to the machinery, operators without willful or moral participation? In his meditation on collective and individual forms of power, Canetti offers an apt description of the disquieting evacuation of intention that accompanies the growth of complex tools:

> It is this mechanical destructiveness of the hands, now grown to a complex system of technology, which, whenever it is linked with a real intention to kill, supplies the automatic element of the resulting process, that empty mindlessness which is so particularly disquieting. No one actually intends anything; it all happens, as it were, of itself.[38]

Severed hand stories respond implicitly to this problem, exposing the complex alienations of automatic processes—emotional, industrial, and corporate—and drawing analogies among them. In "The Monkey's Paw," for example, the scene in which Herbert's parents receive the news of his death sets their horrified grief against the impassiveness of the electric company and its agent.

> "The firm wished me to convey their sincere sympathy with you in your great loss," he said, without looking round. "I beg that you will understand that I am only their servant and merely obeying orders."
> There was no reply; the old woman's face was white, her eyes staring, and her breath inaudible; on the husband's face was a look such as his friend the sergeant might have carried into his first action.
> "I was to say that Maw and Meggins disclaim all responsibility," continued the other. "They admit no liability at all, but in consideration of your son's services, they wish to present you with a certain sum as compensation."

Mr. White dropped his wife's hand, and rising to his feet, gazed
with a look of horror at his visitor. His dry lips shaped the words,
"How much?"

"Two hundred pounds," was the answer. (Jacobs, 38–39)

Interjecting bleak descriptions of the parents' grief, the story aligns
the emotional alienation of the company agent with the firm's dis-
claimer and the occult substitution of two hundred pounds for their
son. Worse, after this sentimental challenge to the moral detach-
ment of Maw and Meggins, the story proceeds gruesomely to literalize Herbert's ephemeral relation to the company and its machines.
Mrs. White uses the monkey's paw to call her son back from the
dead. When she does, a "thing outside" comes frantically knocking
on the front door until Mr. White can use the third and last wish to
return it whence it came (Jacobs, 42).

The subtext of industrial work surfaces in the figure of the severed hand in the 1880s, perhaps in response to the intensified activity of European labor movements toward the end of the nineteenth
century. The relatively high incidence of hand injuries as a percent-
age of factory accidents lent a particular charge to the motif that was
well in place before Jacobs used it.[39] In these precursors to "The
Monkey's Paw," the representation of labor relations is more partial
and vexed than in Jacobs's story, but because of this, they more
clearly illuminate the rhetorical operations within the trope of the
severed hand and the difficulties it presents to moral analysis. In
Fortune Du Boisgobey's *La Main Coupée* (1880), for example, the
dangers of factory work show up briefly and unexpectedly at the
end of the novel. Until that point, the novel pursues a mystery surrounding the severed hand of a thief, unfolding its detective plot
against the background of a nihilist conspiracy. The severed hand is
traced to a Polish countess. She, we learn, is mistakenly involved
with the anarchists, who eventually poison her when she betrays
their conspiracy. These actions frame a novel largely concerned
with the conflicts between aristocratic and bourgeois social values
and with sensational scenes of Parisian night life—for which the
mystery of the theft and mutilation serves as a pretext. When the
countess dies, however, she leaves an odd legacy. And for the first

time Du Boisgobey offers an explicit connection between his bourgeois politics and the figure of the severed hand. With a kind of beneficent mortmain, the countess's real property goes to redress injuries to industrial laborers. Interestingly, this bequest happens by proxy: she leaves the bulk of her wealth to the man unjustly accused of—and dishonored by—her theft:

> Robert de Carnoël only accepted the heritage of Madame Yalta to bestow it upon the poor. The Avenue de Friedland house is for sale, and the proceeds of the sale are to be devoted to a hospital for those disabled by accident. The workman mutilated in a factory will owe an asylum to the woman of the severed hand.[40]

This passage just glances toward the frequent incidence of injury in early factory labor, connecting it to the countess's unintended generosity as if this constituted a necessary gesture of redress. But this glance is fleeting, for the debt is immediately realigned and recouped as aristocratic largesse. The workman *owes her* an asylum. Weirdly, just at the point where what is notoriously invisible in an industrial economy—the experience of individual laborers—becomes momentarily visible, the countess's hand bears out Adam Smith's conviction of the inevitable redistribution of "the necessaries of life" by a ruling class "led by an invisible hand."[41] Still, it is worth emphasizing how strongly words like "mutilation" register the threat of injury and how odd the conversion of the countess's guilt to the workman's debt appears in that context. Though the logic of the passage is almost as perverse as the famous parable of the happy beggar in which Smith's resonant phrase appears, it fails to contain completely the disturbing inequities of risk and dependency that Smith's feudal scene more or less fends off.

The substitutions in this passage and the reorientation of accountability that takes place within the countess's legacy are characteristic of the way the trope of dismemberment works in Gothic fiction. The manner in which intention seems to float freely within the figure of the severed hand here, calling attention to the symbolic transfer of agency, makes more sense in the broader context of the narrative. Early in the novel the hand is amputated by the machinery of a safe. It is this motivated and guilty act that the detective plot pursues. Yet, the closer the novel gets to matching the hand of the one-handed thief to the mysteriously ailing and gloved countess, the less she appears to be an independent actor. With each revelation by the detective, the novel progressively sentimentalizes her motives, making her the unwitting instrument of a nihilist mastermind whose own motives have little to do with her ideals. (It turns out that she attempted the theft in order to protect her anarchist comrades; she wants to emancipate the working class and restore exiles to their homeland, both personified in her old family retainers.) When the problem of industrial labor arises for the first time in the closing passage, it does so immediately after the countess renounces her anarchist ties and emerges fully as a sentimental heroine, driven by personal honor, loyalty, and noblesse oblige. Thus, the involuntary bequest concludes a narrative process that both mystifies and legitimizes the system that produces her wealth, making her less and less an intentional agent of any injury to property or person.

However, the insistent pursuit of the severed hand in the detective plot endows the figure with such a strong presumption of moral agency that despite the sentimentalizing narrative, despite the insistence on accidental and indirect causalities in this passage, intention still clings to it. This is what makes it possible, in fact, for Du Boisgobey to reconstruct the countess as accountable—albeit in a positive sense—for the benefits conferred by her legacy. The severed hand undergoes a symbolic translation when he aligns her mutilation by machinery with the experience of an injured factory worker. This odd equation makes her legacy seem a double restitution—for her transgression and for the injuries at the factory. At the same time, it paradoxically refigures her as the object rather than the agent of injury. The novel's anxious prospect of an association between labor causes and radical politics sustains these contradictory translations. By transferring the sense of obligation from the countess to the anonymous worker—by reconfiguring her guilt in the form of his debt—the trope of the severed hand quiets these anxieties and reasserts a stable class order. What first looked like the threatening hand of an aristocrat-turned-anarchist turns out, reassuringly, to be the dependent hand of a worker. Even more reassuringly, for Du Boisgobey's middle-class audience, the oppressive legacy of the one and the increasingly forceful presence of the other are directed toward each other, and neither shows much vigor.

At the center of the occult substitutions of intention and agency in these stories, as the examples above show, is something loosely identifiable as the experience of disability: usually the sentimentalized experience of physical and psychic helplessness; often, as with the sudden appearance of Du Boisgobey's "workman mutilated in a factory," associated with work. The corrective impulse coded in this experience, whether radical or conservative, suggests a similar kind of impulse behind the reading effect troped by the clutching hand. Indeed, the similarity between these moments of horrified recognition is striking: the automatic emotional response that literally drains the blood in Keats's poem is echoed in the shocked, white-faced grief that grips Mr. and Mrs. White when they learn of Herbert's death. In "beast with five fingers" stories what triggers this response is very specific: the vivid agility and mobility of the hands themselves. Their dexterity and animation precipitates a corresponding immobility in their victims, characterized by the classic physiognomy and physiology of horror: starting eyes, fixed grimace, rigid extremities usually followed by hysteria, madness, and death. The engraving that accompanied a reprint of Maupassant's "La Main" in 1885 illustrates this reaction (see Figure 12), as does the condition of the victim at the end of "La Main d'écorché": "His eyes starting open, his pupils dilated, seemed to stare fixedly with an inexpressible dread at something horrible and strange, his fingers were clenched. . . ." (Maupassant, 5). When the local paper describes the scene, it offers a similar prospect to those who first discover the victim:

> A horrible spectacle is offered to their eyes, the furniture was overturned, everything suggesting that a terrible struggle took place between the victim and the malefactor. In the middle of the room, on his back, legs and arms rigid and his face livid, his eyes horribly dilated, the young Pierre B . . . lay motionless; he bore the deep prints of five fingers on his throat. (5)

FIGURE 12. Illustration by Edouard Zier for "La Main," by Guy
de Maupassant, in *La Vie populaire*, 10 May 1885.

Pierre B. never recovers his reason, but rants deliriously, fixed on
the notion "that he was constantly pursued by a spectre" and falling
dead when he imagines himself strangled by it (6).

These encounters inspire an acute sense—familiar from Keats—
of having been worked on through one's own proper faculties. This
goes further than a gruesome literalization of the moral that the victims bring their fate on themselves by misappropriating the severed
parts (though this is one implication of "La Main d'écorché"). The

hands in these stories appropriate the qualities and functions that ought to distinguish humans as willful and effective. By alienating those same characteristics from their victims, they profoundly threaten that distinction. When they act, they demonstrate the kind of alert, capable dexterity that Herbert the "electrician" prides himself in. Yet their uncanny mobility and their looseness from any "cool head" defy the proper, obedient stillness of his hands. In the worst of cases, as with Nerval's ambitious young apprentice, one's *own* hand perpetuates this experience, stretching and cracking under its own power and then deftly dispatching its proper attachments. This transfer of agency and intention, from what should be part of a person to a grotesquely animated object, induces an acute social and psychic estrangement, manifested in frenzy, hospitalization, and eventual death. As the hands pursue their mysterious rages, they reduce their victims to the automatic responses characteristic of animals—and then finally, to the inertia of things. The helplessness that precipitates quickly into mania and death thus offers an affective account of the experience of objectification: a recognition of the self as instrumental object, subjected to things that behave like intentional agents but lack any moral design. This is precisely the uncanny dynamic that reproduces Herbert White as a "thing outside," and it resonates in the nomenclature of later dead hands. Charles Addams wittily gestures to this idiom in his cartoon Gothic when he names the most mobile and personable of beasts with five fingers "Thing."

Thus, the shock produced and represented by this trope emerges in these stories as a profoundly interested and strategic effect, a kind of social uncanny that pushes readers to ask whose motives or interests are served by such conversions of person to thing. In this respect, "beast with five fingers" stories use aesthetic experience—specifically the experience of horror—with apparently radical aims. "The Monkey's Paw," for example, mobilizes the effects of horror toward economic self-consciousness, but it is not clear that the story promises, *pace* Marx, that class recognitions will catalyze historical action. If not, then what is the point of this focused attention on the condition of sudden amazement and self-conscious helplessness? For Marx and Engels, to come to consciousness in history is to come to consciousness of oneself as a member of an economic class; and class experience, identified as such, illuminates and enfranchises the worker. As E. P. Thompson puts it in *The Poverty of Theory*, "Classes arise because men and women, in determinative productive relations, identify their antagonistic interests, and come to struggle, to think and to value in class ways; thus the process of class formation is a process of self-making, although under conditions which are 'given' " (297–98).

As Perry Anderson points out in his critique of this analysis, Thompson founds his argument on two kinds of "experience"—affective and practical—without always being explicit about the difference between them. "Beasts with five fingers" cross these two orders with the express purpose of distinguishing them. To see why, a brief sketch of Anderson's critique of Thompson is useful. Althusserian accounts of historical agency, Thompson argues, overlook the crucial role of class experience in the process of self-making because it is "through the missing term 'experience' that structure is transmuted into process" (E. Thompson, 362). Anderson summarizes the strategy behind Thompson's use of the term "experience" here, connecting it to the double colloquial sense of the word.[42] Experience is the affective consequence of passing events—"the mental and emotional response, whether of an individual or a social group, to many interrelated events or to many repetitions of the same kind of event" (P. Anderson, 199). It is also the result of "practical acquaintance" and trial. This latter meaning evokes the sense of "experiment" that the word "experience" held in the nineteenth century, associated with wisdom and habitual practice. For Thompson, experience has been "generated in 'material life', has been structured in class ways, and hence 'social being has determined 'social consciousness' . . . [and] for any living generation, in any 'now', the ways in which they 'handle' experience defies prediction and escapes from any narrow definition of determination" (E. Thompson, 393). Thus Thompson deploys the two senses of experience, shifting from singular to group consciousness, in order to reveal the real animation within the apparently automatic processes of histori-

cal change. And Anderson takes Thompson to task for this: for ro-
manticizing the Marxist paradox of historical agency by "transferring the virtues and powers" of the rational, reflective, and controlling order of experience to the emotional, immediate, and passive.
Finessing the difference this way, Thompson produces a "simple dialectic between suffering and resistance whose whole movement is
internal to the subjectivity of the class" (P. Anderson, 30).

If Thompson drifts unconsciously between these senses of "experience," as Anderson argues, "beast with five fingers" stories mix
them deliberately, compressing the diachronic process of "handling"
events into the lyric "now" of its reading effect. They do this in
order to probe the disparity between the two orders of experience.
The results are anarchic on several levels. As in Keats's poem, moments of uncanny recognition precipitated by the "beast with five
fingers" remain belated and helplessly retrospective. To come to
consciousness in these stories is to come to consciousness of oneself
as "handled" rather than handling; furthermore, the affective experience in which the self is made, for Thompson and Engels, becomes in these stories the handle for such social manipulations.
Thus, the interest of these stories is less how or whether a person
can effect historical change, than the politics behind the division of
experience on which claims for or against historical change are
staked.

Joseph Sheridan Le Fanu's "Ghost Stories of the Tiled House"
offers the subtlest and most illuminating account of the function of
such horrified recognitions, as they operate both within the narrative and at the level of textual effect. In these two tales, the moment
of shocked recognition, in which the self emerges as the source of
"unforeseen effects and uncontrolled forces," does the work of a deterministic class system. It sustains a reductive and destructive division of intellectual labor between classes. At the same time, it offers
a critique of such divisions, carrying the oppressive experience of
being "handled" across class boundaries in a subtle fantasy of revenge and pointing out the unequal distribution of the shock and
entertainment offered by ghost stories. More vividly than the later
writers, Le Fanu demonstrates the peculiar way such moments ap-

peal beyond the frame of immediate historical context, while at the same time insisting on the immediacy of that context.

Domestic Service, Amusement, and the Master's Touch

> Alongside of modern evils, a whole series of inherited evils oppress us, arising from the passive survival of antiquated modes of production, with their inevitable train of social and political anachronisms. We suffer not only from the living, but from the dead. *Le mort saisit le vif!*
>
> —Karl Marx, Preface to *Capital*

The trope that resolved toward the turn of the century into a vehicle for mechanical and industrial estrangement emerged from domestic Gothic: in particular, fiction concerned with the increasingly alienated relations of domestic service. Le Fanu's paired tales of the haunting of the Tiled House, which first appeared as chapters 8 and 9 of *The House by the Churchyard: A Souvenir of Chapelizod* (1861–63), deploy their ghosts in this manner, presenting a Gothic analysis of labor relations. The stories are structurally and thematically connected to the novel that sprawls around them, but very obliquely. Indeed, they seem designed to set the scene and displace the social tensions that the novel opens with and looks back from: the disturbing transformation of Chapelizod from a pastoral suburb to a grim factory town.[43] Yet the alienations of an industrial economy, which would seem to be left behind with the narrator's departure from the present, surface in the domestic arrangements of the Tiled House: in the anxieties felt by a servant-employing class at the loss of control that delegated labor entails; in the uncertain dependencies of servants on the fortunes of an employer; in the intellectual division of labor between servants and their masters. As one would expect from a Gothic account of labor relations, these stories call into question the essential differences between employers and employed. They capsize the experience of rational control and orderly existence characterized as "mastery"—and define it as a fantastic and nefarious ideal. But surprisingly, they offer little like the charged glimpse of factory injury in Du Boisgobey or the macabre subtext of Jacobs. Instead of declaring the central role of serving classes in the organization of society or advancement of history, they challenge the underlying presumption of labor as explicable, rational action. Conjuring detached, inexplicable, ghostly hands, they mock the commonplace that labor relations can be systematically analyzed to reveal the causal connections between authority, agent, instrument, and product.

In a seminal essay on agency in the novel, Bruce Robbins describes the division of intellectual labor prevailing in mid-Victorian domestic relations. He quotes George Eliot's short essay "Servant's Logic" (1865) to epitomize the proverbial subrationality of domestic servants. According to Eliot's comic but repressive scenarios, servants' logic is digressive, associative, and emotional. Rational communication with one's domestic employees is worse than useless:

> Reason about things with your servants, consult them, give them the suffrage and you produce no other effect in them than a sense of anarchy in the house, a suspicion of irresoluteness in you, the most opposed to that spirit of order and promptitude which can alone enable them to fill their places well and make their lives respectable.[44]

Reminding us of the commonplace use of domestic servants as "handy representative figures of the working classes in general," Robbins traces the complex set of anxieties worked out in Eliot's essay: concerns about the enfranchisement of industrial workers, their growing power since the Industrial Revolution, and the rational intelligibility of the historical progress that they threaten anarchically to interrupt (B. Robbins, 86). If servants' logic is unintelligible, those in authority are nevertheless profoundly dependent on their labor: "We may look to the next century for the triumph of our ideas, but it is impossible to look there for our dinners," Eliot writes (Pinney, 391–92). As Robbins shows, the apparatus of rational advancement is here comically, but necessarily, at odds with the actions that sustain it; Eliot advocates abandoning the principle of rational explanation for direct command, if one is to obtain the desired results from one's cook (Pinney, 88).

The two stories embedded in *The House by the Churchyard* slyly

overturn these precepts. The novel, published serially during the
first years of Fenianism, takes up the complex relations of employers, employed, land agents, and leasers within the context of the
emergence of modern Irish nationalism. Le Fanu grew up an
Anglican, early supporting and later rejecting the nationalist movements; his ambivalent and changing feelings are recorded in the
editorials of the *Dublin University Magazine*, which he owned and
edited for a time. He cultivated a difficult mixture of audiences:
the small, Anglo-Irish, Protestant readership of the magazine, in
which *The House by the Churchyard* first appeared, and the more lu-
crative London market for which he reprinted it with less success
than hoped for.[45] The ghost stories embedded in the early chapters
of the novel thus seem both as abstract as fairy tales and strikingly
local. They weave specifically Irish conditions of dispossession into
the popular fare of the folk tale. For the latter, they particularly
evoke the Hand of Glory tradition, with its plots of invasion and
theft and its history of literary appropriation and marketing—
both of which suit the reading traps Le Fanu sets for his mixed
audience.

The two stories follow similar narrative patterns. They frame
anecdotes about the Tiled House ghosts with long preambles that
concern the transmission of incredible stories by servants. Although
only the second story describes the ghost of a hand, they should be
read as a diptych concerned with spectral labor relations. The first
story details the Gothic experience of service defined by communication with an impossible master; the second reduces sober, rational, middle-class employers—who first insist "that some domestic traitor held the thread of the conspiracy" perpetrated by a
mysterious hand—to the terrified, credulous, and enthralled condition of their servants. Together, the diptych challenges the division
of intellectual labor described in "Servant's Logic." These stories
suggest that "anarchy in the house" originates in this division itself,
and they implicate the servant-employing class that maintains it.
Servant's logic takes over the Tiled House, but not—as the master
first supposes—in organized revolution. Rather, it reproduces the
conditions of service pervasively in the form of dominating, self-

estranging Gothic terror. What is estranged from the servants in the Tiled House—and then from their masters—is the sense, logic, or rationale that animates their actions. The ghostly hand comes to symbolize that logic: first as the servants experience it, second as their experience is extended to the skeptical employers, and third as it extends—through the complex trope of amusement—to us as rational readers.

The first tale of the Tiled House opens on a quiet domestic scene that establishes the dialectic of master and servant George Eliot describes. Old Sally the nurse lulls her young mistress Lilias to sleep at Lilias's request, with tales of the dead earl's haunted residence: "And now, Sally, I'm safe in bed. Stir the fire, my old darling. . . . And tell me all about the Tiled House again, and frighten me out of my wits" (Le Fanu, 398). This is the only real service Sally still offers, for as the story tells us in its opening lines, Lilias no longer needs her attentions; she "only troubled the good old creature enough to prevent her thinking herself grown old and useless" (397). The stories Sally tells are not frightening, for in addition to this gentle, half-affectionate devaluation of her labor, the narrator emphasizes her "garrulous" credulity and aimless style. Sally's young mistress "sometimes listened with a smile, and sometimes lost a good five minutes together of her gentle prattle" (397) while "good old Sally, whose faith in such matters was a religion, went off over the well-known ground in a gentle little amble—sometimes subsiding into a walk as she approached some special horror, and pulling up altogether" (398). Faith of a more powerful kind maintains its rational presence in the background of these dilations and digressions, as Lilias falls asleep: "For there was no danger while old Sally sat knitting there by the fire, and the sound of the rector's mounting upon his chairs, as was his wont, and taking down and putting up his books in the study beneath, though muffled and faint, gave evidence that that good and loving influence was awake and busy" (397).

Sally's tales fail to scare, not because they are not intrinsically frightening, but because the narrator sets the scene with such assurances of the lovable errancy of the old nurse. Yet these repeated assertions suggest a disturbing subtext in their very alignment of employer's affection and servant's credulity. They remind us that Sally's continued place remains a matter of fondness and forbearance on the part of her mistress, something over which the servant has limited control and which has little value in other employment. Despite the domestic coziness of this opening scene, it is precisely the uncertain dependencies of Sally's condition that return to haunt the Tiled House, in the person of the ghostly earl. Le Fanu offhandedly calls Sally's story a "parable," slipping the word unobtrusively into a description of windy special effects on the night of the earl's death (399), but its didactic connotations resonate. The ghost stories Sally tells suggest a cautionary relation between the vague financial "troubles" that beset the earl and anxiety of the servants who await his return. If the master's "troubles [are] nearly over," as the earl predicts with unconscious irony on the night of his death, the troubles of his staff intensify with this event (399). As if to emphasize this point, the earl's ghost almost exclusively haunts servants: first the butler and manservant who admit it into the house, and then two housemaids, one of whom later dies of fright.

The way the earl's ghost haunts his servants, precipitating encounters similar to those described by Eliot in "Servant's Logic," underlines their dangerous dependency. What Le Fanu describes is the mirror image of Eliot's scene: cautious, reasoned servants caught in a communication crisis with an irrational, incomprehensible master. The earl's letters are cryptic, his words garbled, and his manner terrifyingly self-absorbed; he wanders unpredictably, "tumbling about boxes and pulling open drawers and talking and sighing to himself" (400). He is insistent but unintelligible, immune to delicate deflections or reasonable protest, and encounters with him are both frightening and humiliating. In the central encounter, the ghost approaches a housemaid's bed, in a creepy parody of the seductive master, just as she is about to fall asleep:

> In he comes, a fine man, in a sort of loose silk morning-dress an' no wig, but a velvet cap on, and to the windy with him quiet and aisy, and she makes a turn in the bed to let him know there was some one there, thinking he'd go away, but instead of that, over he comes to the side of the bed, looking very bad, and says something to her—but his

speech was thick and queer, like a dummy's that id be trying to spake—and she grew very frightened, and says she, "I ask your honour's pardon, sir, but I can't hear you right," and with that he stretches up his neck high out of his cravat, turning his face up towards the ceiling, and—grace between us and harm!—his throat was cut across like another mouth, wide open, laughing at her. (400–401)

Le Fanu takes his story on a humorous turn here that works subtly to ironize the reader's perception of the ludicrous even as it pokes fun at Old Sally. Sally's well-timed interjection—"grace between us and harm!"—reflects folk superstition that sounds comically like the faith that protects Lilias. We can't help smiling, but as we do, Le Fanu makes it clear that the aesthetics of improbable melodrama are inflected by the decorum of class difference. Indeed, the terrified housemaid is funny because she remains unfailingly polite; she fears to insult the ghost as much as misunderstand him. Yet, though her protest is genuine (not the polite incomprehension that a maid might pretend in order to deflect such advances), it does not protect her. The burden of carrying out unintelligible demands, and the dependency that does not permit her to object, depart, or send him away sends her into hysterical, staring immobility. Within six weeks of this encounter, Old Sally tells us in conclusion, the maid wasted away into fever and death.

Thus, the first turn of Le Fanu's screw is the ghostly earl himself, whose behavior when dead appears to follow the pattern of his life: always already absent and inexplicable, the burden of which mysterious existence is passed on in the anxious uncertainty of his servants. The second is a trap for the amused reader: one that provokes amusement and having done so, calls us to task for feeling it. As we are entertained by the maid's encounter, so we are aligned with the relationship between Lilias and her dependent storyteller, Old Sally. The earl's wide open smile, wickedly anticipating our own, associates the audience with the "shame and guilt" that keeps him walking. When Le Fanu slyly lampoons our amusement in this ghostly smile he also implies, more seriously, that our disbelief is implicated in the housemaid's humiliation—as if the presumption that her experience is incredible animates the earl's ghost, haunting her. Indeed, as a narrative device, the housemaid's reaction serves to lend the earl more substance: in aesthetic terms, it shifts the burden of his irrational and improbable existence to his servant by emphasizing her submissive credulity in the place of his unlikely apparition. As with the sensational reporting of the attack on Pierre B., or the punning grasp of the letter of the text in Keats's poem, her shocked response is offered as a textual effect. But in this case, Le Fanu's interest is specifically the economics of that effect. Where Keats uses the trope of the dead hand to reflect on the conversion of personal history to literary subjectivity—and the literary success attendant on that conversion—Le Fanu emphasizes the transaction between reader and writer that enables such success. Thus, the bedroom scene produces an aesthetic division of labor, along lines of class, that it also indicts. The sensational details of the housemaid's fatal illness suggest a melodramatic, but also genuinely dark, conclusion for Le Fanu's readers: that it is the dependency of her role as irrational servant—and our complicit pleasure in it—that humiliates her into a feverish death. The mix of terror and seduction in this scene reminds us of the pervasive eroticization of class transgression in contemporary fiction, from *Pamela* to the *Turn of the Screw*.[46] Yet if, as Robbins shows, "the collapse of class otherness is erotically charged with pleasure as well as negatively charged with threat" (B. Robbins, 201), Le Fanu directs our attention to the polyvalence of that pleasure, its unequal consequences, and most interestingly, to its production and exchange.

The second of the "Ghost Stories of the Tiled House" takes place a generation later, bringing a respectable middle-class family into the Tiled House and confirming the essentially bourgeois subtext of the service relations in the first tale. Charles de Cresserons, the narrator of *The House by the Churchyard*, excerpts a letter from his aunt: "dated late in the autumn of 1753," which "gives a minute and curious relation" of a dispute between the heir's steward, Lord Castlemallard, and a Mr. Alderman Harper of Highstreet, Dublin, over the lease of the Tiled House (Le Fanu, 401). Acting for his daughter and son-in-law, Alderman Harper agrees to a lease of the house and furnishes it for them:

Mr. and Mrs. Prosser came there some time in June, and after having parted with a good many servants in the interval, she made up her mind that she could not live in the house, and her father waited on Lord Castlemallard and told him plainly that he would not take out the lease because the house was subjected to annoyances which he could not explain. In plain terms, he said it was haunted, and that no servants would live there more than a few weeks, and that after what his son-in-law's family had suffered there, . . . [he should] be excused from taking a lease of it. (402)

Lord Castlemallard refuses to release Mr. Harper and files "a bill in the Equity side of Exchequer to compel [him] to perform his contract." But the alderman supplies Castlemallard "seven long affidavits" in support of his side and "rather than compel him to place them upon the file of the court," Lord Castlemallard settles. "I am sorry the cause did not proceed at least far enough to place upon the records of the court the very authentic and unaccountable story which Miss Rebecca relates," says the narrator (Le Fanu, 402). Here the incredible account stops just short of encroaching on formal evidentiary procedures of the court by presenting a "cause" that cannot be explained—but it does succeed in breaking the lease. As Robbins argues, to acknowledge the authority of servants' experience is, within this framework, to admit that inexplicable and apparently purposeless actions drive institutions and events (B. Robbins, 86). And, as the story goes on to show, such actions force the rational and "hard-headed" Mr. Prosser to admit an alternative explanation when he literally admits the ghost.

The Prosser household is haunted by a "puffy," "pudgy" hand: "rather short, but handsomely formed, and white and plump . . . not a very young hand, but one aged, somewhere above forty"—as Mrs. Prosser conjectures when she first sees it, lurking on a windowsill (Le Fanu, 402). The "honest, sober" cook—a witness suited to disrupt Eliot's conventions of lucidity—describes it as a "fat, but aristocratic-looking hand" after finding it moving slowly up and down a window pane, "as if feeling carefully for some inequality in its surface" (403). The precise but oddly neutral vocabulary of touch that characterizes the actions of the hand here sets off slight resonances between words like "aristocratic" and "inequality" that might come into the same field of diction in another context. But what such resonances call attention to, instead, is the work required to pull them into a meaningful, argumentative group. As the story proceeds, the actions of the hand call for and frustrate such interpretive analysis with increasing violence:

> After this, for a great many nights, there came at first a low, and afterwards an angry rapping, as it seemed with a set of clenched knuckles, at the back-door. And the servant-man would not open it, but called to know who was there; and there came no answer, only a sound as if the palm of the hand was placed against it, and drawn slowly from side to side, with a sort of soft, groping motion. (403)

This hand is as insistent and opaque as Cathy's icy hand in *Wuthering Heights*. It moves around the house as if seeking entry, first at the back door, then at the window, and finally at the hall door, rapping, "sometimes very low and furtive, like a clandestine signal, and at others sudden and so loud as to threaten the breaking of the pane" (403). The character of the "summons" keeps changing: first a soft and regular beating, "with the flat of the hand," next an impatient "patting," which "assumed the rhythm and emphasis of a series of double-knocks" (404). All of these behaviors appear to be meaningful, and the urgent, inimical purpose they suggest calls for translation or decoding. What makes them frightening, however, is that they remain both imperative and arbitrary. They appear *as if* designed, always in simile: "like a clandestine signal," "as if in search," "as it might be with the hollow of a hand" (404). But they evidence no explicit purpose. Despite the specific detail of these encounters, the ghostly hand absolutely resists rational explication.

This is especially evident in the affidavits of haunting that the alderman gathers. These are based on ghostly evidence that mimics the increasingly popular forensic practice of manual identification. When the hand declares its presence in the house by leaving an impression "in the dust of the 'little parlour' table" for the servants to find, Mr. Prosser conducts an experiment. "[The servants] were by this time all nervous, and some of them half crazed, about the hand" (405). And though he, too, has by this time lost his peace of mind, Mr. Prosser puts the impression to a legalistic examination.

He directs every member of the household to make similar palm prints on the table,

> and his "affidavit" deposed that the formation of the hand so impressed differed altogether from those of the living inhabitants of the house, and corresponded exactly with that of the hand seen by Mrs. Prosser and by the cook.
>
> Whoever or whatever the owner of that hand might be, they all felt this subtle demonstration to mean that it was declared he was no longer out of doors, but had established himself in the house. (405)

Immediately, the hand advances a hostile investigation of its own—a campaign for inimical, oppressive control. Having laid siege to the house, it now intrudes, working its way into closets and bedrooms, and finally impressing itself horribly—by a kind of hypnotic trance—into the minds and souls of Mrs. Prosser and her children. In this way, the ghost forces the Prossers into an uncertain condition remarkably like the wasting ailment of the earl's housemaid: oppressed and disabled by inexplicable but undeniable demands. Prosser's palm-print test bears special relevance to this breakdown of the proper boundaries between class experience. I shall have more to say in the next chapter about the ways in which technologies like Bertillonage, finger- or palm-printing were used to fix social boundaries—particularly the differences between property owners, dependents, and property itself. For the moment, it is useful to note that historically, those printed were defined as both disenfranchised and criminal: natives of colonial India, Indians in South America, black slaves, and later political subversives in the United States. Ironically, Prosser's examination disturbs such clear alignments of social character; if his experiment proves the evil agency definitively to be other, it also, paradoxically, establishes it to be in the house. Despite his suspicions, Prosser's disenfranchised dependents are not the immediate source of hostile opposition; on the contrary, as it turns out, they are we, and we they. Thus, as the alderman's affidavit reprises that perennial nineteenth-century complaint about not being able to keep good domestic help, it also collapses the social distinctions that the complaint sustains. The Prossers suffer both because they cannot keep their servants and because they inhabit—

are made to perform—the irrational role otherwise delegated to servants.

In its ironic treatment of evidence like the palm print, "Ghost Stories of the Tiled House" straddles the fence between the Radcliffean tradition of Gothic—bent on exposing the machinery of the supernatural—and the antienlightenment tradition of Walpole and Lewis. Sally's tales are based on eyewitness accounts, in particular, the accounts of a second housemaid who survived her encounters with the dead earl. If Old Sally's tales are "marvels, fabulae, what our ancestors call winter's tales—which gathered details from every narrator and dilated in the act of narration" (Le Fanu, 401), yet, the narrator teases, "Under all this smoke there smouldered just a little spark of truth—an authenticated mystery, for the solution of which some of my readers may possibly suggest a theory, though I confess I can't" (401). Prosser himself maintains the only theory that the tale explicitly advances, "believing that some domestic traitor held the thread of the conspiracy" (404). This is a theory that has the weight of literary history—in the form of countless haunted Irish Big Houses—behind it, and though the story ultimately rejects it strongly, it is worth pursuing in order to understand why.[47]

Read in the context of Eliot's essay, Prosser's theory explains the haunting as an allegory of Irish dispossession and disenfranchisement: the working Irish hand, its estrangement figured in a ghostly synecdoche, retaliates against those who exploit its labor and alienate its possessions. Julian Moynahan cites a lively contemporary anecdote, from Summerville and Ross's collection *Some Experiences of an Irish R. M.* (1899). The experience of one Major Yeates gives a sense of the currency of Prosser's gloss. Locals encourage him to believe they are ghosts so they can more easily poach and steal on his property.

In this context, haunting connotes both the dispossession and the social invisibility of the landless, native Irish. While, to be haunted, as Yeates and Prosser are, is to be confirmed in a position of authority and power. The proper explanation of Yeates's ghosts—as Jonathan Arac writes of Dickensian specters—is social: "[They] arise from displacements in social relations: undervaluing close relationships or overvaluing distant ones" (Arac, 127). By explaining the hand as a harbinger of anarchy in the house, Prosser debunks the haunting, confirms his position as master, and paradoxically admits a motive for revenge. The retaliation coded by haunting is action outside the proper rule of law and hence anarchic—yet action with a logic—the logic of social displacement and restitution. Thus, the hand that invades the Tiled House reverses the relation Canetti draws between "the fear of a sudden and unexpected clutch out of the darkness" and the social "distances" or hierarchies it dictates ("the house in which he shuts himself and his property, the positions he holds, the rank he desires").[48] Those distances produce that clutch and condition the fear of it.

In this context, it is fitting that the hand appears to Prosser's servants precisely when they are engaged in domestic duties: cooking and unpacking delft.[49] And at first glance, it seems to act out precisely the alien and powerful mastery characterized in Marx's early description of estranged labor as a kind of social uncanny: "Thus, if the product of his labour, his labour *objectified*, is for him an *alien*, hostile, powerful object independent of him, then his position towards it is such that someone else is master of this object, someone who is alien, hostile, powerful, and independent of him" (Tucker, 78).

However, its fatness and puffiness suggest an unwholesome sensuality that links it to the ghostly earl, and its other qualities are exactly opposite to the characteristic signs of nineteenth-century labor: where the hands of domestics are red, these "aristocratic" hands are white; where domestics' hands are rough and chapped, these are soft.[50] To the extent that its actions are characterized distinctly, they seem directed by the master: aimless, insistent, unreasoning, but carrying a sense of inimical authority. Thus, by associating the hand with the earl's ghost and explicitly discrediting Prosser's hypothesis, Le Fanu begins to complicate the usual patterns of colonial haunting: to be the master is to haunt, as much as be haunted.

Having pursued Prosser's theory, it's important to remember

that he is wrong about the hand in several ways. Whether one interprets like Marx or Eliot, labor—estranged and natural—is imagined to be in service to some person or authority. So a hand that moves stealthily on a windowsill or leaves marks on a parlor table must express some aim and interest. Yet, the story quite firmly discredits both Prosser's theory—there are, after all, no domestic traitors—and his assumptions—devoting considerable exposition to showing that the actions of this hand cannot be traced definitively to any person or purpose. Instead, gleefully extending the experience of self-estrangement to both masters and servants, Le Fanu conjures up a condition in which reasonable purpose and action cannot be linked through service relations. In fact, attempts to debunk the ghost ultimately make it more dangerous and less visible. Mr. Prosser finds this out when—angry with superstitious fools and certain he is about to accost the harrasser—he opens the door and gives it entry:

> Looking, he saw nothing; but his arm was jerked up oddly, as it might be with the hollow of a hand, and something passed under it, with a kind of gentle squeeze. The servant neither saw nor felt any thing, and did not know why his master looked back so hastily, and shut the door with so sudden a slam. (Le Fanu, 404)

In its insistent, noisy harassment, the hand acts out precisely the combination of unreasoning but powerful agency that Eliot ascribes to domestic servants—an effect that has no tangible cause. Thus, the legal cause that begins with a familiar domestic complaint—we cannot keep the house because we cannot keep the servants—reveals a more unsettling challenge to the fundamental causalities inscribed in service relations. The Prossers' experience of the ghostly hand in the second tale of the Tiled House becomes more and more like the fearful uncertainty of the hysterical maid in the first tale. In this way, the paired stories stage a subtle revenge against the division of intellectual labor epitomized in "Servant's Logic." The condition of irrational existence, the recognition of self as the source of "unforeseen effects and uncontrolled forces," crosses class boundaries, offering a revised syllogism of the domestic occult. To be the master is both to haunt and be haunted: to experience events as a servant. In this sense, the ghostly hand emerges from the division of rational labor itself—the split between reasoning intention and unreasoned performance entrenched by the servant-owning class—a division apparent in the earl's haunting laughter and the housemaid's submissive wasting away.

When hands take on a separate life, as independent parts of the world of objects rather than dependent parts of the body, they occult the lines of guilt and responsibility, making ethical analysis of their actions difficult. This is the charge—whether fleeting and oblique, as in *La Main Coupée*, or extended and direct, as in "The Monkey's Paw"—that the labor plots of severed-hand stories bring against the technological and social systems that produce workers as synecdochic hands. The most interesting and ethically complex versions of this charge are—like Le Fanu's pointed, ghostly grin—directed at the reader's own participation in this alienating economy. *Pudd'nhead Wilson*, Mark Twain's novel of fingerprint detection and twinning, directs precisely this kind of disturbing, humorous look back at relations of labor and service in the American slave economy still vestigially present in the 1890s. Twain's objects, characteristically, are both reader and author. Invoking the bloody daggers, ghosts, and murderous hands of Jacobean revenge tragedy, Twain employs the imagery of the dead hand in order to expose the structures of revenge and uncanny return inherent in American notions of property relations. For Twain, the newly evolving sciences of forensic identification and motor neurology that seek to explain and codify bodily evidence internalize rather than resolve anxieties about volition and identity posed by race slavery. The principle of self-possession in these discourses—epitomized by the analysis of fingerprints and motor control—absorbs a peculiar notion of involuntary action from the legal and economic system that defines certain actors—slaves—as nonpersons. This principle is itself internalized by the emerging American justice system, through the institution of the Fingerprint Division of J. Edgar Hoover's Federal Bureau of Investigation. In the complicated rhetoric used by Hoover and the forensic professionals before him—all deeply invested in *Pudd'nhead Wilson*—Twain's analysis of the conditions of self-possession moves like a persistent and compelling ghost.

Chapter Five

Involuntary Confession: Pudd'nhead Wilson and Law-Enforcement Mythology

> There is no prejudice to be overcome in procuring these most trustworthy sign-manuals, no vanity to be pacified, no untruths to be guarded against.
>
> —Francis Galton, *Finger Prints*

> Property is nothing more than the mind's enhancement of the body's limitation.
>
> —Patricia Williams, *The Alchemy of Race and Rights*

In *Fingerprinting: A Manual of Identification*, 1941, Charles Edward Chapel recounts the 1903 case of Will West and William West: a benchmark case of confused identities that appears in numerous histories of forensic identification. Published about a decade earlier, *Pudd'nhead Wilson*—Mark Twain's novel of fingerprint detection and cradle switching—seems both to anticipate and explain the social and legal logic of the West case history. Both the prison story and the novel mark epiphanies in the internal history of the Federal Bureau of Investigation's Identification Division. In law-enforcement folklore, Twain's novel helped transform the popular conception of fingerprint evidence as a hoax or fad. Its courtroom scenes seemed to affirm the transcendence of fingerprinting over earlier kinds of physical identification, and this affirmation carried the aesthetic and cultural force of an authentic American voice. What Twain's writing affirms for the FBI, the West anecdote confirms: the essential and physical nature of identity. Yet both sto-

ries trouble the certainties they seem to exemplify. Together they illuminate the way material traces of criminal actions were reimagined at the turn of the twentieth century as "involuntary confessions." That is, as evidence free from willful deception that proves
willful action. In the works considered below, Mark Twain draws on
forensic conventions of agency to expose the contradictions in contemporary notions of effective action. For Twain the metaphor of
the body social posed particular difficulties in the constitution of
authorial agency, difficulties expressed through fictions of physical
disability, racial exclusion, and self-alienation. Together, *Pudd'nhead
Wilson*, its sibling story *Those Extraordinary Twins*, and Twain's wry
self-analysis in "How to Tell a Story" offer deeply skeptical accounts
of the connection between intention and act. They disrupt any easy
continuity between an acting person, the gestures of his or her
hands, and the material traces hands leave. In doing so, they call into
question the fictions that support the forensic theory and practice of
fingerprinting: that the unchanging physical marks of fingerprints
admit no interpretive error or interest; that the ability willfully to
control one's actions is an essential physical faculty.

Chapel's version of the West case, something between re-
portage and fictional account, is striking enough to quote at length:

> In 1903, Will West, a Negro, was committed to the U.S. Penitentiary
> at Leavenworth, Kansas, where he was measured and photographed
> according to the Bertillon system of personal identification, then in
> general use throughout the civilized world. During his physical ex-
> amination, the clerks who were measuring him said that he looked
> familiar, and asked West if he had not been confined there before, but
> he insisted that this was his first time in Leavenworth. At the end of
> the examination, he was assigned a prison number, 3426, and was
> then taken to the chief record clerk.
>
> "West," said the chief clerk, "you've been here before; there is no
> use denying it; we have your photograph and description here in our
> file of Bertillon records."
>
> "No, sir, boss," answered West, "I ain't been here before."
>
> The chief clerk turned to the records, searched through the cards
> for a few minutes, and then handed West a card bearing a photograph
> which very closely resembled that just taken, and the name "William
> West," with the prison number of 2626.

"Do you still deny that you've been here before?" asked the chief clerk.

"No, sir, just like I tells you, I ain't been here before and I ain't had no picture taken before today, but that sure does look like me."

Puzzled, the chief clerk turned the card over and found written on the back the words, "Committed to this institution on September 9, 1901; Charge—Murder."

This entry meant but one thing, that there was another man with practically the same Bertillon measurements and with almost the same facial features who was still confined in the prison, for the old record card did not show any statement that the prisoner had been released. The prisoner, William West, number 2626, was sent for and when he arrived at the record office he was compared with Will West, the new prisoner, number 3426. When they put on hats, the experienced identification experts could not tell one from the other, but without their hats one of the older men thought that he could distinguish between the two men by a very slight difference in the shape of their heads, although this difference was one which would not be reflected in the Bertillon measurements and could not be scientifically measured or described.[1]

The anecdote concludes by demonstrating that the fingerprints of the two William Wests were distinctly different. Chapel reproduces photos of the prisoners with their print records to illustrate this point. Of the different versions of this story, Chapel's is the longest and most dramatic, and it diverges from other accounts in minor details. But the moral of this case in all its versions is the same: the superiority of fingerprint identification over the Bertillon system of anthropometry.[2] Despite their variances, the West Bertillon records appeared to describe one "William West" until comparison of fingerprints showed them to be the measurements of two. In what had become the celebratory formula, Chapel concludes, "Where photographs and body measurements had failed, fingerprints had succeeded because no two men ever have the same fingerprints, and fingerprints do not change from the cradle to the grave" (Chapel, 13).

For the Federal Bureau of Investigation in particular, this story takes a central place in the myth of origin of the Identification Division, the core agency from which J. Edgar Hoover later built the FBI. A synopsis of the case (using what appear to be the same photos that Chapel uses) introduces the FBI pamphlet *Fingerprint Identification*, which offers a brief history of fingerprinting and of the Identification Division (Figure 13).[3] A wall-sized version of the synopsis graces the visitor circuit of the Hoover Building in Washington, D.C. The West story is transmitted by the FBI in the mode of folklore: in an anonymously compiled digest, reprinted from pamphlet to pamphlet. No source materials are documented in any of the versions I have been able to locate—including Chapel's and the FBI's. Yet most of the accounts credit the warden of Leavenworth with immediately understanding the implications of the clerk's misrecognition of West and with taking prompt action. Chapel's version concludes when the warden applies for official permission to adopt fingerprinting in place of Bertillonage, setting a new law-enforcement standard.

Pudd'nhead Wilson precedes the official institution of this new forensic relation between agency and identity by about a decade, yet it has a powerful proleptic quality. It anatomizes the difficulties in managing fingerprint evidence—recording, storing, indexing, and transmitting prints—that permit the willful manipulation and careless misreadings that haunt case histories and detective novels in the decades to follow. The novel unfolds the changeling history of a slave child and the master's son. Both "blue-eyed and flaxen curled," they are switched in the cradle by their respective mother and nurse, Roxana (one-sixteenth "black" and equally blond), in order that her son not be sold down the river. Woven into this story is the plot of the eponymous young lawyer, David Wilson, who—in the course of pursuing his fingerprinting hobby—solves a murder committed by the false heir, Tom Driscoll, and reveals the switch. This detective story precipitates a dramatic trial scene, in which the efficacy of forensic fingerprinting is eloquently demonstrated and then ironically effaced: Tom Driscoll is pardoned on a technicality in order to be sold down the river to recoup damages to the estate he "usurped."

The influence of *Pudd'nhead Wilson* on the developing institution of fingerprinting in the FBI depends in part on a strategically

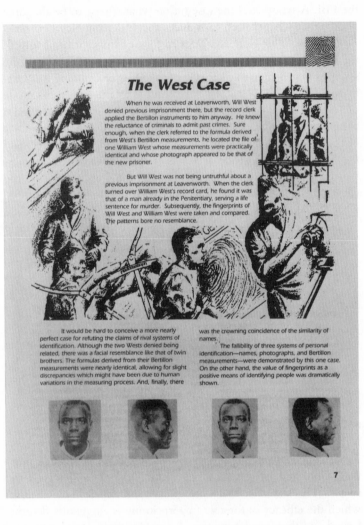

The West Case

When he was received at Leavenworth, Will West denied previous imprisonment there, but the record clerk applied the Bertillon instruments to him anyway. He knew the reluctance of criminals to admit past crimes. Sure enough, when the clerk referred to the formula derived from West's Bertillon measurements, he located the file of one William West whose measurements were practically identical and whose photograph appeared to be that of the new prisoner.

But Will West was not being untruthful about a previous imprisonment at Leavenworth. When the clerk turned over William West's record card, he found it was that of a man already in the Penitentiary, serving a life sentence for murder. Subsequently, the fingerprints of Will West and William West were taken and compared. The patterns bore no resemblance.

It would be hard to conceive a more nearly perfect case for refuting the claims of rival systems of identification. Although the two Wests denied being related, there was a facial resemblance like that of twin brothers. The formulas derived from their Bertillon measurements were nearly identical, allowing for slight discrepancies which might have been due to human variations in the measuring process. And, finally, there was the crowning coincidence of the similarity of names.

The fallibility of three systems of personal identification—names, photographs, and Bertillon measurements—were demonstrated by this one case. On the other hand, the value of fingerprints as a positive means of identifying people was dramatically shown.

7

FIGURE 13. The West Case. From *Fingerprint Identification*, U.S. Department of Justice, 1991.

narrow reading of Twain's trial scene. Like the West case, *Pudd'nhead Wilson* addresses the descriptive and definitive limitations of scientific measures of difference. Where FBI myth, however, confidently answers uncertainties about physical identity by recourse to newer technology, David Wilson's tragicomic, successful failure in fingerprint detection contests the essential nature of the identity that technology confers.[4] Wilson succeeds because he finds a murderer and simultaneously proves that his fad is truly a science. He fails because the murderer, shown to be a slave and redefined as property, is legally evacuated of moral agency. The fault, we learn, is in an "erroneous inventory" taken at the earlier death of his putative father, Percy Driscoll. The inventory failed to take account of Tom-as-property; had it done so, he might have been sold off earlier and the murder prevented.

What makes this legal reversal possible is not only the sophistic logic of race slavery, which denominates a class of individuals as nonpersons, but also the complicated status of prints themselves. Fingerprints are legal evidence of both the uniqueness and persistence of identity and of action that establishes physical presence. Most importantly, their efficacy in legal argument depends on their status as concomitant acts: the unwilled, careless by-products of the central actions in dispute (a stabbing or a forgery, for example). They register physical presence, the facts of certain gestures. But they record neither an intentional relation to their own impression nor evidence per se of the intentions behind the act that incidentally produces them (picking up a knife or pen). The moment that they enter into a plot of intentional creation they become suspect.[5] Thus, fingerprints signify a curious kind of involuntary agency: action necessarily amputated from intention. In *Pudd'nhead Wilson* and elsewhere, Twain meditates on the split between volition and agency that this differentiation within the notion of legal person depends on. His writings illuminate this split in a way that prepared contemporary law enforcement to recognize its usefulness in the West case. Yet Twain pursues imaginative consequences that early advocates of forensic fingerprinting could not envision and that legal precedent has since obscured: if the acts that define identity are involuntary, what sense of self do they produce? If a criminal cannot be said to intend the traces his hand leaves, whose intentions inhabit those traces and what kind of morality do they carry?

Twain suggests the direction of this last speculation when he makes the work of fingerprints a supplement and corrective to the erroneous inventory: the essential interests and structures of both accounting systems are institutional. Wilson's collection fulfills the promises of early advocates like Sir Francis Galton (from whose 1892 treatise *Finger Prints* Twain derives much of his technical language): his prints provide "the thoroughness of the differentiation of each man from all the rest of the human species [that] is multiplied to an extent far beyond the capacity of human imagination."[6] For Galton's peers Henry Faulds and Sir William Herschel, this promise spoke directly to problems of institutional control (specifically in the British colonial administration). Their work records crises of imposture and false witness, inflected by race, that both threaten emerging central bureaucracies and give them their reason and occasion.

Suggestively parallel stories of fraud and forensic resolution dominate the rhetoric of American law enforcement from the turn of the century into the late 1920s—the period in which innovations in law-enforcement administration were most intense. The emergence of a central federal law-enforcement bureaucracy in the 1920s and 1930s reflects what historians have described as the "organizational synthesis" of American institutions, which began in the late nineteenth century. Louis Galambos distills this process:

> Some of the most (if not the single most) important changes which have taken place in modern America have centered about a shift from small-scale, informal, locally or regionally oriented groups to large-scale, national, formal organizations. The new organizations are characterized by a bureaucratic structure of authority. The shift in organization cuts across the traditional boundaries of political, economic and social history. Businesses, reform groups, professional and labor organizations—all developed along somewhat similar lines.[7]

The crises of imposture long recognized as Twain's characteristic concern has a broad cultural context in these organizational shifts. Gillman, Michael Rogin, and others have shown the contradictions Twain finds in this science of identity; less attention has been paid to the institutional history of this science and his complicated relation to it.[8] *Pudd'nhead Wilson* illuminates the rhetorical continuity between those early experiments in forensic fingerprinting and the emerging bureaucracy of federal law enforcement. The concerns of Faulds and Herschel, translated into American terms in the West case, take national form in the speeches of J. Edgar Hoover and persist ghostily in early court precedents. Fingerprinting succeeded as a technology because it offered a theoretically pure, physical index of identity in the face of social and criminal imposture. As Twain's novel suggests, however, it succeeded as a forensic institution because of the interests it introduces in practice: specifically, because of the peculiar shift of agency and intention, from criminal to governing bureau, that it makes possible. Thus, Twain writes from a middle point ideologically, as well as historically. His ironic response to such crises of imposture, throughout the different works considered below, is mixed. He celebrates the new technology anxiously, suspicious of the institutional interests it serves, warily anticipating the felt presence of an emerging state. This suspicion propels Twain's interest in what it might feel like to inhabit a body that regularly performs the intentions of others. But it appears most clearly in his preoccupation with bodies that only evidence intention—write, testify, or confess—involuntarily. Twain's writings reflect and reflect on turn-of-the-century discourse of forensic identification, and they illuminate the way this odd form of involuntary agency has become naturalized in institutional practice and popular commonplace.

"Sign Manuals" and the Long Arm of the FBI

The last decade of the nineteenth century brought an explosion of forensic innovation in anthropometry and other scientific means of determining identity. Fingerprinting evolved out of scientific projects that were at once bureaucratic and ethnographic, finally displacing the unwieldy Bertillon system in America in the

first decade of the twentieth century. The earliest official, public—
and well-publicized—application of fingerprinting was instituted by
Sir William Herschel, British administrator of the Hooghly district
of Bengal. In 1859 Herschel drew up a contract for road construction with a "native," Rajyadhar Konai; "On impulse," he asked for
Konai's hand-impression in ink in lieu of signature—vaguely attributing his impulse to the conviction that Konai would feel mys-
tically and ritually bound to a document that bore the impression of
his hand. In the following years, as magistrate and collector in
Nuddea, Herschel took up fingerprinting as a direct response to
"the Indigo disturbances" in his district: "Violence, litigation, and
fraud; forgery and perjury were rampant," along with imposture in
the collection of pensions and the confirmation of leases.[9]
Recognizing its efficacy in verifying identity, he made several un-
successful efforts during his tenure to have his system officially established throughout India. From 1860 to 1913 Herschel collected
the "sign-manuals" (a card with ten finger prints) that later figured
as evidence in the work of Sir Francis Galton. Galton, a noted an-
thropologist, proponent of eugenics, and cousin of Charles Darwin,
was the first scientist to confirm by extensive analysis the two qualities that give fingerprints such efficacy in forensic use: the persistence of patterns throughout a person's life and their uniqueness.

Both Herschel's and Galton's analyses were deeply embedded
in the discourse of colonial bureaucracy. Galton's descriptive metaphors display an enthusiasm for neatly described boundaries and
contained world making: "We shall see that they form patterns,
considerable in size and of a curious variety of shape, whose boundaries can be firmly outlined, and which are little worlds in themselves" (Galton, 2).[10] Recalling Herschel's project, Galton sums up
the ambiguities of colonial identity that prompted his search for a
means of "differentiating between a man and his fellows":

> In civil as well as in criminal cases, the need of some such system is
> shown to be greatly felt in many of our dependencies; where the fea-
> tures of natives are distinguished with difficulty; where there is but lit-
> tle variety of surnames; where there are strong motives for prevarica-
> tion, especially connected with land-tenure and pensions, and a
> proverbial prevalence of unveracity. (14)

Herschel's own statement, published by Galton, is equally concerned with ambiguities of character determined by race: "The uniformity in the colour of hair, eyes, and complexion of the Indian races renders identification far from easy, and the difficulty of recording the description of an individual, so that he may afterwards be recognised, is very great. . . . Personation was most difficult to detect" (Galton, 152). As Herschel describes it in a letter to Galton, racial physiognomy and handwriting are alike "devoid of character and [give] but little help towards identification." The extent to which such troubling observations depend on the colonial appropriation and legal construction of land right is clear in the bemusement of Herschel's next paragraph: "The tenacity with which a native of India cleaves to his ancestral land, his innate desire to acquire more and more, and the obligation that accrues to him at birth of safeguarding that which has already been acquired, amounts to a religion, and passes the comprehension of the ordinary Western mind" (Galton, 150).

In our popular lexicon, the term "fingerprinting" reigns as a standard of forensic certainty that seems very far from these origins. It is sometimes adopted for DNA analysis, for example, because it imparts a sense of incontrovertibility that the newer technology still lacks. The discourse affirms an essential, immutable quality of identity. In displacing Bertillon's physical codes, fingerprints signify a kind of testimony that is irrefutable because it is both physically permanent and unwilled. In this they were found greatly superior to Bertillon measurements, which were vulnerable to various kinds of "trickery" on the part of the subject measured (Chapel, 16–17). Yet the use of "fingerprint" as a commonplace obscures uncertainties then and still present in forensic identification. If DNA "fingerprinting" cannot establish the absolute uniqueness of an individual, conventional fingerprinting has failed to provide the genetic determinants of descent and personality that Herschel and Galton sought. In practical terms, fingerprint files have always been as vulnerable as other kinds of physical evidence: at one time the federal prison in Leavenworth, Kansas, employed inmates to catalogue their Bertillon and fingerprint records. The fragility of physical evidence has led to ever more rigorous conventions of crime-scene preservation, and technical and management innovations have minimized error in the collection, distribution, and storage of prints. Nevertheless, trial use of fingerprints today still prompts questions about the security of prints in collection, transmission, and testing.

In both theory and practice, then, fingerprint identification developed in response to profound cultural anxieties about fraudulent representation and administrative authority. In order to resolve such epistemological crises as imposture and forgery, fingerprints were defined by forensic historians as outside the realm of human intention and control. For Henry Faulds, fingerprints are "nature-prints," for example.[11] Chapel opens his *Manual of Identification* with an epigraph from Job 37:7: "He sealeth up the hand of every man; that all men may know his work" (Chapel, 3). Here Chapel echoes many criminologists in attributing the persistence and uniqueness of fingerprints to an ultimately divine origin. Frederic Brayley's 1910 reference manual is more explicit:

> "God's finger-print language," the voiceless speech, and the indelible writing imprinted on the fingers, hand palms, and foot soles of humanity by the Allwise Creator for some good and useful purpose in the structure, regulation, and well being of the human body . . . and who shall say it is not part of the plan of the Creator for the ultimate elimination of crime by means of surrounding the evilly-disposed by safe-guards of prevention; and for the unquestionable evidence of identity.[12]

Likewise, in the history of jurisprudence no intentions except those of the law-enforcement apparatus are said to be involved in finger impressions. The analogy of fingerprinting to Fifth Amendment rights against self-incrimination is said to be false on exactly these grounds. Similarly, the notion that fingerprinting a suspect might constitute undue constraint or forced confession is rejected. According to *People v. Sallow* (New York, 1917), the earliest, widely referenced U.S. precedent:

> The requirement that the defendant's fingerprints be taken for the purpose of establishing identity is not objectionable in principle. There is neither torture nor volition nor chance of error. . . .

No volition—that is, no act of willing—on the part of the mind of the defendant is required. Finger prints of an unconscious person, or even a dead person are as accurate as are those of the living. . . . By the requirement that the defendant's finger prints be taken there is no danger that the defendant will be required to give false testimony. The witness does not testify. The physical facts speak for themselves; no fears, no hopes, no will of the prisoner to falsify or to exaggerate could produce or create a resemblance of her finger prints or change them in one line, and therefore there is no danger of error being committed or untruth told.[13]

In this finding, then, the court established an implicit association between the abstract nature of prints—persistent, unique, and free from the equivocations of false testimony or disguise—and their practical interpretation. Yet in forensic practice as well as in literary deployment fingerprints are relational indices, as Gillman, Rogin, and others have pointed out. They signify nothing in and of themselves except the possibility of structural similarity or difference. As Twain emphasizes in his courtroom scene, they are meaningful only in comparison to other prints. They are often fragile in transmission, vulnerable to their handling—to erasure, mislabeling, misindexing—but only significant if handled—"lifted," "rolled," "transferred," or "impressed." It is the exigencies of handling prints and the opportunities this handling offers that give latent prints their peculiar and powerful status: they define agency simultaneously in terms of individual and corporate persons.

The emerging technology of fingerprinting produced institutional conventions about the distribution of authority in American law enforcement that parallel the legal conventions of volition established in *People v. Sallow*. If no willful intervention by the criminal can alter fingerprint evidence, no insidious agency can mislead the proper operation of FBI personnel armed with this tool. This analogy emerges in decades of addresses and articles by J. Edgar Hoover, the passionate, aggressive force behind the bureaucratization of forensic identification. It involves several characteristic rhetorical moves: personification of the fingerprint; a hyperbolic appeal to heroic contest and demonization of the opponent (the "chieftains" of the law oppose "sob-sisters," "legal vermin," and "human rats"); and an allegory of law enforcement authority as manual prowess. Together, these tropes evoke a new sense of the presence of federal government, felt in the dominating pressure of the arm of the law.

Hoover's descriptions of fingerprints celebrate the involuntary nature of finger impressions. "That the finger ridges, man's immutable marks of identification—also have the capacity to leave their impressions as incontrovertible testimony that their possessor was once at a particular place and touched certain objects there seems providential—at least to the law enforcement officer."[14] But this logic is more slippery than it first appears: the apparent agency of providence is less important than the fact that finger ridges themselves leave the prints, with little relation to the intention and volition of "their possessor." Possession is imagined here as a relation of distance and alienation: finger ridges and the fingers that touch certain objects are set in subtle opposition on the basis of willful action. Further, the "persons" for whom fingerprints are truly instrumental, it turns out, are the officer and the law enforcement agency who employ them. In an address to the New York Chamber of Commerce in 1935, Hoover explicitly elaborated the transfer of control, from criminal to law enforcement agent, afforded by fingerprints:

> Thus the work goes on endlessly, protecting a winter resort from persons of bad reputation, keeping a police force clean, establishing the past of a criminal who seeks to plead a previously unsullied record— these fingerprints are silent policemen, on guard twenty-four hours of the day. What they do to strike fear into the heart of a criminal, they also can do to give peace of mind to the honest citizen.[15]

The colonialist anxiety about a clear separation between unknowable stranger and known self echoes in Hoover's isolationist nostalgia for a "local" security defined by self-evident criminality. Hoover's nostalgia reflects the rise of large and centralized national institutions and the erosion of social experience shaped by "island communities," to use historian Robert H. Wiebe's definitive phrase:[16]

> In times past . . . crime or the criminal was a more or less local issue. Our local or neighborhood criminal was known, his haunts could be

watched, his associates shadowed, the method and nature of the crime often bore within itself the recognizable identity of the criminal. . . . Every stranger was a marked man, every newcomer aroused suspicion.[17]

Thus, for Hoover, fingerprint technology answers the profound threat to this insular vision of America as a kind of Dawson's Landing, the fictional small town in which *Puddin'head Wilson* is set. The "chieftains of the army of law enforcement" staunchly battle against the wary criminals of today, whose world "offers almost endless means and channels of escape" (Hoover 1925, 1, 3). These scenes evoke the passing of isolated, local communities under the complex pressures of industrialism and the end of isolation, changes that demanded the intervention of officials like Hoover and shaped new administrative forms.[18]

Hoover's speeches point to some of the conflicts raised by the gradual shift from decentralized to federal law-enforcement administration, obstacles to his expanding grasp. Careful negotiations are embedded in his anxious logic of community knowledge as community security: "Compelled by an historical enmity toward centralized political—particularly police—power, the American experience produced an intricate array of law enforcement agencies whose jurisdictions honored the profuse political and geographical areas that emerged in the country's expansion westward."[19] Speaking year after year before the annual convention of the International Association of Chiefs of Police, Hoover had to tread his ground lightly. He did, figuring the contest for jurisdiction as an "honorable" territorial imperative. His rhetoric expands with the efforts of protesting that a federal enforcement agency will naturally share control with local authority. In a speech a few months after his "silent policemen" address, Hoover repeatedly assures his audience of their community of understanding: "I know that we stand upon a common ground. I know that I speak to my own people . . . I feel that here I am bulwarked among friends, all of us sworn to stand against a group of dangerous enemies, who consistently attack efficient law-enforcement."[20] Significantly, he imagines the conflict of jurisdiction as primarily one of manual control: "[Local police] should be able to arrest a man when they want to arrest him, and not have their arm stayed by the more powerful hand of some town or county or State politician."[21] Finally, he strategically displaces anxiety about the competing claims of local and federal law onto a common enemy: the political "allies" of crime who "have paralyzed the arms of the law and allowed a criminal a sense of protection greater than that of the citizen upon whom he preys" (Hoover 1934, 1). Silent policemen step in to mediate this struggle, embodying the combined agency of federal and local authority.

Hoover's most generous, overflowing moments in lecture are those when he lists the expanding number of submissions, requests for prints, and requests for comparisons that flood toward his central "library." He celebrates the growing files as a kind of reference work: a "Library of Cooperation," "American Encyclopedia of Criminals" (Hoover 1934, 5), and a "Who's Who in the Field of Crime" (Hoover 1933, 7). Here, the fiction that fingerprints function as neutral, inert information, easily exchanged, conceals the power of possession and dispensation they also represent to Hoover. Over the course of two decades, Hoover's speeches open by listing the current statistics of the Identification Division: the number of employees, the number of agents, the number of cases resolved, and the number of criminals apprehended as a result, concluding with the number of prints processed. One can hear his tone become more expansive over this period as these numbers increase. For Hoover, such figures clearly establish the centrality of his "Identification Agency," despite his attempts to define that agency as a cooperative labor. In 1933 he spoke appeasingly to the International Association of Chiefs of Police, using a favorite cliché:

> "United we stand, divided we fall". . . . Cooperation—complete, coordinated, self-sacrificing cooperation, must continue to be our motto and our daily endeavor. . . .
>
> I do not need to impress upon any person here present that it is not my desire at any time to intrude upon the authority or functions of any individual police force. I am of the opinion, however, that the Federal Government, as represented by the Bureau of Investigation, may render some assistance in this type of case and our offer is made in the spirit of cooperation and we are honored in being privileged

to join forces with you. We do not want to come to you in these cases with empty hands but with a full desire to make plans with you, to work with you, and to offer the full resources of our Identification Division, our crime laboratory and the cooperation of our Special Agents who are stationed in every section of the nation. These problems of relationship will, I am certain, be amicably solved along mutually profitable lines in every instance.[22]

But what this relationship evolved into was a structure much more centralized than his ideal: personified in the G-Men and in the "silent policemen," whose long arms have a local grasp. Hoover formed the Identification Division, using the Leavenworth files that Will West's prints inaugurated, only six weeks after he was appointed director of the FBI in 1924. The relational nature of the indices his agency is founded on—the fact that fingerprints require complex manipulations, comparisons, and a large repository to be powerfully deployed—effectively shifted control from the local margins of law enforcement to his federal bureaucracy.[23]

Hoover's compound metaphor of fingerprinting as the arm of the law signals a figurative shift that occurs persistently in the manual symbology of fingerprinting. Like Herschel's notion of indexed "sign-manuals," the trope works as a kind of lever across which agency can be shifted and amplified. Each fingerprint stands in metonymic relation to the finger that made it: significant through a momentary proximity of hand and object to which it continues to testify. Likewise, the finger that leaves a print stands for its hand, and the hand for body, and the body for person, in a sequence of metonymic attachments. (Herschel's notion of a mystical and ritual moment of touch, to which he credits the impulse to take Konai's hand print, depends on such metonymic identity.) However, the mobility and reproducibility of the mark, and of collected records, stretches and attenuates these metonymies. Herschel's "sign-manual" represents a peculiar compound of manual activities: making prints, collecting prints, and indexing prints into a "manual" for later reference or transfer. "Sign-manuals" evidence the agency of other hands than the ones that left their prints, as well as the corporate agency of the institution that compels and manages those prints. Thus, they represent an idea of agency based on transfer and appropriation, like Konai's hand, mailed in facsimile to Galton along with Herschel's manuals, reproduced on both covers of Herschel's book and in numerous later works (Figure 14). "The decisiveness of a finger-print is now one of the most powerful aids to Justice," Herschel wrote. He closed with a modestly oblique reference to his own labor: "Our possession of it derives from the impression of Konai's hand in 1858" (Herschel, 9). Perhaps in tribute to Herschel's tract (or as an assertion of his own extended reach?) one of Hoover's last essays carries a large hand print on its title page (Hoover 1973, 22). These hands look like emblems of self-evident identity—invitations to the mystical physiognomy of chiromancy—but they record an idea of self produced in comparison and transmission, separated from individual intention. The agency they represent, for both Herschel and Hoover, is also a corporate, administrative one.

The relation between Hoover's customary topoi of local security and the anxieties about personation expressed by Herschel and Galton brings us back to the West story. Case histories of fingerprinting and the Hoover vision alike carry over from their colonial sources traces of the urge to displace anxieties about identity onto the person of an ethnically differentiated other. In this discourse, the West case seems to represent a transitional moment: fingerprinting in the process of assimilating one set of social constructions—the Negro and native—to another—the criminal. The peculiar uncanniness of the Leavenworth prisoners looking so alike and sharing a name generates consistent interest in most versions of the story. Several accounts conclude from the common surname that despite their protestations to the contrary, Will and William West must have been twins, separated in infancy. This argument tacitly explains the arrival of two men with similar names and faces at the same prison as a matter of heredity (a theory of criminal offense very important to Hoover). If the Leavenworth prisoners can be shown to be twins it becomes "natural," not uncanny, that two William Wests, both black, should be criminals in the same place. Thus, what begins as a practical interpretation based on received notions of race, kinship, and criminality is explained by a technology that is in theory abstracted from social systems, value free.

In Chapel's story, as in the work of Herschel and Galton, the

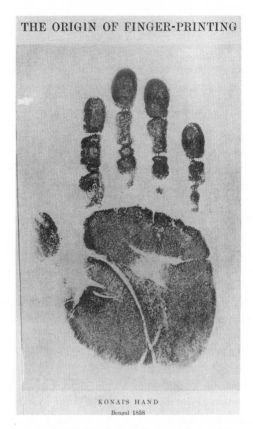

FIGURE 14. Konai's Hand, Bengal, 1858. Cover plate to Sir William Herschel, *The Origin of Fingerprinting*. Oxford University Press, 1916.

problem of physical differentiation expressed as a function of race depends on a fundamental unreliability of oral testimony. This becomes clear in the complicated way in which the anecdote treats West's own account of himself, contrasting formal effects with the prison staff's evaluation of his story. West's assertion that he had never been to Leavenworth before turns out to be accurate, in the sense that it is confirmed by the institutional apparatus (the writing on the back of the card for prisoner 2626 and the evidence of different fingerprints). Further, the story itself anticipates this ending by evoking a formal gesture from fairy tale: the triple assertion of a truth. Three times, West repeats his statement that he had never been to Leavenworth before. Each time, his story is dismissed by the chief clerk, who assumes that the prison records controvert it and suggests that convicts instinctively lie: "West . . . you've been here before, there's no use denying it." Yet the question of whether his statements are true is implicitly reinforced in the anecdote by another formal effect: the use of "black" dialect for his dialogue. Paradoxically, if his words are not to be trusted, his dialect offers evidence as trustworthy as fingerprints. The involuntary and physical nature of dialect, however, substantiates West's race and class, and by extension, moral character. In West's speech, the qualities of blackness and criminality converge—a convergence reflected in other fingerprint case histories. Blackness and criminality become generically equivalent signs of the dangerous ambiguities in oral and physical evidence that fingerprinting is meant to resolve. This complicated evacuation and reinvestment of intention in involuntary physical qualities gains an accidental irony from Will West's name. Except for his name, all the qualities particular to West's person, like the sound of his voice, confirm his inability to exercise his own will.

The dialectical qualities of West's speech are the only oral evidence Chapel's anecdote acknowledges. This testimony imprisons without narrative consequence: it implies authenticity—aural detail—in the account, but it also testifies to narrative and personal ellipsis. Despite his realist diction and apparent attention to detail, Chapel omits any interior account of what it might feel like to encounter an unfamiliar double. The uncanny experience so central to nineteenth-century explorations of self has no part here: the meeting of Will West and William West is recounted as a comparison of records. Missing also is the story of their criminal history and what happens after they enter Leavenworth: a story that appears to have no bearing on the accuracy and reliability of fingerprinting.[24] By contrast, it is precisely questions of history and outcome that Twain emphasizes in his remarkable trial of fingerprint technology and makes the focus of a darkly ironic indictment of race slavery. If the absence of West's story seems not to call attention to itself, the absence of Chambers's story is unavoidable and discomfiting: the narrator explicitly withholds it, a "curious fate" and a "long story" that he refuses to tell.[25]

For Twain, the analogy between dialect and fingerprints calls into question the assertion that "physical facts speak for them-selves," suggesting that fingerprints, like speech patterns, express culturally determined signs of identity. Furthermore, when physical facts speak, they seem always to speak for someone else. Thus, at the end of *Pudd'nhead Wilson*, the "real" Driscoll heir—switched in the cradle with the slave "Chambers" and raised in his place—finds himself suddenly restored to his estate and to whiteness. But he re-mains imprisoned in the social and domestic spaces defined by slave-holding custom and manners:

> He could neither read nor write, and his speech was the basest dialect of the negro quarter. His gait, his attitudes, his gestures, his bearing, his laugh—all were vulgar and uncouth; his manners were the man-ners of a slave . . . The family pew was a misery to him, yet he could nevermore enter into the solacing refuge of the "nigger gallery"— that was closed to him for good and all. But we cannot follow his cu-rious fate further—that would be a long story. (*PW*, 167)

Linking the involuntary and inescapable qualities of Chambers's dialect and his untellable history, this passage illuminates the com-plex agency relations represented by fingerprints in the West case. At the same time, it raises questions about the institutional interests that impel this evacuation of intention from personal history. What is at stake when the West anecdote shifts evidentiary value from nar-rative to the materials of narrative expression? For law enforcement, of course, the answer at least in part is a system of identification that the enforcement agency can secure and control. Yet for Twain, this shift carries anxieties about personation into the physical evidence that seems to resolve them. As Chambers's predicament makes clear, fingerprinting produces whiteness, but in a tenuous way. Con-versely, as several critics have argued, what counts for evidence of race in a slave society can—and in this nightmare family romance does—make anyone black. The ambiguities typed by blackness and criminality in the discourse of fingerprinting thus become general conditions of action and identity in the novel. Drawing connections between fingerprinting and the economies of possession expressed in race slavery, Twain shows their paradoxical dependence on a pervasive loss of self-control. When physical facts speak for themselves, in his writing, they testify to an experience of helplessness and uncanny self-division. To see this, it is first useful to take a closer look at Wilson's description of fingerprints and to compare its reception by early forensic and legal practitioners with the responses it elicits inside Twain's fictional courtroom.

Proprioception: The Physiology of Self-possession

The Federal Bureau of Investigation has for years fixed on *Pudd'nhead Wilson* as the "prophetic" catalyst of the law enforcement institution of fingerprinting in the United States. For the anonymous historians of the Identification Division, the novel marks a decisive turning point in American law enforcement practice and in public acceptance of that practice. Published at a moment of enthusiastic forensic exploration in anthropometry in Europe and America, *Pudd'nhead Wilson* seemed almost magically to anticipate the efficacy of fingerprint identification. The driving force of the novel in the Justice Department's internal history is its "striking exposition of the infallibility of fingerprint identification."[26] Criminologists Bert Wentworth and Harris Hawthorne Wilder are more hyperbolic in asserting that Twain "spread among the people correct ideas concerning the new system, and thus became a true 'prophet to the Gentiles' in the subject."[27] Chapel's 1941 manual invokes Twain's lawyer as a spiritual guide, among other ghostly fathers of the profession; to the novice seeking professional employment, he conjures, "May the spirits of Faulds, Herschel, Galton, Henry, and even Pudd'nhead Wilson, smooth your path!" (Chapel, 10). Mark Twain, "beloved author," is included among the authorities in at least one court precedent, *State v. Kuhl et al.* (42 Nev. 185), 1918 (Wilton, 225). The second edition of John Henry Wigmore's seminal textbook, *The Principles of Judicial Proof*

(1931), praises Wilson's exemplary speech to the jury and lists Twain among the useful authorities and references.[28] More recently, Robert D. Foote's widely circulated monograph, a survey of current technology in the 1970s, celebrates Wilson's charge to the jury as "one of the most accurate and convincing descriptions of the significance of fingerprinting."[29] After quoting several hundred words of Twain's famous "physiological autograph" passage, Foote concludes, "This fictional work probably did as much to arouse interest in the United States about fingerprinting as any other single factor."[30] He follows these conclusions with an anecdote from the early life of Superintendent Albert G. Perrott, Indianapolis Bureau of Identification, the "acknowledged dean" of American fingerprint experts. Perrott's first epiphany with fingerprinting reportedly occurred in 1896, while attending a dramatic adaptation of the novel.

What aspects of *Pudd'nhead Wilson* account for this influence? One wishes for memos on Twain in J. Edgar Hoover's files, but these are perhaps more appealing than required. The canonization of the novel appeals to a larger cultural mythology that figures "Mark Twain" as the symbol of unique, if eccentric Americanness, relentless exposure of humbug, and above all, *authentic* individuality. The irony of electing the works of a self-described "talent for imposture" as the perfect expression and invisible motive force of the identification industry is acute. Twain's Penelopean unfashioning of authentic self, his lifelong struggle for copyright control, and his deep sense of his own creative practice as a kind of automatic writing contradicts the central metaphor for fingerprints used by Herschel, Galton, and Hoover: the signature or "natal autograph." For Twain, signature epitomized a comic dispossession of self and expression. His corpus is full of tongue-in-cheek, hopeful gestures toward authenticity, like the frontispiece to the Authorized Edition: a handwritten and signed statement that affirms: "This is the Authorized Uniform Edition of all my books."[31] But for each of these assertions an acutely alienated expression can be found, as in his famous reflection: "I am not acquainted with my double, my partner in duality, the other and wholly independent personage who resides in me . . . and signs [his name] in a hand which has no resemblance to mine when he takes possession of our partnership body and goes off on mysterious trips."[32] The kind of internal displacement theorized by Derrida in "Signature/Event/Context" seems apt to this sense of autography: "By definition, a written signature implies the actual or empirical nonpresence of the signer."[33] For all that his writings suggest a deep ambivalence about this double self, however, the public "Mark Twain," the scourge of all humbug, embodies imposture and makes it visible, identifiable, and recoverable. The thieving, jackleg novelist reliably unmasks duplicity and humbug—confessing especially his own. For the FBI, peculiarly, the Twain persona thus serves as a kind of fetish: enabling an institutional desire for fixed identities by embodying and warding off anxieties of personation. To forensic historians, Twain's doubleness seems comfortably transparent. "Strangely enough," Robert Foote writes, "fingerprints as an identification medium were introduced in the fiction of one of our best known authors, Samuel Clemens, or as he is better known, Mark Twain" (Foote, 6).

The success of Wilson's courtroom speech in law-enforcement mythology depends obviously, in part, on a loss of context and resistance to irony. Like Shylock's famous humanistic appeal, "Hath not a Jew . . . ," the famous "physiological autograph" passage has had a life of its own, outside the complex and disconcerting context of the rest of the story. Yet the canonization of this passage in forensic literature depends on more than a simple misreading and appropriation of catchy terms. To see this, we need to look more closely at Wilson's charge to the jury:

> "Every human being carries with him from his cradle to his grave certain physical marks which do not change their character, and by which he can always be identified—and that without shade of doubt or question. These marks are his signature, his physiological autograph, so to speak, and this autograph can not be counterfeited, nor can he disguise it or hide it away, nor can it become illegible by the wear and mutations of time. This signature is not his face—age can change that beyond recognition; it is not his hair, for that can fall out; it is not his height, for duplicates of that exist; it is not his form, for duplicates of that exist also, whereas this signature is each man's very own—there is no duplicate of it among the swarming populations of the globe! [The audience were interested once more.]

"This autograph consists of the delicate lines or corrugations with which Nature marks the insides of the hands and the soles of the feet. If you will look at the balls of your fingers . . . you will observe that these dainty curving lines lie close together, like those that indicate the borders of oceans in maps . . . there was never a twin born into this world that did not carry from birth to death a sure identifier in this mysterious and marvelous natal autograph. That once known to you, his fellow-twin could never personate him and deceive you."

Wilson stopped and stood silent. Inattention dies a quick and sure death when a speaker does that. The stillness gives warning that something is coming. All palms and finger-balls went down now, all slouching forms straightened, all heads came up, all eyes were fastened upon Wilson's face. He waited yet one, two, three moments, to let his pause complete and perfect its spell upon the house; then, when through the profound hush he could hear the ticking of the clock on the wall, he put out his hand and took the Indian knife by the blade and held it aloft where all could see the sinister spots upon its ivory handle; . . .

"Upon this haft stands the assassin's natal autograph, written in the blood of that helpless and unoffending old man who loved you and whom you all loved. There is but one man in the whole earth whose hand can duplicate that crimson sign." (*PW*, 108–9)

Wilson's exuberant tone certainly inspires satisfaction. He systematically checks off the familiar characteristics measured by Bertillonage—face, hair, height, etc.—and asserts the superiority of fingerprints in each respect. Yet the passage does more than provide a compelling phrase. It illuminates the "physiological autograph" in a way that anticipates the terms of *People v. Sallow*: emphasizing the essential, physical, and involuntary nature of concomitant evidence. At the same time, as the passage makes clear, if fingerprints establish identity, they do not belong to the person identified but to those who make them legible. Wilson's dramatic pause and lifted knife demonstrate the alienable character of this essential evidence and the shift in control from criminal to legal practitioner that its portability affords. It is precisely the mixed character of latent prints, essential but alienable, involuntary but powerfully instrumental, that enabled Hoover's Identification Division and that forensic technology has systematically evolved itself to protect.[34]

Thus, the scene of collection, indexing, and public comparison

of fingerprints that takes place in Twain's courtroom is as important
to understanding the persistence of this passage in law-enforcement
literature as the definitions it offers. What readers from Hoover to
Chapel miss, not surprisingly, is the ironizing context for such du-
plications. Twain's vision of the portable, instrumental character of
latent prints complicates here, offering more of Derrida than
Hoover. The contingent relation of finger to print reveals a problem
of mimesis in Wilson's technique: the patterns without double must
be duplicated on the panes of glass in the courtroom window to
prove their uniqueness. While unique in themselves, they are useless unless transposed, and in that moment of transposition the
difference between unduplicated pattern and the mark it makes introduces the possibility of misdirection, manipulation, and appropriation. Print and finger are "close by a minute difference," in
which the fingerprint originates: like the gesture that generates sign
for Derrida, "that small difference—visibility, spacing, death"
opened up by writing.[35] Subsequent to duplication, the vulnerability of other signs of identity to disguise—face, hair, height—can easily mislead fingerprint comparison. Thus, when Tom commits his
crimes in female dress, this disguise leads Wilson to review only the
women's print records in his collection, "grubbing and groping
after that woman that don't exist" (*PW*, 102).

For Twain, the requirement of duplication invites specifically
literary tropes of transmission and interpretation. As in palmistry
and fortune telling (both involved in the detective processes of
Pudd'nhead Wilson) the delicate patterns record a story:

> "Caesar's ghost!" commented Tom, with astonishment. "It beats any-
> thing that was ever heard of! Why, a man's own hand is his deadliest
> enemy! Just think of that—a man's own hand keeps a record of the
> deepest and fatalest secrets of his life, and is treacherously ready to ex-
> pose him to any black-magic stranger that comes along. But what do
> you let a person look at your hand for, with that awful thing printed
> on it?" (*PW*, 52)

Here, the histories a hand carries appear to be essential. Recalling
Wilson's charge to the jury in this context, the metonymic chain
from bloody hand to "crimson sign" to scripted dagger seems to es-

tablish a seamless semiotic teleology: physical contiguity that signifies the unity of act and identity, proof that the trace of a print signifies not only the presence of the actor but the character of that actor. Accordingly, Tom Driscoll's trial contests not only his innocence or guilt, but also his character: "assassin" or "poor bereaved youth."

But the print that incriminates Tom is carried on a dagger inscribed with a murderous history that seems to deconstruct this essential logic. The story engraved on the dagger suggests both the temporary, contingent nature of signs of identity and the inherent treachery of such signs. Finger marks are dangerous, Tom intuits, because they constitute a kind of narrative of the self that one cannot control, that is always about to turn against oneself. In both its shape and the story it tells, the dagger confirms this:

> The devices engraved on it are the ciphers or names of its long line of possessors—I had Luigi's name added in Roman letters, myself, with our coat of arms, as you see. You notice what a curious handle the thing has. It is solid ivory, polished like a mirror, and is four or five inches long—round, and as thick as a large man's wrist, with the end squared off flat, for your thumb to rest on. (*PW*, 52–53)

Designed for use as well as elegance, "with the end squared off flat for your thumb," the dagger serves as a symbolic and actual link between the hand that holds it and the object world it acts on. Furthermore, its handle, as thick as "a large man's wrist," suggests an identity between its symbolic and instrumental functions: as if it displaces the hand that wields it. Like the fingerprint it carries, it collapses the gap between body and sign, agent and instrument: so much so that Angelo can attribute to the dagger, rather than Luigi, the burden of guilt. Like fingerprints, the instrumentality of this sign is both powerful and dangerous. As if fulfilling Tom Driscoll's premonition, it precipitates internal contest: it opens up the possibility of the self undoing itself, betraying its own secrets, inviting treachery, and most importantly, inviting theft. Thus the dagger's ciphered inscriptions record a cumulative history of dispossessions. Significantly, each name listed in its "long line of possessors" records a person who faced assassination or assassinated in order to keep it:

> The knife was to blame [for the homicide]. A native servant slipped
> into our room in the palace in the night, to kill us and steal the knife
> on account of the fortune encrusted on its sheath. . . . Suddenly that
> native rose at the bedside and bent over me with his right hand lifted
> and a dirk in it aimed at my throat, but Luigi grabbed his wrist, pulled
> him downward, and drove his own knife into the man's neck. That is
> the whole story. (*PW*, 53)

Luigi earns his inscription on the dagger this way. But the history it
records allows Tom to frame him for Judge Driscoll's murder. To
own this dagger, to be identified by it, is by definition to have committed murder—as indeed, Tom's use of it to kill Judge Driscoll
demonstrates. By stealing the dagger afterward and keeping it, Tom
amplifies the fiction of Luigi as assassin and fraud. It becomes generally accepted that Luigi must secretly still possess the dagger that
bears his name, must accordingly have killed Judge Driscoll, and for
this he risks hanging. The tenuous links in this logic—besides the
fact that it is specious—are the presumption that identity and intentions can be established by physical possession of such a sign and
that identity constituted this way is somehow essential.

The dagger's lineage of possessors, together with the plots it sets
in motion, immediately invoke the broader context of Twain's critique of race slavery in which slaves are "daily robbed" of "ines-
timable treasure—[their] liberty" (*PW*, 12). When the signs of identity are established in physiology, he suggests, they become more,
rather than less, vulnerable: just as owning this dagger makes one
more, rather than less, likely to lose one's life. Like the dagger, the
latent print it carries records a history of transmission that is fraught.
If it must be lifted, transferred, and read in order legally to establish
Tom's presence and identity, it remains a kind of property never
possessed by the person it is proper to—conditioned by and result-
ing in dispossession. For Twain, as Gillman has argued, this construction of criminal agency incorporates the paradoxes of slave
labor: the legal fiction of possession that makes a fingerprint the
sign of unequivocal presence of the subject paradoxically signifies
the social absence of subjectivity and authenticity. It does so because
the manufacture of presence depends on a physical stability, a sense
of self-possession that Twain's post–Civil War notions of physiology

cannot ensure. The infamous dog joke that opens *Pudd'nhead Wilson* and that anoints David Wilson a pudd'nhead makes this clear.

> [Wilson] made his fatal remark the first day he spent in the village, and it "gauged" him. He had just made the acquaintance of a group of citizens when an invisible dog began to yelp and snarl and howl and make himself very comprehensively disagreeable, whereupon young Wilson said, much as one who is thinking aloud:
> "I wish I owned half of that dog."
> "Why?" somebody asked.
> "Because, I would kill my half."
> The group searched his face with curiosity, with anxiety even, but found no light there, no expression that they could read. (*PW*, 5)

Whether you kill one half of the "general dog" or one end of the dog—the citizens of Dawson's Landing reason—if you kill one half you kill the whole dog. Wilson's version of the invisible dog appears divisible in terms of a legal and economic logic of ownership; the townsfolk interpret his comment only in terms of their holistic logic of physiology, predicated on its indivisibility and viability. After a lengthy "rational" analysis they confirm the complete illogic of one system in terms of the other, missing the intersection of systems on which Wilson's irony is predicated. Apparently wishing to own only half the dog and kill it, and thus responsible for killing the hypothetical half he doesn't own, Wilson is judged a pudd'nhead by the town and loses his first name (*PW*, 6).

As several critics have pointed out, this joke exemplifies the absurd fiction of "black" and "white" fractions of identity that sustained Jim Crow laws: to own one part in sixteen of an individual like Roxy is to own all of Roxy and to condemn all of her to social death. By analogy, such self-division ironically deconstructs the use of fingerprints as natural signs of character, personality, or intention. Like his first public failure, Wilson's dramatic courtroom show demonstrates the failure of an essential, value-free system for determining identity.[36] Yet, in addition to its dialectics of master and slave, of naturally and culturally constructed person, the dog joke clearly suggests a third problem. It exemplifies the failure of possession as a metaphor for embodiment and consequently the failure of embodiment as the means of effective action. As an allegory of physiology, the fate of Wilson and the dog together make the point that we inhabit a body we do not own and that we cannot predictably control.

Like Twain's comic sketch of the Siamese twins Chang and Eng, who fight on opposite sides of the Civil War and take each other prisoner, the dog joke represents a kind of postwar exemplum of the limits of physiologically determinate self-possession.[37] Their Civil War backdrop points directly to contemporary developments in neurophysiology on which they depend. The high frequency of amputation in the Civil War, usually attributed to the predominance of fighting with infantry, gave rise to innovations in the science of self-perception. Silas Weir Mitchell, a physician whose detailed postwar studies of phantom limb phenomena and reflex paralysis were widely read in the 1870s, contributed to popular interest in the medical theory of motor disorders. His famous story "The Case of George Dedlow" rehearses a loss of a bodily sense of self: one that eerily echoes the conditions of impersonation that generated Herschel's work in India. Dedlow, whose limbs are successively amputated during the Civil War, dictates his experiences of phantom pain and, as it fades, his fading sense of self: "I have so little surety of being myself, that I doubt my own honesty in drawing my pension." He attends a seance during which he calls up two spirits who identify themselves as "UNITED STATES ARMY MEDICAL MUSEUM, Nos. 3486, 3487." "They are my *legs! my legs!*" he cries in sudden recognition. The phantom parts temporarily restore to Dedlow his vanished sense of self: "I felt a strange return of my self-consciousness, I was re-individualized, so to speak." He rises, and "staggering a little, walked across the room on limbs invisible to them or me." "It was no wonder I staggered," he says, slyly reminding us that these are spirit parts, "for, as I briefly reflected, my legs had been nine months in the strongest alcohol."[38]

In the 1890s, neurologist C. S. Sherrington, also working with amputees, pioneered the concept of the "sixth" perceptual faculty Dedlow had lost. He defined it as "proprio-ception," an integrative neurological faculty of being-in-the-body, the experience of embodiment as a whole, inalienable, and essentially continuous self-possession. This "secret sense" "that we feel our bodies as proper to us, as our 'property,' as our own," produces phantom limbs of a mutilated or lost part, or disappears from a limb as a result of neurological damage.[39] Most importantly for understanding Twain, however, Sherrington theorized this sense in the negative. Proprioception is observable primarily in cases of injury, amputation, or suspension: recognized as a result of loss.

Following these explorations in motor control, Twain suggests that legal and social notions of self-possession produce just such experiences of partial proprioception and lost control. Dispossession and involuntary surrender characterize both physical and social agency in *Pudd'nhead Wilson*, and these conditions are reflected in the props and tools at the center of the action. So, for example, the Indian knife ironically incarnates Macbeth's floating dagger, recalling the early modern stage props of a patricide. But Twain twists dramatic tradition, making the knife threaten an unacknowledged patrimony through the fiction of a false one: if it exposes Tom's false paternity, might it not expose his real one? Yet what seems to be the instrument of a powerful usurpation turns out to be legally nonexistent—a kind of ghost prosthesis that only simulates murderous agency—when Tom is pardoned in order to be sold down the river. Thus, the knife translates Tom's fingerprints into a legal discourse of agency and intention that makes its instrumentality a handicap: the phantom of a body never proper to itself.

It is important to note that this condition of dispossession attends Tom and Chambers from the cradle to the grave, as their fingerprints do. After Roxana switches the children in their cradles, Tom's "usurpation" and the "fiction" of his reign emerge in such fetishizing enhancements. From his earliest years Tom engages in a kind of fort-da game of manual control, attempting to confirm his mastery of the world and of his mother:

> When he got to be old enough to begin to toddle about, and say broken words, and get an idea of what his hands were for, he was a more consummate pest than ever. Roxy got no rest while he was awake. He would call for anything and everything he saw, simply saying, "Awnt

it!" (want it), which was a command. When it was brought, he said, in a frenzy, and motioning it away with his hands, "Don't awnt it! don't awnt it!" and the moment it was gone he set up frantic yells of "Awnt it! awnt it!" and Roxy had to give wings to her heels to get that thing back to him again before he could get time to carry out his intention of going into convulsions about it. . . . The moment Roxy's back was turned he would toddle to the presence of the tongs and say, "Like it!" and cock his eye to one side to see if Roxy was observing; then, "Awnt it!" and cock his eye again; then, "Hab it!" with another furtive glance; and finally, "Take it!"—and the prize was his. (*PW*, 18)

A few pages later we learn that as he grows older, Tom requires more purchase on his world than the tongs supply. In an allegory of the labor relations of slavery, Chambers becomes his "proxy" hands: stealing, fighting, and finally saving his life for him when he cannot act for himself. Not privileged to "lift his hands" against Tom, Chambers keeps them in his pockets. Those pockets remain symbolically empty of anything but equally empty hands; although Chambers plays "keeps" with marbles for Tom, Tom takes "all the winnings away" (*PW*, 20). But without Chambers, Tom is socially helpless. Finding the former unconscious at one point, "several of Tom's ancient adversaries saw that their long-desired opportunity was come, and they gave the false heir such a drubbing that with Chambers's best help he was hardly able to drag himself home afterward" (*PW*, 20). After Chambers saves Tom from drowning, the boys taunt him with a phrase that confirms the contingency of his strength by proxy: they call Chambers the "author" of Tom's "new being" (*PW*, 21). Thus Tom's mastery, social and personal, remains one of supplementation: dependent on a transitional object that signifies only tenuous control over the world.

The economic relation between Tom and Chambers thus expresses itself in physical disability: a loss of self-possession that results from the constitution of identity in terms of property. Their complex mutual dependence is embodied in more profoundly confusing form in the Siamese brothers brought to trial in *Those Extraordinary Twins*. In this curious fragment of *Pudd'nhead Wilson*, the separate Italian twins, Luigi and Angelo, share a Siamese body with four arms and two legs. Here, the dangers inherent in instrumental signs of identity, suggested by the Indian dagger, become the central problem of knowledge—explored in a body that exists in a permanent state of prosthesis. As in *Pudd'nhead Wilson*, the twins are continually described as a conundrum of "possession," "owner-ship," and "control." Yet self-possession cannot be determined in a double body never proper to "itselves," as the novel terms them. The peculiar system by which the brothers share control of their single torso confirms this. "If our legs tried to obey two wills," Angelo argues, "how could we ever get anywhere?" (*PW*, 138). "By a mysterious law of our being, each of us has utter and indisputable command of our body a week at a time, turn and turn about" (*PW*, 139). This command shifts instantaneously and involuntarily: "In that instant the one brother's power over the body vanishes and the other brother takes possession, asleep or awake." Luigi declares that this exchange is a mechanism more perfect than clockwork:

> So exactly to the instant does the change come, that during our stay in many of the great cities of the world, the public clocks were reg-ulated by it; and as hundreds of thousands of private clocks and watches were set and corrected in accordance with the public clocks, we really furnished the standard time for the entire city. (*PW*, 139)

Yet their means of transferring control turns out to be less definitive than Luigi maintains, a kind of Cartesian dualism with the connec-tions gone badly awry. Later, when Luigi meets Judge Driscoll in a duel—an action Angelo morally abhors—Angelo continually and apparently spontaneously disrupts Luigi's aim. He faints, he starts—putting Luigi off balance—and finally dodges out of the line of fire. Yet Luigi is supposed to be "in control" of their body at this time, and Angelo present "only by courtesy, . . . without official recogni-tion" (*PW*, 156). Significantly, Angelo's mournful description of the condition of proprioception in which the twins exist invokes the phantom limbs of George Dedlow:

> A week's possession at a time seems so little that we can't bear to spare a minute of it [to a twin who want's to "borrow" control]. People who have the use of their legs all the time never think of what a bless-ing it is, of course. It never occurs to them; it's just their natural or-dinary condition, and so it does not excite them at all. But when I

wake up, on Sunday morning, and it's my week and I feel the power
all through me, oh, such a wave of exultation and thanksgiving goes
surging over me, and I want to shout "I can walk! I can walk!" (*PW*,
140)

Will and embodiment are so disjoint in this pair that Luigi and
Angelo cannot even organize their involuntary physical responses.
When Luigi sits smoking in bed, Angelo coughs, and when Luigi
drinks alcohol he feels no effects, but Angelo, a teetotaler, gets
drunk (*PW*, 128). In turn, when Angelo puts too much sugar in his
tea, Luigi gets indigestion (*PW*, 132). In this admixed physiology,
the tenuous instrumentality displayed by props like the dagger extends into the body itself. As they sidle through Patsy Cooper's
door, the twins appear as a confusion of agent body parts, "just a
wormy squirming of arms in the air" (*PW*, 126). When they eat,
"the commingling arms feed potatoes into one mouth and coffee
into the other at the same time," an exchange of services that their
hostess, transfixed, cannot trace (*PW*, 131).

Like *Pudd'nhead Wilson*, the plot of *Those Extraordinary Twins*
revolves around a legal debate about the signs of bodily agency. The
kick that Luigi is fined for in the former novel becomes Wilson's
first legal exercise in the latter. When Tom takes the twins to court
for kicking him off a stage, Wilson's defense depends on the un-
solvable problem of proprioception they represent. The law protects the twins from testifying against themselves as to which
brother had control of their shared leg at the time of the kick. Since
"which of them was in possession of the legs . . . would of course
indicate where the guilt of the assault belongs," and since the pros-
ecution cannot determine a single possessor of the leg that kicks
Tom, neither twin can be legally understood to be guilty of assault
(*PW*, 150).

The legal fiction that finds Tom Driscoll not guilty of a murder to which his fingerprints testify takes temporarily comic form
in *Those Extraordinary Twins*. By the end of the novel, however, the
community brings a second trial against the twins and hangs both
brothers—like the invisible, indivisible dog—by hanging Luigi.
Protected by their Fifth Amendment rights against self-incrimina-

tion, the Siamese twins represent the nightmare of a legal apparatus unable to make their physiology testify for them. It is significant that the fingerprint plot plays no part in this version of Wilson's trial. The extraordinary, radical uniqueness of their body, which fingerprints *could* evidence, would not in any way evidence the secure, determinable agency of one twin or another in such a confusing physiology. The evidence given by the fingerprints of such "commingling" hands could never be used to determine which twin retains self-possession.

Ironically, the involuntary, inconstant proprioception that protects them in this first trial comes back to haunt the twins in the second. The judge closes their first trial with words that sound eerily like Hoover's, galvanizing the anxious community to hang the brothers and thus resolve the indeterminate personation they represent:

> You have set adrift, unadmonished, in this community, two men endowed with . . . a power by which each in his turn may commit crime after crime of the most heinous character, and no man be able to tell which is the guilty or which the innocent party in any case of them all. Look to your homes—look to your property—look to your lives—for you have need! (*PW*, 154)

Framing his fingerprint plot with these gothic histories of self-alienation and disability, Twain explores the experience that the West case veers away from. The persistent and ambivalent sense of dispossession written into these doubled bodies offers a radical revision of the Cartesian mechanics of the body. For Twain, the distance between animating will and instrument, like the distance between finger and latent print, widens to invite other, often nefarious interests. The mixed and shifting agencies defined by fingerprinting reemerge in the courtroom scene of *Pudd'nhead Wilson* as a problem of narrative control. Wilson's success there depends as much on his skills as a storyteller as on the essential accuracy of fingerprints in determining identity. His success depends in particular on his mastery of the dramatic pause, the stunning impression it makes on his audience, and the involuntary response it elicits from Tom. Yet Twain plays on the term "impression" in the jury speech, linking the evidence of finger impressions and the impressions made on Wilson's audience in a way that shows the lawyer to be as helpless as Tom and Chambers. To see this, it is useful to turn briefly to Twain's rare manifesto, "How to Tell a Story," in which he theorizes the problem of narrative impression in terms that reprise Wilson's lecture to the court. Here, the dramatic pause seems to establish a dialectic between the mechanical, dependent, and involuntary actions of a machine and consummate authorial control. Yet the essay develops this argument through equivocal fictions of amputation and ghostly prosthesis that seem to reflect back on the narrator. Like *Pudd'nhead Wilson*, this is a confidence story, meant to show as much technical skill in duping its audience as any Jamesian trap for the sophisticated reader. But unlike James, Twain always imagines *himself* to be caught by the trap of his story, maintaining that both storyteller and audience share an uncertain, equivocal command of themselves and their tale.

Finger Impressions, Involuntary Confession, and How to Tell a Story

"How to Tell a Story" proceeds through two anecdotes, "The Wounded Soldier" and "The Golden Arm," making a distinction between badly produced "comic stories" and skillfully produced "humorous stories" that largely depends on the persona of the storyteller.[40] Twain's "humorous" speaker dissembles disingenuously, digressing along in his innocent, pleased way while the audience laughs "until they are exhausted" ("HTS," 8). Playing a "dull-witted old farmer," he forgets his joke, "gets all mixed up and wanders helplessly round and round, putting in tedious details that don't belong" ("HTS," 7). The "comic" narrator, in contrast, stumbles through bragging lines, loudly explaining and repeating the nub of his joke. Twain describes the subtler skills of the humorist as follows: "The simplicity and innocence and sincerity and unconsciousness of the old farmer are perfectly simulated, and the result is a performance which is thoroughly charming and delicious. This is art—and fine and beautiful, and only a master can compass it; but

a machine could tell the other story" ("HTS," 8). Calling this mastery that is not a machine's "the basis of the American art," the
speaker goes on to assert that it depends on the grasp of the well-
timed pause. ". . . A dainty thing, and delicate, and also uncertain
and treacherous," the pause is the hinge on which Twain's equivocal argument about the storyteller's control swings:

> On the platform I used to tell a negro ghost story that had a pause in
> front of the snapper on the end, and that pause was the most impor-
> tant thing in the whole story. If I got it the right length precisely, I
> could spring the finishing ejaculation with effect enough to make
> some impressible girl deliver a startled little yelp and jump out of her
> seat—and that was what I was after. . . . You can practice with it your-
> self—and mind you look out for the pause and get it right. ("HTS,"
> 9–10)

This analysis of the pause leads into the second tale in a way
that seems to reinforce the dialectic of masterful storyteller and automatic machine. In her reading of Twain's lecture persona, Susan
Gillman elucidates this metaphor and its complicated relationship to
the pause. Following Justin Kaplan, she calls the machine Twain's
bête noire, relating it to his adversarial relationship with his audience:
"If the performer Mark Twain, for example, 'used to play with the
pause,' he remembered in 1907, 'as other children play with a toy,'
it was the audience who determined the length of the pause and
therefore controlled his play" (Gillman, 31). Gillman goes on to cite
his contradictory observation that, "An audience is that machine's
twin; it can measure a pause down to that vanishing fraction." The
pause is treacherous, it turns out, because it shifts control away from
the performer at exactly the point Twain wants to assert narrative
authority. Thus, no clear-cut authority emerges in this dialectic: like
Tom Driscoll's uneasy fort-da game, Twain's "toy" with the pause
acquires an air of uncertain mastery.[41]

This equivocal role is the one that David Wilson oddly inhabits during his courtroom demonstration of fingerprinting and that
Twain assigns him explicitly. In a famous letter to Olivia Langdon,
Twain declares, "I have never thought of Pudd'nhead as a character
but only as a piece of machinery—a button, or crank or lever, with

a useful function to perform in a machine, but with no dignity
above that."[42] In calling Wilson "mechanical," Twain means to
define him as "acting or performed without the exercise of thought
or volition."[43] In this sense, he is a useful contrivance resembling
Melville's grotesque carpenter, whose brain "if he had ever had one,
must have early oozed along into the muscles of his fingers" and
who assumes the exterior of "a common pocket knife, but containing, not only blades of various sizes, but also screw-drivers,
corkscrews, tweezers, awls, pens, rulers."[44] In this context the term
"mechanical" recalls its early modern sense: rustic, vulgar, mean,
and defined by manual labor.[45] Thus, with Wilson, as in "How to
Tell a Story," Twain characteristically differentiates between vernac-
ular storyteller and the author of "high and delicate art" in terms of
their degree of motor control.

Yet in the preface to *Those Extraordinary Twins*, Wilson appears
quite slyly willful and dexterous. The preface weaves a darkly
whimsical account of the birth of the Siamese story from which
Pudd'nhead Wilson was extracted, and in it Wilson emerges as an en-
trepreneur who—along with Tom Driscoll and Roxana—usurps
Twain's authorial rights and powers:

> The tale kept spreading along and spreading along . . . Before the
> book was half finished those three [Wilson, Tom, Roxana] were tak-
> ing things entirely into their own hands and working the whole tale
> as a private venture of their own—a tale which they had nothing at
> all to do with, by rights. (*PW*, 120)

Here, the Wilson machine embodies for Twain his familiar self-description as a lazy amanuensis to his own books. Twain's relationship
with this character looks forward to the enterprising grotesques of
Sherwood Anderson's preface to *Winesburg, Ohio*, and to Anderson's
equally powerful sense of alienation from the work of his writing
hands, under the pressures of industrial mechanization. As a substitute and usurping agent, Wilson embodies the potential of automatic writing out of control: less like a Cartesian mind-body machine than a "black box" that produces unexpected results and
wrests its material from its rightful owner, more a handicap than a
lever. In this sense, Twain's grotesques are not so much character

types as narrative operations—operations, moreover, that are reversible—apt to take over the animate and make it automatic.[46]

The failed joke that begins "How to Tell a Story" seems to connect the dangerous prospect of mechanical storytelling to the radical challenge to self-possession embodied in Twain's grotesque twins. "The Wounded Soldier" takes place in a Civil War scene, in the middle of "a certain battle" with "bullets and cannon-balls . . . flying in all directions" ("HTS," 6). A soldier whose leg has been shot off asks a comrade for aid; the able soldier picks up the injured one and runs for the rear, not noticing that in the course of his flight a cannonball has decapitated the fellow. "Where are you going with that carcass?" his officer asks.

> "To the rear, sir—he's lost his leg!"
> "His leg, forsooth?" responded the astonished officer; "you mean his head, you booby."
> Whereupon the solder dispossessed himself of his burden, and stood looking down upon it in great perplexity. At length he said:
> "It is true, sir, just as you have said." Then after a pause he added, *"But he* TOLD *me* IT WAS HIS LEG!!!!!" ("HTS," 6)

Told by the unskilled narrator, who cannot control his pause, this joke sounds like a parody of the "Case of George Dedlow." The apparent confusion of head and leg—momentary and absurd—emphasizes the vulnerability of the body that intends and acts. Oddly disembodied, the dead soldier's testimony returns—"He told me it was his leg!" However, this turns out to be phantom testimony, that cannot reanimate his corpse or restore a lost sense of self as the phantom limbs restore Dedlow. Reading a kind of practical morality into the scene, we might imagine that the heroic soldier benefits from the attempted rescue by interposing another body between his own and the cannonfire. However, the "booby" who fled so speedily differs very little from the soldier whose head was blown off in his place. The peculiar humor of the story lies in the astonishment of the second soldier, but his shock also registers the futility of asking for or giving aid in an environment that turns most of the combatants into corpses.

A "Negro ghost-story," told by the successful narrator, follows

"The Wounded Soldier." It concludes "How to Tell a Story," and ostensibly demonstrates the consummate narrative control that "only a master can compass" ("HTS," 8). Twain learned this story as a child on his uncle's farm in Missouri; he performed it in lecture with great success for decades, but saw it also as a cautionary tale, one fraught with a sense of failure (Kaplan, 309). "The Golden Arm" is a classic tale of uncanny return. A "monsus mean" man, living all alone out in the prairie, returns to his wife's grave on the stormy night of her burial to dig up her golden arm, "all solid gold, fum de shoulder down" ("HTS," 10). The narrative builds suspense as the dead wife follows her husband back through the storm, into the house, and up to the bedroom, calling, "W-h-o—g-o-t—m-y— g-o-l-d-e-n *a-r-m*?" ("HTS," 12). At the last moment, when the voice intones right at the husband's "year," the narrator springs the carefully timed punch line directly at his audience—"You've got it!" ("HTS," 12). The folk origins of this tale go back to Beowulf's encounter with Grendal, and analogs abound in Western folklore. They generally take the form of cautionary stories: stories about mistaken notions of value (that center around the symbolic connotations of gold and prosthetic limbs) or about mistaken notions of exchange (that center around the burial of signs of value). [47] Twain's ghost story differs in at least two significant respects from these earlier versions. First, it admits little analysis of the relation of the arm to its "proper" owner: it is hard to ask, for example, why the wife in the story has a golden arm, where it came from, what history of accident or disability it represents. Second, the story conveys no sense that burying the arm is wrong, a caution often central to tales of gift exchange. Instead of imparting a warning the tale enacts one, repeatedly reminding us—its audience of novice storytellers—to "look out for the pause and get it right."

> Den de voice say, *right at his year*—"W-h-o—g-o-t—m-y—g-o-l-d-e-n *arm*?" (You must wail it out very plaintively and accusingly; then you stare steadily and impressively into the face of the farthest-gone auditor—a girl, preferably—and let that awe-inspiring pause begin to build itself in the deep hush. When it has reached exactly the right length, jump suddenly at that girl and yell, *"You've got it!"*

If you've got the *pause* right, she'll fetch a dear little yelp and spring right out of her shoes. But you *must* get the pause right; and you will find it the most troublesome and aggravating and uncertain thing you ever undertook.) ("HTS," 12)

For a story that is supposed to model narrative control, getting the pause right turns out to be surprisingly difficult. And the authorial parenthesis with which Twain concludes the essay (playing his confidence game on the audience) suggests that one source of anxiety is the snapper itself—"You've got it"—not just classic performance hazards like timing.[48] The themes of dispossession and dismemberment that underwrite "The Golden Arm" thus convert to accusation in the punch line, as the audience gets—understands? possesses?—something illicit. To paraphrase Walter Benjamin, the arm at the center of "How to Tell a Story"—a mixed symbol of value and disability—passes figuratively from the didactic narrator to his audience. In Benjamin's famous analogy: "[The story] embeds [itself] in the life of the storyteller in order to pass it on as experience to those listening. It thus bears the marks of the storyteller much as the earthen vessel bears the marks of the potter's hand."[49] But the experience embedded and passed on in "The Golden Arm," is one of lost control, involuntary response, and guilt. The storyteller resembles the ghostly wife he ventriloquizes—burdened with a prosthesis whose value is inversely proportional to its utility, that he does not control, but that calls him helplessly in pursuit. The audience's "yelp" suggests both confession and displacement, for if it controls the pause that haunts the storyteller, it does so involuntarily.

Suggestively, Twain embeds both of his anecdotes in cultural contexts that simultaneously name and mystify the object of their anxious humor. He gives each story a history that controverts its apparent origins and internal allusions. In this way, he transfers the European genealogy of "The Golden Arm" to "The Wounded Soldier": a story that "has been popular all over the world for twelve or fifteen hundred years" (9). The violent causes of the Civil War, in turn, are worked out in "The Golden Arm": now a "Negro ghost-story" that advertises its local origins in broad dialectic print (12).

These are playful substitutions, but they suggest the hybrid cultural origins of American narrative and undermine the overt claims of the essay. And they also call attention to the shared topoi of these anecdotes: the vulnerability of bodies as a locus of political identity, and their violent transformation, objectification, and circulation. To read "The Golden Arm" as a "Negro ghost-story" as well as an ancient folk tale is to recognize race slavery as its subject and parable as its method. Indeed, its first descriptive phrase repeats a familiar fictional epithet for slaveholders: the "monsus mean man" is as miserly, culpable, and unnatural as any plantation owner in a Charles Chestnutt story. This monstrous husband appears as an American Bluebeard: commodifying and stealing the value of his wife's body in a Gothic marriage that allegorizes the systematic appropriations of the slave economy. Thus his thieving raises the specter of a social death that haunts the tale. And it interprets the familiar dispossessions represented in the wife's prosthetic arm: the radical alienation of slave labor and its products; the alienation of propriety and consent in persons bound by contracts that define them as nonpersons. As the golden arm passes figuratively from speaker to "impressible" girl, the manipulations it symbolizes—far from naturalizing artistic labor like Benjamin's potter's mark—turn out to be clumsy and illicit. Twain's "impressively" held pause remains "the most troublesome and aggravating and uncertain thing you ever undertook" (12). The cost of simulating "simplicity and innocence and sincerity and unconsciousness" for the American storyteller is to be haunted by the repressed conditions of mastery—and the guilty fictions of possession on which such mastery depends (11).

The analogies between manual and oral kinds of impressions explored in "The Golden Arm," seem nonintuitive ones, but Twain pursues them at length in his analysis of the pause in *Pudd'nhead Wilson*. As in "How to Tell a Story," the pause exemplifies a problematic relation between the speaker's intentions and narrative control, and it enters the novel at a crucial point in the trial—exactly as Wilson unveils his fingerprint evidence—interrupting the famous explication of latent prints. Here Twain begins repeatedly to play on the word "impression," tying together the evidence of fingerprints, storytelling, and the girlish yelp of confession. His play on the word derives at least in part from his acute ear for terms of art: "impression" is Francis Galton's preferred designation for an inked or latent print. Along with "mark" and, less often, "seal," it remains synonymous with "print" throughout the forensic literature.[50] In this context, Wilson's timing in the courtroom scene draws a dramatic parallel between the evidence given by prints and the evidence given by storytelling. Repeatedly, Twain begins with the lawyer's pause "to give impressiveness to what he was about to say" (*PW*, 106). When Wilson dramatically interrupts his explication of the prints, Twain's prose dilates as the pause does, echoing his description of the technique in "How to Tell a Story." Like the audience in "How to Tell a Story," the courtroom bursts from astonished hush into somatic and vocal spasms when Wilson declares he will reveal the murderer before the clock strikes noon. "Stunned, distraught, unconscious of its own movement, the house half rose, as if expecting to see the murderer appear at the door, and a breeze of muttered ejaculations swept the place" (*PW*, 109). Tom Driscoll's involuntary, silent faint likewise confirms the potency of Wilson's impressive delivery. The helplessness of his response associates him with the impressible girl of "The Golden Arm," while Wilson's rhetorical command aligns him with the storyteller. Commanded to "make upon the window the fingerprints that will hang" him,

> Tom turned his ashen face imploringly toward the speaker, made some impotent movements with his white lips, then slid limp and lifeless to the floor.
> Wilson broke the awed silence with the words:
> "There is no need. He has confessed." (*PW*, 113)

The numerous echoes of "How to Tell a Story" illuminate the ambivalent and complicated logic of such unconscious testimony. Tom's collapse reprises the rhetoric of involuntary confession that appears throughout contemporary accounts of fingerprinting, from Brayley's "voiceless speech" to Hoover's "silent policemen." From its earliest expression in the discourse of forensic identification, the involuntary, concomitant nature of this physical evidence establishes the truth of criminal identity. Recalling *People v. Sallow*, we remember "There is neither torture nor volition nor chance of error. . . . The witness does not testify. The physical facts speak for themselves." Because it can be compelled or invented, the precedent implies, oral testimony is not reliable as a means of epistemological detection. Yet, the cases recounted in turn-of-the-century manuals and histories of fingerprinting rehearse this trope with a curious addition. Each time they describe the use of fingerprinting to resolve some acute dilemma of criminal deception, they assert that the criminal confessed—confirming evidence that by definition need not be orally confirmed.[51] Indeed, in *Pudd'nhead Wilson*, Roxy's own confession of having switched the children is soon to come. Spontaneous physical response appears to solve the problem of oral evidence by assimilating confession to the class of involuntary physiological signs legally defined by fingerprints. But it is precisely this kind of confirmation, spontaneous and apparently involuntary, that is most uncertain in Twain's estimation: "the most troublesome and aggravating and uncertain thing" ever undertaken. In early histories of fingerprinting, the generic gesture that supplements fingerprints with an apparently willing confession suggests a lingering uncertainty about the assimilation of oral and physical "confessions."

As it concludes—as well as it proceeds—Wilson's triumphant courtroom narration turns out to be as founded on uncertain contingencies as that of the short story. Numerous readers have observed that the logic of moral agency that he authoritatively constructs turns out to be a legal fiction. Echoing Angelo's assertion that "the knife was to blame," the court agrees with Tom's creditors that he cannot be guilty:

> . . . the creditors [of the Driscoll estate] came forward, now [after Tom's confession], and complained that inasmuch as through an error for which *they* were in no way to blame the false heir was not inventoried [when Driscoll died] with the rest of the property, great wrong and loss had thereby been inflicted upon them . . . that if [Tom] had been delivered up to them in the first place they would have sold him and he could not have murdered Judge Driscoll, therefore it was not he that had really committed the murder, the guilt lay with the erroneous inventory. (*PW*, 115)

Believing in the existence of a "Valet de Chambre" who will be hanged for murder, Wilson is in a sense elected "Pudd'nhead" twice when his murderer turns out never to have had legal existence as an intending person. After twenty years of "compulsory leisure" as a lawyer-manqué, his superb litigation confirms him "a made man for good." "All his sentences were golden," we learn (hearing a ghostly trace of the stolen arm) (*PW*, 114). But the "roaring gangs of enthusiasts" who come to this conclusion hardly seem models of probity. His professional debut in fingerprinting exposes the cross-purposes inherent in legal conventions that use bodily evidence both as the sign of inalienable, individual self-possession (in the case of fingerprints) and as the sign of dispossession and social death (in the case of blackness). It also exposes again the mechanical function of Wilson's own role in this system, serving institutional interests even at the moment when he seems most heroically self-determined.

Twainian physiology deeply complicates the notion of person constructed through ownership and of government founded on such a notion. In *Those Extraordinary Twins*, the effort required to maintain such laborious political fictions is caricatured in Angelo and Luigi's contest for self-possession. Should one brother fail to cede control and become officially nonexistent (as Angelo fails in the duel), they both "couldn't dress, couldn't stand up, couldn't sit down, couldn't even cross [their] legs, without calling a meeting first, and explaining the case, and passing resolutions, and getting consent" (*PW*, 156, 138). This condition might be termed a kind of dispossesive individualism, founded on a lack of proprioception that mirrors the social dispossessions of slavery. Its central recognition is the fact that being in a body may give only fragile coherence to the experience of self-possession. Thus, at the end of the novel, Roxy sits in the courtroom during Wilson's performance, "her bill of sale in her pocket. It was her most precious possession, and she never parted with it, day or night" (*PW*, 99). Here Roxy's pocket uncomfortably recalls Chambers's earlier empty pockets and his figuratively empty hands. The document that constitutes evidence that she owns herself must be gripped as tightly as possible; but no matter how closely she holds it, it still records an identity constituted in exchange, transmission, and dispossession.

By 1924, when Hoover's Identification Division took organizational shape, the technological superiority of fingerprints, figured as involuntary physical confession, gave the new federal agency its necessary moral authority. In the context of this institutional history, the gift of Twain's fictional stories of dispossession and amputation is two-fold. They make the disjunction of intention and agency within this concept more visible, and they question its implications. Like Will West's account of himself, like Chambers's imprisoning dialect, like the "dear little yelp" in "How to Tell a Story," it may be the degree of inarticulation that testifies to the truth of physical and social experience.

Epilogue

Writing in his journal in the 1920s, Sherwood Anderson sums up the Gothic threat posed by technological and industrial progress in the early twentieth century. He begins with his growing sense of estrangement from his body, felt most acutely in his writing:

> My own hands had not served me very well. Nothing they had done with words had satisfied me. There was not finesse enough in my fingers. All sorts of thoughts and emotions came to me that would not creep down my arms and out through my fingers upon the paper. How much was I to blame for that? How much could fairly be blamed to the civilization in which I had lived? I presume I wanted very much to blame something other than myself if I could.[1]

In the impulse to blame, to trace moral responsibility, Anderson maps the modern interpenetration of organic and mechanical action:

> The thoughts that came to me were something like this: "Suppose," I suggested to myself, "that the giving of itself by an entire generation to mechanical things were really making all men impotent. . . . Was the desire all modern peoples had for a greater navy, a greater army, taller public buildings, but a sign of growing impotence? Was there a growing race of people in the world who had no use for their hands and were the hands paying them back by becoming ineffectual? Was

the Modern after all but the man who had begun faintly to realize what I was then realizing and were all his efforts but at bottom the attempt to get his hands back on the ends of his arms?" (Anderson, 376)

Anderson's meditation inherits Twain's suspicions of an emergent state infrastructure, elaborating its mechanical and bureaucratic dispossessions on a grand scale. As with Twain, the symptoms of Anderson's postindustrial anomie are simultaneously physical (the palpable clumsiness of hands that resist their service to feeling and thought), professional (he writes here in some anguish about hostile critical reception), and cultural. What begins as a self-accusing complaint expands beyond the thematics of inscription to the thematics of physical performance, prowess, and work. For Anderson, the work of writing is representative: one of a set of bodily practices that ratify (or in this case fail to ratify) the forceful presence of the modern individual in a civil world. Intimate failures of dexterity trope similar alienations in the grotesque characters of his best-known fiction, *Winesburg, Ohio*. Vague lassitudes and uncertain frenzies of manual activity overcome the characters in his opening stories, conjuring a collective failure of proprioception that oppresses the fictional "writer" and his cast. In the Twainian preamble to this collection, for example, a dream-vision pageant of grotesques usurps the author's role. In the next story, "Hands," the helpless and wayward gestures of the isolated central character suggest a late-industrial George Dedlow. The grotesque emotional landscapes of *Winesburg, Ohio*, like those in Anderson's journal, manifest cultural change as intimate psychosomatic experience.

The recognition of such dynamism in apparently essential bodily experiences troubles Anderson as much or more than his own writer's block. For a literary scholar at the end of the twentieth century, such accounts of proprioceptive failure are worth pursuing not to confirm or contest their troubling nature or even to rehearse the uncertain moral environment they frame for us. From Shakespeare's stage dismemberments to Le Fanu's witty domestic horrors, these fictions do this very effectively for themselves. Viewed longitudinally, such conventional dismemberments stretch our understanding of the essentialist strategies that underwrite Western concepts of autonomous, dependent, and corporate action. Such a view invites us to look with critical interest at a category of thought, essentialist argument, that remains pervasive and surprisingly complex in its different historical inflections—if not always morally admirable.

With all its constituent inscriptions—movement, tactile contact, social encounter, and making—the trope of the dead hand concentrates our attention on what Victor Turner calls the "oretic" or sensory qualities of its symbolic operations. In this respect, the device provocatively emphasizes both the constructedness of the body as cultural form—described so powerfully in the work of Michel Foucault—and its persisting physicality. As in the theater, even the most text-based versions of this trope—"beast with five fingers" stories, Keats's "Living Hand"—conjure performance effects on readers imagined as members of a responsive, present-time audience. In texts that are performative—didactic, theatrical, epiphanic, or ecstatic—the apparent opposition between the artifice of culturally constructed symbols and the essence of physiology loses its force. As Caroline Bynum puts it in her seminal study of the medieval body, "However we construct it and whatever it stands for to us, body is what we've got. . . . All evidence for the doing of history opens out beyond itself to an intractable physicality. . . . What we study—what we can study—is culturally constructed. But we know we are more than culture. We are body. And, as body, we die."[2]

It is this very certainty that generates such contested accounts of death and disintegration in medieval theology—the vital matter for Bynum's analysis. Foucault's insight, as her work reminds us, is that the intractability of "being in a body" makes the varied experiences of bodies more, rather than less, available for cultural work. (And, as Keats's lyrical mortmain confirms, there is little more culturally available for lively artifice than the intractability of death.) The career of the disembodied hand illuminates the complex nature of what is appealed to when one set of intractable but plastic facts—the faculties of the hand—are marshaled to ratify a dynamic cultural fiction—the changing notion of what it means to be an acting person.

Every *grand recit* of such changes—like the reimagined proprieties of Lockean political theory or the subjection of the body to mechanism in Carlyle's "Mechanical Age"—prints a totalizing pattern over a loose historical weave of multiple narratives of performance and action. One of the purposes of this study has been to describe the multiple threads of iconographic and textual tradition drawn through the recurring trope of the disembodied hand, at local moments and in local contexts. A second has been to record the reconfiguration of these threads as the new conditions of work and social affiliation described by such *grands récits* change the questions the trope addresses. The delight and strangeness of a complex trope is both the *longue durée* of its available, constitutive referents, and their multiplicity.

Looking forward, this discursive variety can be provisionally mapped in the manual iconography of emerging digital technologies. Historians of digital industries, for example, invoke both Andersonian and neo-Aristotelian metaphors of the hand to describe the experience of electronic labor. The dead hands of industrial Gothic echo in E. F. Schumacher's classic economic study, *Small Is Beautiful* (1973), as he regrets the misdirections of modern industrial design and prophecies the technological future:

> The type of work which modern technology is most successful in reducing or even eliminating is skillful, productive work of human hands, in touch with real materials of one kind or another. In an advanced industrial society, such work has become exceedingly rare, and to make a living by doing such work has become virtually impossible. A great part of the modern neurosis may be due to this very fact.[3]

Yet in recent studies of digital information design, such Andersonian nostalgia has given way to optimistic accounts of the possibilities of electronic cottage industries. And along with the vision of an electronic uncanny, scholars increasingly employ a vocabulary of virtual handiwork. Thus Malcolm McCullough describes information technology not as a late industrial extension of modernist modes of production, but as virtual "handicraft."[4] In popular discourse and in practice, he shows that digital production began in the late twentieth century to acquire the Benjaminian "quality of being 'thrown,' that is, executed at a particular moment, with a particular degree of skill, and with particular idiosyncrasy to the result"

(McCullough, 8). A digital artifact may "not bear the mark of some-one's hands, as a clay pot does," McCullough acknowledges, but,

Neither is it the product of a standardized industrial process, like an aluminum skillet. It is individual, and reveals authorship at the level of its internal organization. It is unique, for although flawless copies can be made, nobody is going to make another just like it unless by copy-ing. It is abstract: a symbolic structure, a workable construction, in a digital medium, showing the effects of manipulation by software tools. (McCullough, 155)

McCullough's history traces the invention of graphical tools for "direct manipulation"—like the arrow pointer and pointing hand with which we negotiate computer interfaces—as they "developed grips and intrinsic operations, such as selecting, stretching and repli-cating" (McCullough, 23). For McCullough, the instruments for virtual exploration, manipulation, invention, and play serve as seamless electronic prostheses; they coordinate hand and eye mo-tions sufficiently well that we handle "things" in virtual environ-ments with efficacy. In this context, icons like the pointing virtual hand renovate Aristotelian assumptions about the immanence of spirit in the motions of the hand. Although disembodied, they abide biddably, inertly, not uncannily. In practice, McCullough ac-knowledges, graphical tools and figures remain limited: functionally fixed in certain ways and oretically or sensorily impoverished.[5] But in theory, the only handiwork in a virtual environment is the work of thinking: selecting, addressing, composing, and revising.[6]

The manual metaphors of this new media manifest a long iconographic history. Peter Stallybrass notes, for example, the ways graphical hands conjure the medieval manuscript index, associated with readerly intervention and interpretation.[7] Thus the mixed and sometimes conflicting rhetorics of electronic design evoke earlier conventions of manual action in competing ways. Their multiple renovations—of modern, early modern, and medieval tropes—sug-gest the volatile character of late twentieth-century experiences of electronic work and expression. But they also illustrate the flexible and layered fabric of the Western body that articulates, conjures, and performs agency relations.

Notes

Preface

1. Brontë, 67.
2. "Historical Epistemology," 282. Daston credits the recent work of Ian Hacking (" 'Style' for Historians and Philosophers") and Arnold Davidson ("The Horror of Monsters") for innovations in this genre. I am indebted to her own powerful version of this kind of work: the history of the conceptual categories of fact and evidence outlined in "Marvelous Facts," 244.
3. See, for example, Frank R. Wilson's recent study of human intelligence and manual performance, *The Hand: How Its Use Shapes the Brain*.
4. F. Wilson, 288.

Introduction

1. Bulwer, 7. Hereafter cited parenthetically in the text, by page numbers to Cleary's edition.
2. For a recent example, see Sorell.
3. For a history of innovations in hand surgery, see Boyes.
4. See Bell; Bertillon.
5. See Le Bot; Simmel.
6. Hertz.
7. See *Beowulf*, ed. Klaeber, 833–36; 980–90.
8. Galen, 71. Hereafter cited parenthetically in the text, by page number to May's edition. May (71, n. 12), Lynch (33), and Goldberg (14) all comment on the double sense of the phrase "instrument of instruments."

9. See the key terms "presence-at-hand" and "ready-to-hand" in *Being and Time*, and the famous claim that "thinking itself is man's simplest, and for that reason hardest, handwork" (Heidegger, 16–17).

10. G. E. Moore's phrase "here is one hand, and here is another" is the starting place for Wittgenstein's meditation on the language games of common sense epistemology. See Wittgenstein, 2e.

11. "There is no way of deducing from a knowledge of physiology, however thorough, that there is a rule in our society to the effect that an extended hand means 'I am about to turn to the right.'" Passmore, 530.

12. See Bernstein, 280, for this summary of the central dichotomies identified by R. S. Peters, A. I. Melden, and Charles Taylor. These have been refined in turn by Charles Landesman, Donald Davidson (in his influential study of action descriptions, "Action, Reasons, and Causes"), and many others. For the example of signing a contract, see Peters, 13; for raising the arm, see Melden, 56. Bernstein's chapter 4 offers a lucid survey of the main issues addressed in contemporary analytic philosophy. See also Care and Landesman's *Readings in the Theory of Action*.

13. Augustine, 8.8. David Aers ("A Whisper") points to the historical continuity of Augustinian subjectivity through the early modern period. Elaine Scarry draws even longer connections between Augustine's writings on the will and later philosophical accounts of willful motions ("Consent and the Body," 875).

14. Augustine, 8.9. William James seems to have this passage in mind in his chapter on the will in *The Principles of Psychology*; there, he repeatedly turns to the example of lifting an arm or clenching a fist, and to counter-examples of palsied or paraplegic limbs to make the point that volition is a "psychic or moral fact pure and simple" (499, 560–61).

15. Scarry, "The Merging of Bodies," 85; hereafter cited parenthetically, by page number. Meditating on stories that describe a relationship between dolls and artificial limbs, "the doll/limb hybrid," Scarry summarizes the earlier version of this argument, found in Scarry, "Consent and the Body."

16. And this is part of what makes her work continuously interesting, for she seeks out discourses and genres that articulate a contrarian eagerness and sense of certainty about the ways cultural artifacts remake us, from the medical engineering of prosthetic limbs, to product liability law, to marriage law.

17. Scarry makes a related point about the centrality of motion in the philosophy of volition: "In philosophic writings about the will, the enactment of freedom is often couched in terms of physical movement" (875).

18. See Macpherson, 77–78, 106, 200.

19. Locke, "The Second Treatise of Civil Government," section 27, in *Two Treatises of Government*, 134.

20. See Maine. For a more recent assessment of the changes in English common law in this period, see Simpson. Don Wayne's influential essay, "Drama and Society in the Age of Jonson," interpreted the changing status of the Jacobean playhouse in the light of Maine's argument. Luke Wilson has elaborated the importance of early concepts of contract in understanding problems in early seventeenth-century drama; see Wilson, "Ben Jonson and the Law of Contract" and "Promissory Performances." I am indebted to his thinking about the rise of assumpsit in this period.

21. See Wayne, 115.

22. For a detailed survey of the contest between ecclesiastical and secular property law, from the medieval period to the present, see H. D. Hazeltine's history of dead hand law in Europe, "Mortmain."

23. *Oxford English Dictionary*, 2d ed. Oxford Clarendon Press, 1989. "Agent," *sb.* 4. Hereafter cited as OED.

24. See Charles Taylor's history of the "webs of interlocution" that shape the modern sense of subjectivity, in *Sources of the Self*. David Aers has applied Taylor's ideas to medieval studies (see the introduction to *Culture and History*), and Elizabeth Fowler invokes them in her study of medieval models of agency in "Civil Death and the Maiden."

25. See Braunmuller.

26. Burke, x. Hereafter cited parenthetically in the text.

27. P. Anderson, 18.

28. On agency and history see Callinicos; and in a literary context, Bruce Robbins, "The Butler Did It." On agency and the law, see Hart and Honore.

29. P. Anderson, 16, 54, 58; paraphrasing Althusser, 183, and quoting E. P. Thompson, 280.

30. OED, *sb.* 5.

31. Bolton, 295; Defoe, 32.

32. See Bernstein's introduction, ix–x, for these definitions of *praxis* and *poesis*.

33. Bernstein, 303.

34. Giddens, 54–55. For Giddens, these are the central lacunae of analytic philosophy in the 1960s and 1970s: missing from the work of G. E. M. Anscombe, Theodore Mischel, Richard Taylor, Arthur C. Danto, R. S. Peters, and Donald Davidson. Alvin I. Goldman's *A Theory of Human Action* is the exception that addresses something like unintended consequences. In contrast, he argues, Marxist theory does a better job of theorizing institutions and addressing the politics of social practices (n. 268).

35. In this, Giddens's point is similar to arguments made by Peters, Melden, and Taylor.

36. B. Williams, 20.

37. For the phrase "deeply accidental," see B. Williams, 28.

Chapter 1

1. On marital handclasps, see Randall. On feudal handclasps, see Lynch. For a history of the Renaissance handshake, see Roodenburg; see also Spicer. On raising the right hand, see Bulwer, "Juro," 48, "Suffragor," 49. Jonathan Goldberg's study of early modern hand writing, *Writing Matter*, addresses a related set of visual conventions, the disembodied hands that illustrate correct hand posture and style in writing manuals. Like Goldberg, I take seriously the idea that actions comprise the iconographic and literary *semes* of the hand. And like him, I am particularly interested in texts that offer both a theory and practice of a specific kind of manual activity. Where Goldberg reads the inscription of institutional violence in the visual synecdoches employed in writing manuals, I am interested in their contemporary iconographic contexts. The visual traditions for representing God's hand, adapted to secular writing practices, represent mixed, layered, and sometimes contested agencies working in a single bodily instrument. In the context of Biblical metonymy, Goldberg's Foucauldian figures of "disciplinary submission" might equally be read as appropriating and participating in authority. Furthermore, the diligent practice emphasized in these manuals registers the real difficulties of writing legibly and transcribing accurately. These difficulties remind us of the traditionally errant nature of writing by hand—which remains as imaginatively powerful as the practices that seek to regularize it. As Harold Love has shown, the very errors inherent in manuscript publication, which marked the human limitations of medieval scribes, began to gain new meanings, associated with liberal community and individualism, in the seventeenth century (Love, 155–56).

2. John of Salisbury, 104–5.

3. In *Nature's Work of Art* (86), Leonard Barkan comments on the repetition of "hand" in John of Salisbury's passage. As Barkan shows, the microcosmic metaphor has mixed motives in the classical tradition; it can be used to argue for the primacy of the citizen and mutual protection of parts of society or for their obligation to subordinate to the larger good of the whole (65–66). But he also notes, "As far back as the Timaeus the limbs have been an image of the mortal diversity—rather than the divine essence and unity—of man" (123). The dissection discussed below is striking for the way in which it adapts the hand's conventional separateness and mobility to an argument about divine coherence, yet it retains the seeds of conflict suggested by such mortal diversity. Elaine Scarry points out that "In philosophic writings about the will, the enactment of freedom is often

couched in terms of physical movement" ("The Merging of Bodies," 85); but this claim can be made more precisely. The limbs that are an image of mortal diversity are *the* locus of political resistance, as John of Salisbury's graft-given officers or as in the ancient parable of the belly, with its rebellious hands.

4. Specific early modern discourses that feature the hand, such as chiromancy, have been addressed as follows. On chiromancy (palmistry) see Thorndike. On the Arabic influence of *khamsa* amulets (the so-called Hand of Fatima), see Hildburgh. On the mnemonic devices of Annahands and Marienhands in prayer, see Bruckner; and Engel, 32–47. Michael Neill surveys the wide range of manual symbolism on the Renaissance stage in "Amphitheatres in the Body."

5. On early modern theories of agency in the law, see Braunmuller. Luke Wilson discusses legal and economic notions of agency in contract in "Ben Jonson and the Law of Contract."

6. See, for example, Crooke's extended analysis of this vocabulary in the light of Aristotelean theory of the senses, 6.

7. The persistence of Aristotelian-Galenic thought in the seventeenth-century biological sciences is a larger phenomenon in itself, of course. See Wollock for an account of the influence of Paduan Aristotelianism on English medical theory in this period.

8. Banister, fol. 60v.

9. Jonathan Sawday's study of the culture of dissection, *The Body Emblazoned*, advances these arguments in compelling ways; he also traces the history of dualist discourses in the culture of dissection. As I hope to show here, the dissection of the hand is in some senses anomalous—a hybrid or holdout in the shift toward Cartesian and Harveian mechanics.

10. The work was reprinted twice by 1618 and published again (corrected, enlarged, and largely outdated) in 1631. As the title page makes clear, Crooke compiles and translates the best of the authorities of the previous century, notably Andreas Laurentius and Caspar Bauhin. He set out to describe the best of current practice (drawing verbatim from Bauhin) and to survey historical controversies (opining in the more conservative voice of Laurentius); the numerous illustrations derive mostly from Vesalius's *Fabrica* (see O'Malley, "Helkiah Crooke," 5, 8). According to O'Malley, Crooke's work contributed little to the scientific advancement of anatomy, but significantly to its practice in England (12).

11. See Schupbach, 28, and Sawday for historical analysis of the order of dissection.

12. Crooke, 784. Hereafter cited in parentheses by page number.

13. See Schupbach's discussion of the use of this dissection in anatomy lectures in the Netherlands during the early sixteenth century for a similar

argument. The deep connection between formal and symbolic properties of the hand and early modern mnemonics can be seen in any chiromancy; these themes are illustrated in Engel, 12–67.

14. Like Crooke, Banister cites Realdus Columbus's *De re anatomica* (1559) on this point, as if it is an especially compelling one: "This member is most notable, and worthy longest to be borne in mynde. The muscles whereof (sayth Columbus) will, in dissection, the longest endure uncorrupted" (Banister, fol. 60v).

15. Aristotle, *De Anima*, 3.8.432[a]1. *The Complete Works of Aristotle*.

16. For the preceeding account, see Schupbach, 17–19. I am indebted especially to his appendix 2, "The Special Significance of the Hand" (56–65), which excerpts the relevant anatomical literature, from Aristotle to *Gray's Anatomy*.

17. Vesalius, fol. 2r–v. Translated in C. D. O'Malley, *Andreas Vesalius*, 317–20.

18. O'Malley ("Helkiah Crooke") and Sawday (225–26) both give fuller accounts of the publication controversy.

19. See especially the detail of an engraving from Heironymus Fabricius Aquapendente, *De visione voci auditu* (Venice, 1600) discussed by Schupbach (19); here Anatomia herself pulls back the superficial flexor-muscles of a dissected arm. Other examples of the use of the severed hand as an emblem of anatomical practice can be found in the title page of Bidloo's *Anatomia humani corporis* (lower right corner, a severed hand on the title page of an anatomy text that two putti open curiously) and in the decorated initial letters of Valverde's *Historia de la composicion del cuerpo humano* (Rome, 1556) where putti hold up a severed hand (19r).

20. Dilwyn Knox glosses the spread-fingered, open-palmed gesture more specifically as one of invitation. He cites a fifteenth-century Florentine illustration of an innkeeper making this gesture, accompanied by an explanatory caption; see 104.

21. See Sawday's analysis of écorché gestures—the fullest to date—in his chapter 5. See also Wilson; and Glenn Harcourt. K. B. Roberts and J. D. W. Tomlinson provide a history of these aesthetics in *The Fabric of the Body*. In *Literature After Dissection in Early Modern England*, forthcoming, John G. Norman discusses emerging representational strategies of the anatomy theater.

22. Harcourt, 49.

23. See "Posture, Expression and Decorum" in Kemp, 144. The visual tradition that associates gestures of the hand with expressions of intention is a very old one. Jean-Claude Schmitt summarizes the medieval theories of gesture that Leonardo and his contemporaries drew on and that animate anatomical illustration (59–70).

24. Wilson, "William Harvey's *Prelectiones*," 81.

25. Of the manual terms for linear measure in England and Scotland (cubit, ell, hand, span, palm, nail or thumb, and finger), many were still in practical use in the sixteenth century. The cloth measures, ell and thumb, lasted even longer: Elizabeth I's Exchequer standard ell (forty-five inches) remained the *de facto* standard until 1824 (Connor, 95). Fabric is still available at retail in standard bolts of forty-four to forty-five inches.

26. Barkan, *Nature's Work of Art*, 142. For the architectural system of human proportions, Barkan refers us to Vitruvius's influential *De Architectura* and Giovanni Paolo Lomazzo's *Trattato dell' arte della pittura*, translated by Richard Haydock (London, 1598). According to Lomazzo, "from the proportions of man's body (the most absolute of all God's creatures) is that measure taken which is called Brachium, wherewith all things are most exactly measured, being drawne from the similitude of a mans Arme, which is the third part of his length and breadth, and the Arme containeth 3 heads or spans" (108). The simultaneously practical and mystical character of these similitudes was preserved in the etymology of *cubit* and *ell*, which identifies these bones as essential units of measure and measure as an essential activity of the arm. These commonplaces persist in seventeenth-century debates about the standardization of measure. See, for example, John Greaves's scathing objection to the application of Vitruvius; it is impractical "Unless, as some fancy, that the cubit of the Sanctuary, was taken from the cubit of *Adam*, he being created in an excellent state of perfection" (9).

27. Scholz, 62–63. Hereafter cited parenthetically in the text. Scholz reminds us of the Mosaic injunction against pictorial representation of God, adopted by the early Christian Fathers, noting that inscriptions of God's hand pun on the Hebrew word *yad*, which means both "hand" and "power" (258–59).

28. Scholz points out that this figure is rarely treated as a key motif in emblem books, as if it lacks its own "symbolic relevance" to their authors and audience (259). However, while the emblem books themselves may not index the motif, their audience certainly registered this complicated metonymic occlusion of "cut off" as symbolically relevant. Contemporary literary allusions to the motif often develop dismemberment as a dramatic, narrative, and aesthetic problem (see Chapters 2 and 3).

Chapter 2

1. For a lucid account of the problems modern productions encounter in staging the mutilations, see Dessen, *Titus Andronicus*. On the violent disjunction between action and language in the play, see Tricomi; Hulse; and

Kendall. David Willbern's "Rape and Revenge in *Titus Andronicus*" is one of the earliest psychoanalytic readings.

2. Hobbes, 125. Hereafter cited parenthetically in the text.

3. See Braunmuller on the criminal and civil jurisprudence concerning the various kinds of principal and agent.

4. Plowden, 98.

5. Marjorie Garber remarks on the uncanny persistence of the trope of dismemberment in editorial and critical commentary on the play (23–24). Describing the "textual effect" that the search for a ghostly author inevitably produces, Garber observes that in the case of "hands," "body parts and parts of speech seem inextricably intertwined" for editors of the play. Gillian Kendall discusses this inextricability of rhetorical figure and dramatic dismemberment in complex detail; she is particularly interested in the interpretive and dramatic consequences of the way the play literalizes rhetorical conventions. My aim is the inverse: to explain the extraliterary symbolic systems in which stage dismemberments operate.

6. Berry, xxxvi. Stubbs confirmed Camden's account in a later letter to Sir Christopher Hatton (Berry, 111). The Stubbs anecdote carries interesting resonances in relation to a play concerned with the right manner of constituting sovereignty. Frances Yates was among the first to point out that the play is primarily concerned with the problem of defining just Empire, by drawing a connection between Elizabeth I and the references to Astraea and Virgo during Titus's peculiar arrow-shooting scene (*Astraea*, 74–76). Yates reads the scene as a cryptic appeal for the restoration of "justice" to Rome, in the conventional figure of Virgo as Justice. She concludes that Lucius (who has hit Virgo "in her lap" with his arrow) shall bring her down to earth and establish the golden age of the Just Virgin. While this leads to an extremely positive reading of the play's ambivalent ending, it draws a thematic connection between Shakespeare's concerns with virginity, sovereignty, and invasion and the anxieties raised by Stubbs at the prospect of the Alençon marriage. In this context one might imagine Lavinia as a kind of antiemblem of the Just Virgin, "lopp'd" of the iconic hands that might hold scales and sword and made the center of a vengeful demand for justice. For a rich account of Shakespeare's concern with the theme of westering Empire in this play, see James, *Shakespeare's Troy*. In "Getting It All Right," Naomi Conn Liebler nails down the historical context for the play's subtext of imperial decline and dissolution, Herodian's *History*.

7. A history of scholarly and audience response to these speeches would include most of the essays on *Titus Andronicus* written during this century. See especially Waith, "The Ceremonies of *Titus Andronicus*."

8. Galen, 81; quoted in full in the introduction.

9. All quotations from Shakespeare's plays are taken from *The Riverside Shakespeare*, hereafter cited parenthetically by act, scene, and line number.

10. Menenius's fable of the Belly and its "mutinous parts" tests the right relations between the "instruments" and "agents" of the body in similar ways. In Shakespeare's version of this very old story, the natural anatomical order on which Menenius bases his politics of digestive cooperation are challenged when the plebeian Great Toe develops hungry bellies. Here Shakespeare humorously deconstructs the principle that body parts naturalize political hierarchies. Interestingly, the Variorum *Coriolanus* attributes this parable to several sources that recount a revolt against the belly led principally by the hands.

11. Paradin's collection appeared in 1551 and became one of the most influential and copied collections of the later sixteenth century (Paradin, 1). Henry Green's detailed source study, *Shakespeare and the Emblem Writers* (1870), established the influence of English and continental emblem books on Shakespeare's plays; among the most important were Whitney's influential *A Choice of Emblemes* (1586) and an English translation of Paradin called *The Heroicall Devises of Paradin* (1591). Drawing on the same sources as Whitney, Wither's collection is somewhat belated—as Rosemary Freeman notes in her introduction to *A Collection of Emblemes*. More recent scholarship has shown the general currency and robust influence of continental collections on English art and imagination. Charles Moseley points out that there were ninety editions of the works of Alciato between 1531 and 1600; emblem books and pictures "were translated rapidly and spread across Europe either in translations or, increasingly, in polyglot editions, and the frequency of editions is evidence that the popularity of emblem books was vast and universal" (Moseley, 15).

A number of critics have referred to *Titus Andronicus* in passing as "emblematic"—implicitly responding, I think, to the enigmatic and often stylized quality of its dramatic displays. See comments in Bradbrook, *Shakespeare and Elizabethan Poetry*, and Daly, *The English Emblem Tradition*. Ann Haaker discusses the thematic parallels between emblems and the play in "*Non sine causa*."

12. Unlike the hands in medieval stained glass, for example, they rarely point, bless, or otherwise engage in the wide range of symbolic manual gesture. Perhaps they have their literary roots in the disembodied, sword-wielding hands of Malory and Amadis of Gaul.

13. The importance of gift rituals in the constitution of heroic community goes back at least as far as *Beowulf*. This tradition evolved into the conventions of seignorial largesse central to medieval feudal systems and frequently supplies potent imagery for Shakespeare. See Lynch, 153.

14. Randall, 178.

15. Wither, 13—16, 230. Hereafter cited parenthetically.

16. Critical readings of the play sometimes internalize the pressure of this displacement of attention, most acutely in relation to Lavinia's injuries. However, a number of essays treat this problem at length, as a peculiar effect of the disjunction between the formal language and violent events in the play. See Tricomi; Hulse; Kendall; and Waith, "Metamorphosis of Violence."

17. Yates describes this continental symbol of imperial justice as follows: "Favyn, writing in 1620, when speaking of the origin of the *main de justice* carried before the kings of France—the wand with a hand at the end of it, a derivation from the Roman standard—says that the hand is made of white ivory to denote the 'innocence of the Virgin Astraea.' " (82). Lavinia's hands, like her cheeks, are of course "lily" in color.

18. Cf. Hulse, who argues that Lavinia's fellatio-like actions in the stick-writing scene reenact her rapes (116); also Douglas Green, who elaborates that argument in "Interpreting 'Her Martyr'd Signs,' " 317.

19. S. Freud, "Fetishism," 154. Hereafter cited parenthetically in the text.

20. Titus calls his script for Chiron and Demetrius his "sad decrees" and goes on to assert, as a judge, that "what is written shall be executed" (5.2.11—15).

21. Lucius's description of Titus's "true hand" eerily echoes the language of faithful nationalism used by William Page in his scaffold speech before losing his right hand: "And holding up his right hand, [he] said: 'This hand did I put to the plow and got my living by it many years . . . ': And so [he] laid his hand upon the block and prayed the executioner quickly to dispatch him; and so at two blows his hand was smitten off, and so lifting up the stump, [he] said to the people, 'I have left there a true Englishman's hand,' and so went from the scaffold very stoutly and with a very great courage" (Berry, xxxvi). Despite the ambiguity of Titus's role, it is tempting to read topical criticism of Elizabethan tyranny into the trickery and ingratitude that Lucius decries here: pitting a true nationalist hand against the prospect of an adulterated national heritage threatened by contamination with the Goths or with Alençon. This kind of reading would be in keeping with the complex critique of a waning, corrupt, empirial model James and Liebler find in Titus's Rome.

22. Crooke, 730.

23. See Richard Strier's "Faithful Servants" on humanist debates about faithful disobedience.

Chapter 3

1. Stallybrass, "Reading the Body," 137, citing Bakhtin, 320.
2. See McLuskie, *Renaissance Dramatists*; Jankowski.
3. Bakhtin, 26.
4. "Hermaphrodite or ambidexter would be good names for such men of double estate," "The Lollard Conclusions, 1394," in E. Peters, 279.
5. Maine, 165.
6. See Rider; Cockeram.
7. Constance Jordan pioneered this field; see especially *Renaissance Feminism* and more recently, *Shakespeare's Monarchies*. Literary scholars have most often addressed early modern contractualism in terms of the genre of romance. For an excellent summary of the use of marital consent as a model for political contract, in this generic context, see Victoria Kahn's recent "Margaret Cavendish and the Romance of Contract." On royalist romance see Annabel Patterson, "Paradise Regained," and Lois Potter, *Secret Rites and Secret Writing*. On emergent vocabularies for contract in medieval literature see Fowler, "Civil Death and the Maiden." With the exception of the last, most literary studies of contractualism focus on the midseventeenth century on. I hope to contribute to this work by expanding both its generic and historical field of view.
8. There are important exceptions. A. R. Braunmuller describes such developments in the law of agency in "Second Means. " In "Faithful Servants," Richard Strier maps out the theory of courtly service promulgated in conduct manuals like Castiglione's *The Courtier*. Jonathan Dollimore's reading of social displacement in Webster's *The White Devil* calls attention to the surplus of dispossessed, university-educated men in this period; writers from Bacon to Hobbes pointed to this surplus and consequent discontentment as an important cause of sedition and rebellion. See "The White Devil," in *Radical Tragedy*, 231–46, esp. 242. Earlier scholarship usually addressed these issues in terms of the character of the Malcontent; I hope to shift attention from character type to the structural analysis of service relations that preoccupies these plays. Lawrence Danson's recent discussion of Webster's own concerns about rising professionalism (presented at the 1997 Shakespeare Association of America seminar "Early Modern Drama and the Question of Agency") suggests the new directions this kind of study might take. Danson reads Bosola's divided role as an agent for himself and an agent for others as a reflection of Webster's intense concern with the changing nature of patronage and professional service in this period.

9. John Webster, *The Duchess of Malfi*, 4.1.53–55. Hereafter cited parenthetically by act, scene, and line number of the Oxford *World Classics* edition.

10. Wayne, 115.

11. Webster, *The White Devil*, 2.1. 216–17. Hereafter cited parenthetically by act, scene, and line numbers of the New Mermaid edition.

12. Bulwer, 50.

13. Gataker, 9.

14. This is slightly earlier than the OED places the emergence of this sense of the word, in the 1630s.

15. For a detailed analysis of the marital traditions Webster draws on in this scene, including the anatomical logic symbolized by handfasting, see Randall.

16. The critical note in Brennan's edition glosses the dead man's hand briefly: "A dead man's hand was a powerful charm used in the cure of madness." Brennan's source is M. C. Bradbrook's brief citation of the scene "Two Notes upon Webster." Bradbrook invokes a mixed tradition of folk cures and occult practices to explain the prop, including the Hand of Glory. She notes that dead hands and fingers, often severed, were used in a number of early modern European folk cures, and their use persisted at least into the nineteenth century. Her source, in turn, is George Lyman Kittredge's seminal *Witchcraft in Old and New England*, whose robust bibliography of medicinal and malevolent uses of dead hands is where most editors of the play arrive.

17. Remy seems to have been comparable in reputation to Jean Bodin; his *Demonolatreiae* (1595), which covered trial accounts between 1581 and 1591, was frequently republished and borrowed from. See R. Robbins; Macfarlane.

18. See E. Radford and M. Radford, *The Encyclopedia of Superstitions*, edited and revised by Christina Hole, 179.

19. It is also reflected in several sources and analogues. Lucas cites Herodotus's *Tale of Rhampsinitus* (2.121), which involves two related plots, one of theft from the king's coffers, one of a trick with a severed hand that leads to the marriage of the trickster and the king's haughty daughter. See related examples in Kittredge; Porter; and S. Thompson.

20. Macfarlane, 25.

21. Here, and throughout this book, I am indebted to Caroline Walker Bynum's rich account of late medieval relics and the complex synecdoches they realize. See *Fragmentation and Redemption*, especially chapter 7.

22. Macfarlane also quotes Francis Hutchinson's assertion in his *Historical Essay* (1718) that it was "lawful to give in Evidence Matters that are no

ways relating to that Fact, and done many Years before" (16). A number of scholars including Macfarlane (16) and Newman (54) quote Dalton, *The Countrey Justice* (1619), on this principle (see Note 23, following).

23. Dalton, 251, quoted in R. Robbins, 175. Hereafter cited parenthetically in the text.

24. Ady, 114, 130.

25. Scot, 192.

26. OED, *sb.* 1.

27. See the opening set pieces by Antonio and Bosola, 1.1.11, 1.1.47.

28. See Strier for the theory of faithful disobedience in conduct literature and contemporary political theory.

29. See Curtis.

30. Locke, chapter 7, sec. 85.

31. Agnew describes the "arrival of a new labor standard of value" in *Worlds Apart*, 143.

Chapter 4

1. Dickens, 80. Hereafter cited in parentheses.

2. Walpole, 17. Hereafter cited in parentheses.

3. Duncan, 30. Hereafter cited in parentheses.

4. See, for example, the "invisible agency" that hinders the protagonist in the opening pages of Beckford's *Vathek*, 20. The evocative authority of this idiom is apparent in the proliferation of popular titles like Marie Connor Leighton's *The Hand of the Unseen* (n.d.); Thomas Peckett Prest's *The Death Grasp; or, A Father's Curse* (1842); *The Skeleton Clutch; or The Goblet of Gore* (1842); *The Bloody Hand, or the Fatal Cup* (n. d.).

5. OED, "mortmain" *n.* a, c.

6. Randall.

7. See, for example, the contemporary biscuitware model of the Tomb of Madame de Langhan at Hindelbanck, Switzerland, in the Chatsworth collection. She is breaking out of the tomb with her child, raising her hand (uncertain date).

8. *Night of the Living Dead* (1968), *Dawn of the Dead* (1977), dir. George Romero. *Gothic* (1986) dir. Ken Russell. The television ad for Nikon Cameras, "The Hand with Five Fingers," produced by Scali, McCabe, Sloves appeared in the mid 1980s.

9. Le Fanu, *Wylder's Hand*, 369. The episode renders a wonderfully muddy version of broken tomb scenes like Madame de Langhan's, complete with blackened, decomposing fingers, the motto glimmering ironically on a ring, and "the point of a knee . . . protruding from the peat" (369).

10. Kittredge, 145; Kittredge's note on p. 463 to these folk tales collects the most comprehensive list of the many European cognates. Contemporary accounts of the use of the charm were apparently not uncommon. For example, the *Observer*, 16 January 1831, reported an attempted robbery on 3 January at Loughcrew, Co. Meath in which the burglars "entered the house armed with a dead man's hand, with a lighted candle in it." See Radford and Radford, 179.

11. Hawthorne's peculiar send-up of the dead Romantics, in "P.'s Correspondence" (1845), gives an apt example of the posthumous life of the Keats persona. His narrator, P., apparently delusional, claims to encounter Keats on the London streets and reports: "I stood and watched him, fading away, fading away, along the pavement, and could hardly tell whether he were an actual man, or a thought that had slipped out of my mind, and clothed itself in human form and habiliments, merely to beguile me." (Hawthorne, 374.) For a full account of the story, see Jewett.

12. E. Thompson, 280.

13. Engels, "Introduction," 352–53.

14. The difference between human and animal hands remains a central topos of philosophical meditations on "the human." See for example Canetti, 211–19; Heidegger, Lectures I, II, 3–27; Derrida discusses this difference in "Heidegger's Hand."

15. Korff, 70. Korff traces the evolution of visual imagery of the hand in early labor organizations, from the midnineteenth to early twentieth centuries.

16. Tucker, 767.

17. Giddens, 52. As several scholars have noted, this is an unresolved tension that continues within modern Marxist philosophy: between Althusser's theory of history as "a process without a subject," and the Marxism of Lukacz and Paci in Giddens's discussion (52–53); or between Althusser and E. P. Thompson's liberal Marxism, in Perry Anderson's analysis (16). The conflict between individual agency and social exigency in the Thompson/Althusser debate, as Bruce Robbins has shown, reprises a Victorian one: "The difficulty of combining Comte's global theory of historical stages with Carlyle's incitement to immediate heroic action" ("The Butler Did It," 88).

18. Lévy, 615.

19. Arac, 124. Hereafter cited parenthetically in the text. See also Arac's sources: Mehlman; and Maxwell Jr., 196.

20. "La Main" appeared in *Le Gaulois*, 23 December 1883, reprinted in *Contes du jour et de la nuit* (1885). "La Main d'écorché," Maupassant's first experiment with the Hand of Glory, appeared in 1875 in *L'Almanach lorrain de Pont-à-Mousson*.

21. Godfrey, 83.

22. Maupassant, 226; my translation.

23. Godfrey also makes this connection between Maupassant and Nerval.

24. Nerval, 141; my translations. "La Main de gloire" went through numerous reprintings, appearing first in *Cabinet de lecture* (1832), then as "La Main de gloire: histoire macaronique" in *Revue pittoresque* (1844), again in *Bohème galante* (1855), and then as "La Main enchantée" in *Oevres Complètes*, vol. 1 (Paris, 1868).

25. Harvey, "The Beast with Five Fingers," 20.

26. Dreiser, 55.

27. A much later revision of these stories, Julio Cortázar's "Estación del Mano," reverses the moral valence of literary mortmain. In his evocative, pastoral version of the "beast with five fingers," to presume to or claim ownership of the work of one's hands is a guilty and dangerous act that precipitates the loss of both innocence and poetic invention.

28. Freudian models of repression and displacement, usually in crude or simplistic form, dominate twentieth-century film remakes of the "beast with five fingers." Notable examples include: *The Beast with Five Fingers* (1946), *The Thing* (1951), *The Hand* (1960). Film variations of this motif are legion; Dr. Strangelove's prosthetic hand, that finally strangles him in proper beast with five fingers form, is perhaps the best known example.

29. S. Freud, "The Uncanny," 397.

30. "Story of the Cut-Off Hand" is the last chapter of "The Caravan," a frame tale set in the Egyptian desert. It begins as an embedded tale, told by one of the traveling merchants in the company, but concludes by unraveling the mysteries surrounding the arrival of a strange rider who joins the company in midjourney. He proposes the round of storytelling ostensibly to pass the time, but his real motive is to make amends for his part in a murder-for-hire, for which one of the traveling merchants lost his hand. See Hauff, "The Caravan," in *Tales by Wilhelm Hauff*.

31. Jacobs, "The Monkey's Paw," in *Selected Short Stories*, 33. This story is perhaps Jacobs's most widely read; it has been translated into five languages and circulated in the Trans-Atlantic reading series.

32. Jacobs, *The Monkey's Paw*, adapted by Louis Napoleon Parker for *French's Acting Edition*, 15. The play was performed at the Haymarket Theatre, London, 6 October 1903.

33. In placing Herbert at the electric company, Parker follows Jacobs's lead, for the firm's name plays on the proprietary name of a new electrical testing apparatus, the "Megger," trademarked by Evershed and Vignoles, Ltd., of London, in 1903 (OED, *Megger*).

34. Arac.

35. Carlyle, "Signs of the Times" in *Thomas Carlyle: Selected Writings*, 64.

36. Canetti, "Destructiveness in Monkeys and Men," in *Crowds and Power*, 218.

37. For the argument that late eighteenth- and early nineteenth-century Gothic conventions, together with new modes of scientific holism, offered a "synechdochic sense of shared essence [that] combated a mechanical sense of isolated cause and effect," see Arac, 125.

38. Canetti, "Destructiveness in Monkeys and Men," in *Crowds and Power*, 218.

39. The dramatic increase in named procedures in hand surgery during the late nineteenth century, together with a decline in rates of industrial accident toward the beginning of the twentieth century (presumably due to innovations in risk management), suggest the extent of contemporary interest in industrial working conditions and the serious context behind Herbert White's melodramatic demise. Historians are cautious about drawing conclusions regarding the real incidence of industry-related injuries in nineteenth-century Britain, largely because accident statistics tend to reflect changes in reporting practices legislated by the Factory and Workshops Acts of 1844, 1871, 1891, and 1895 (see especially Bartrip and Fenn, "The Measurement of Safety"). Bartrip and S. B. Burman cautiously find that an increase in fatalities in three major industries (railway, factory/workshop, and coal mining) corresponds to the level of business activity within the country; so, for example, the years 1880–82 and 1887–90 both show brief rises in industrial fatalities along with an easing of the "Great Depression" of 1873–96, after which the level of fatal accidents again increased (Bartrip and Burman, 53). Early statistics on the predominance of hand injuries as opposed to other parts of the body are sparse but telling. The figures on mill accidents treated at Leeds General Infirmary for the year 1840 record 31 persons (probably children) admitted for serious injuries to the arm, hand, thumb, or fingers, out of a total of 33 inpatient admissions; of 228 outpatients, all were apparently admitted for injuries to the arm and hand (Lee, 89). Company accident records in several different kinds of industry, between 1897 and 1923, show that hand injuries (including fingers, elbows, arms) account for between one third, and, in some instances, one half of all reported injuries to workers (Leneman, "Lives and Limbs"). On the history of hand surgery, see Boyes.

40. Du Boisgobey, 541.

41. Smith, 184–85.

42. P. Anderson, 25–26. Hereafter cited parenthetically in the text.

43. The sprawling, Joycean narrative of eighteenth-century Chapelizod, a pastoral "outpost village" of Dublin, begins in a flashback from the grim

prospect of a century of industrial expansion. The pair of stories embedded here remain among Le Fanu's most-read fiction, reprinted and endlessly anthologized as "Ghost Stories of the Tiled House" or "The Narrative of the Ghost of a Hand"; they appeared, for example, in at least eight anthologies between 1931 and 1983.

44. Pinney, 395–96 (cited in B. Robbins, "The Butler Did It," 85). Robbins expands his analysis of fictions of domestic service in *The Servant's Hand*.

45. Wayne Hall's account of the publishing history of *The House by the Churchyard* explicates the complex of economic and emotional motives behind Le Fanu's turn, after this novel, to more explicitly British formulas and settings. See Hall, 65.

46. See the discussions of S. Freud, *My Secret Life*, and James, *The Turn of the Screw* in B. Robbins, *The Servant's Hand*, 196.

47. The politics of possession—by ghosts and of real estate—has been a staple of Le Fanu criticism since Elizabeth Bowen. Bowen famously links Le Fanu's haunted architecture to his family background, poor and Anglican, isolated in a largely Catholic community: "The hermetic solitude and the autocracy of the great country house, the demonic power of the family myth, fatalism, feudalism and the 'ascendancy' outlook are accepted facts of life for the race of hybrids from which Le Fanu sprang. For the psychological background of *Uncle Silas* it was necessary to invent nothing. Rather, he was at once exploiting in art and exploring for its more terrible implications what would have been the norm of his own heredity," cited in McCormack, 141. See also Moynahan.

48. Canetti, "The Fear of being Touched," in *Crowds and Power*, 15, 18.

49. This timing has become a stock feature of "beast with five fingers" stories, and it seems ironically to echo the themes of Eliot's parable of the poisoning cook. In Harvey's story, for example, the hand appears to the scullery maid, as she washes dishes, in a passage that reprises the proverbial empty-mindedness of servants:

"And then Parfit was washing up the dishes in the scullery. She wasn't thinking about anything in particular. It was close on dusk. She took her hands out of the water and was drying them absent-minded like on the roller towel, when she found she was drying someone else's hand as well, only colder than hers." (Harvey, 34)

Charles Addams's "Thing," in keeping with this tradition, is usually found in a soup tureen.

50. See the diary entry of A. J. Munby, barrister and friend of Carlyle and Ruskin, 23 November 1860, which details his fascination with the

hands of female domestics, in this case, of a "coarsemade rustic and red-handed waiting maid" (discussed in B. Robbins, *The Servant's Hand*, 2). The recent movie sequel, *Addams Family Values*, reprises this theme at its most perversely parodic, making "Thing" Uncle Fester's masturbatory toy: the logical extreme of an alienated sex worker.

Chapter 5

1. Chapel, 11–12.

2. Developed by Alphonse Bertillon in the late nineteenth century, the system involved painstaking measurement and codification of a variety of distinguishing physical characteristics: height, weight, length of arm reach, width of the head from the root of the nose to the widest part at the back, length of the left foot, length of the left little finger; the color of eyes, hair, and complexion were matched to standard samples (see Chapel, chapter 2, for a detailed description of the process and tools). These measurements were then converted to a metric sequence for storage and indexing. Most importantly, Bertillon attempted to standardize the terminology of physical description. Like fingerprinting, his system addressed the problem of impersonation and false testimony by establishing a kind of involuntary confession in a procedure he called "Le Portrait Parle."

3. Foote, 7.

4. As Susan Gillman and others have shown, Twain's fingerprinting plot uncovers the contradictions inherent in the economic logic that sustained race slavery and continued in different forms under Jim Crow. For Gillman, these urgent contradictions gave social form to Twain's personal preoccupations with the tenuous, contingent nature of identities based on social fiction; *Pudd'nhead Wilson* begins to articulate epistemological concerns that expand in Twain's dream writings and transvestite tales.

5. Numerous courtroom dramas and detective stories revolve around setups or cover-ups that disguise the events that led to the leaving of fingerprints. For example, a secret enemy incriminates his friend by asking him to cut open a package with a kitchen knife, and then commits a murder using that same knife and wearing gloves; a murderer discovers her victim's hanged body and in the process of cutting it down provides an innocent explanation for the presence of her prints all over the rope.

6. Galton, 11–12. As Gillman explains, Twain "devoured" a copy of Galton's book soon after it came out in 1892, while he was writing *Pudd'nhead Wilson*; he adapted Galton's techniques and terminology, particularly the "A" and "B" notation Wilson uses. Galton gets this terminology

in turn from the work of Sir William Herschel; several criminologists have concluded that Twain must have been familiar with the early 1880s dispute between Herschel and Dr. Faulds in the British journal *Nature*. Discovery rights to the forensic and institutional use of fingerprinting were hotly debated between these two men for decades. See Gillman, and Wigger for the Twain connection; and Wilton, *Fingerprints: History, Law, and Romance*, for the priority debate.

7. Galambos, cited in Brinkley, "Poverty, Depression, and War," 121. Robert H. Wiebe's *The Search for Order, 1877–1920* pioneered the organizational history of America in this period; Galambos and others have extended his work. Theda Skocpol, Kenneth Finegold, and Stephen Skowronek have emphasized the work of American state-building—across areas as disparate as civil administration, the military, and transportation—that resulted in a qualitatively new form of state government.

8. These scholars point out how sardonically Twain treats Galton's attempt to trace racial identity through fingerprints, especially in his trial scene. See Gillman; Rogin; and also Sewell, 124–25. Randall Knoper's recent study *Acting Naturally* draws on this work. Knoper explores the link between involuntary and "authentic" emotion, physical expression, and writing in Twain's work. See his account of the interpretive challenges of indexical and other kinds of evidence, 102.

9. Herschel, 11.

10. This vaguely geographical terminology persisted as late as the 1904 case *Emperor v. Sahdeo*, which set legal precedent in Rajpur, India. The court described ridge-patterns as "origins," "islands," and "enclosures" (Moenssens, 35). Within a few years of that precedent, forensic convention settled on less evocative architectural titles like "Arch," "Whorl," and "Loop."

11. Faulds.

12. Brayley, 13.

13. *People v. Sallow* 1917, cited in Moenssens, 64.

14. Hoover, "The Role of Identification in Law Enforcement," part I, 8–9. Hereafter cited as "Hoover 1973."

15. Hoover, "Law Enforcement and the Citizen," 6.

16. Wiebe, 6.

17. Hoover, "Speech given before the International Association of Chiefs of Police, July 14, 1925," 3. Hereafter cited as "Hoover 1925." The association of fingerprint identification with isolationist politics was a broad one, and threats to the technology are a staple of early, political thrillers. In Owen Fox Jerome's *The Hand of Horror*, for example, an evil

mastermind bent on world empire controls American leaders psychically, committing murder through the hands of others. The novel's Hooverian politics are given a scary rationale in the prospect of fingerprints that prove only the mechanical instrumentality of the person who does the killing, rather than the true identity of the evil genius who controls him.

18. Skowronek, 8–14.

19. "Fingerprinting: A Story of Science vs. Crime," 9.

20. Hoover, "Modern Problems in Law Enforcement," 1.

21. Hoover, "Detection and Apprehension," 2. Hereafter cited as "Hoover 1934."

22. Hoover, "Address read by Inspector James S. Egan," 1, 7.

23. In *G-Men*, Richard Gid Powers gives a more complex account of the forces that centralized Hoover's authority. He argues that the popular fictions that rose around Hoover's FBI conflicted with his personal, and surprisingly populist, theories about crime prevention at communal levels. Yet the "coordinated nation-wide drive against crime" that these speeches envision seems at least, at this early stage, to reflect Hoover's personal investments (Powers, xviii).

24. Chapel alludes to the "Crime—Murder," but only one other historian mentions even this much factual information and then only to assert that it is unclear whether either West was incarcerated for murder or not.

25. Twain, *Pudd'nhead Wilson and Those Extraordinary Twins*, 114. Hereafter cited as "*PW*" in parentheses, by page number. The desire to know what happened to the two Wests, like the desire to know what happened to Chambers, stems in part from the narrative closure that fingerprints promise. In the cliché coined by its early advocates and rehearsed by Wilson, fingerprinting promises a coherent story of identity, a consistent account of the subject "from the cradle to the grave." In withholding the story of Chambers's alienated reinstatement to white, land-owning, self-owning society, the novel emphasizes the failure of the coherent life history promised by Wilson's hobby. In its place Twain offers a particularly gothic version of a life history: exploring the condition of dispossession and self-division that Chapel's version of the West case veers away from.

26. U.S. Department of Justice, *Fingerprint Identification*, 2. This booklet is periodically updated; the publication date is listed with the total number of fingerprints, recorded on the last page. The particular material cited here seems to have been around as long as the booklets have been produced—for several decades at least—and to have remained in substantially the same form.

27. Wentworth and Wilder, 350.

28. Wigmore, 120.

29. Foote, 6.

30. Browne and Brock cite part of the same passage, making similar assertions about the place of Twain in the "roll of pioneers in fingerprint detection," 39.

31. Cover page reproduced in every volume of Mark Twain *Works*.

32. Paine, 349–50; cited in Gillman, 48.

33. Derrida, "Signature/Event/Context," 328.

34. FBI accounts of fingerprinting emphasize the futility of attempts to alter or efface ridge patterns, affirming the involuntary character of prints and their immunity to willful deception. Attempts to tamper with them have included amputation, use of acid, scarring, grafting skin from the torso, coating fingers with plastic film, and creating false latex prints, as well as the time-honored practice of wearing gloves. In most cases, changes in ridge patterns either produce unique marks of their own (scarring, grafting, amputation) or produce material that can likewise be "lifted" for latent prints. Current technology allows the FBI to fingerprint the insides of latex gloves, human skin, and many other unlikely surfaces. Nevertheless, latent prints are delicate marks in practice: prone to decay and smudge and to overlay each other illegibly.

35. Derrida, *Of Grammatology*, 234.

36. For seminal versions of these arguments see Gillman; also Rowe.

37. See Twain, "Personal Habits of the Siamese Twins."

38. Mitchell, 11.

39. Sacks, 43; Sherrington, 129–32, 336–45.

40. Mark Twain, "How to Tell a Story," 266. Hereafter cited in parentheses as "HTS."

41. As Justin Kaplan explains, machines were a deeply ambivalent object for Twain—associated with fraud and economic and domestic disempowerment, as well as fascination. *Pudd'nhead Wilson* was written in the later period of Twain's investment fiascoes with the Paige Typesetter and publishing house. The desperate financial situation that resulted from his compulsive passion for new inventions sent him on a lecture tour in Europe to raise money and precipitated bankruptcy in 1894. In response, counseled by longtime advisor Henry Huttleston Rogers, Twain established his wife Livy as his principal creditor, assigning her in payment of a sixty-thousand-dollar claim all of his copyrights, typesetter stock, and the Hartford house. Twain became "adept at the legal convention of always referring to 'Mrs. Clemens's' copyrights, 'her' books, 'her' typesetter stock, 'her' house and 'her' plans for *Pudd'nhead Wilson*" (Kaplan, 329). It is hard not to read Twain's obsession with mechanical action, from the "Jumping Frog" to *A Connecticut Yankee*, as connected to such formal dispossessions.

42. Morris, xii.

43. OED, *a.* and *sb.*, 4.

44. Melville, 388–89.

45. The OED records the use of "mechanical" in this rarer sense as late as 1880: "Of persons: Engaged in manual labour; belonging to the artisan class. . . . Hence characteristic of this class, mean, vulgar." (OED, *a.* and *sb.*, 2.a). Thus, the "mean" husband and "dull-witted old farmer" are double incarnations of the mechanically writing part. Reading "mechanical" writing as a trope of class illuminates Twain's enigmatic self-characterization as "jack-leg novelist" in the "Author's Note" to *Those Extraordinary Twins*. Twain scholars adopt this phrase as a general synonym for "hack," but it has a complex set of associations. The OED glosses "jackleg" as a pejorative colloquialism used from the midnineteenth century to the present and meaning "Incompetent, unskilled; unscrupulous, dishonest. Freq. used of lawyers and preachers" (OED, *adj.*). Contemporary OED glosses for "jack" import notions of abbreviation, handicap, and mechanical supplementation. "Jack" (like "Moll" or "Joe") is a colloquial moniker for a generic person of lower—artisan, "mechanical"—class; "jack" signifies a support, addition, or mechanical substitute; finally, it can also mean short, small, or deficient. The unscrupulous chicanery Twain always associates with professional writing—especially, as Gillman argues, in his role as impostor lecturer-thief—is a function of writing as supplementation. A jackleg novelist is one who, like Chaucer's Pardoner, must supplement his narrative with ironic self-display. "Would the reader care to know something about the story which I pulled out [by literary Caesarean]?" Twain writes in the "Author's Note"; " . . . won't he let me round and complete his knowledge by telling him how the jack-leg does it?" (*PW*, 119).

46. See Wolfgang Kayser for his seminal definition of the grotesque as animate mechanism.

47. In his study of "The Golden Arm," John A. Burrison documents the past 150 years of the folk tradition in detail.

48. The distinction between storytelling and writing can be an important one for critics to make, except where Twain does not make it himself. In his writings in general, and in these works in particular, the two narrative modes typically reflect and interpret each other. In the early 1890s, for example, Twain suffered from acute rheumatism in his right hand and arm and was forced to write left-handed. Remarking on this condition, "Every pen-stroke gives me the lockjaw," Twain comically compounds the two expressive means in an image of muscular spasm (Kaplan, 307). "How to Tell a Story" displays a similar compound of modes. It frames storytelling in material terms much the same way Chaucer's "Pardoner's Tale" does: intentionally crossing the boundary between verbal and written text in order

to make a point about the vulnerability of both to their material conditions and transmission. Like the Pardoner, Twain's narrator continually tests his chutzpah by exposing the duplicity at the center of his display. The narrative transferal of authority is what makes the hypocrite lecturer both potent and vulnerable; the tokens of that transfer—like the Pardoner's pardons and relics or the golden arm—are susceptible to theft and imitation. The fantasy represented by fingerprint identification is a system of material signs invulnerable to forgery and imitation.

49. Benjamin, "On Some Motifs in Baudelaire," 159. Benjamin first uses this image in "The Storyteller" (1936): "[Storytelling] sinks the thing [experience] into the life of the storyteller, in order to bring it out of him again. Thus traces of the storyteller cling to the story the way the handprints of the potter cling to the clay vessel" (Benjamin, *Illuminations*, 91–92). Returning to this metaphor in "The Work of Art in the Age of Mechanical Reproduction" (1936), and then working it out most fully in "On Some Motifs in Baudelaire," Benjamin employs it to distinguish between storytelling and other modes of communication (reports, novels, etc.). "The replacement of the older narration by information, of information by sensation, reflects the increasing atrophy of experience" (Benjamin, *Illuminations*, 159). In this respect Benjamin's project differs from Twain's. The rhetoric of narrative agency in "How to Tell a Story" extends beyond the limits of the lecture to textual storytelling.

50. See the plate of early Chinese clay seals in Chapel, opposite page 6. And see also Browne and Brock, "finger-impressions employed as a decorative motif in pottery from Laplata Valley, New Mexico (A.D. 900–1100)," plate opposite page 14. The quality of authenticity suggested by Benjamin's image of the hand in clay resonates with law enforcement histories of fingerprint identification. The ancient use of fingerprints in clay—as decoration and as seals on legal contracts—documents a prehistory of the science. It should be noted that Benjamin's reference is not explicitly to fingerprinting, though it represents an idea of narrative authenticity transferred through physical contact, and it seems to invoke this decorative history. He is interested primarily in the way experience is preserved in aesthetic form, through the immediacy of manual labor.

51. For examples in fingerprinting case histories see Wilton, *Fingerprints: History, Law and Romance*; and Cooke, *The Blue Book* and *Fingerprints, Secret Service*. See also the Rojas story, La Plata, Argentina, 1892 (United States Department of Justice, *Fingerprint Identification*, 3). When Wilson's courtroom sermon is cited in fingerprint textbooks, the confession passage is almost always included (see for example Wilton, *Fingerprints: History, Law and Romance*, 146).

Epilogue

1. S. Anderson, note 5, 374–76. Hereafter cited parenthetically by page number.

2. Bynum, 19–20.

3. E. F. Schumacher, *Small Is Beautiful*, 141. Cited in McCullough, 17.

4. See McCullough, "A Short History of Craft," in *Abstracting Craft*, 16–19. Hereafter cited parenthetically by page number. In his condensed but provocative history, McCullough traces the evolution of modern theories of manufacture from ancient and early modern thought. Arguing against it, he sums up the depressing prospect projected onto electronic modes of production from industrial design: "Trends such as managerial command and control, productive efficiency regardless of the social cost, deliberate deskilling, replacing people with machines, and so on, were now given just the leverage they needed to deliver the final blow to any humane aspects of work. The circumstances of working with the technology itself would be harmful in their own right: new class divisions, concessions to the technology providers, antisocial working arrangements, worker surveillance, endless mindnumbing technical detail, and overall sensory deprivation. For the hands, the only prospect would be painful repetitive motion disorders" (17–18).

5. See McCullough's account of developments in "haptic" interfaces that simulate touch (McCullough, 25). As scholars like Richard Lanham have argued, electronic technologies tend to lag behind human needs and uses.

6. Allucquère Roseanne Stone goes even further in maintaining the nonmechanical, intensive (rather than extensive or prosthetic) nature of electronic media. Describing the late twentieth century as the close of Carlyle's "Mechanical Age," she argues that computers "are arenas for social experience and dramatic interaction, a type of media more like public theater, and their output is used for qualitative interaction, dialogue, and conversation" (Stone, 16).

7. See the final comments in Stallybrass, "The Materiality of Reading."

Bibliography

Ady, Thomas. "A Candle in the Dark." In *A Perfect Discovery of Witches*. London: H. Brome, 1661.

Aers, David. "A Whisper." In *Culture and History, 1350–1600: Essays on English Communities, Identities and Writing*, edited by David Aers. 177–202. Detroit: Wayne State University Press, 1992.

———, ed. *Culture and History, 1350–1600: Essays on English Communities, Identities and Writing*. Detroit: Wayne State University Press, 1992.

Agnew, Jean-Christophe. *Worlds Apart: The Market and the Theater in Anglo-American Thought, 1550–1750*. Cambridge, Eng.: Cambridge University Press, 1986.

Althusser, Louis. *Politics and History: Montesquieu, Rousseau, Hegel and Marx*. Trans. Ben Brewster. London: New Left Books, 1972.

"Anatomy of Violence: Violent Have Flat Prints." New York State Identification and Intelligence Systems Newsletter, February 1970, 3.

Anderson, Perry. *Arguments Within English Marxism*. London: New Left Books and Verso Editions, 1980.

Anderson, Sherwood. *A Story Teller's Story*. New York: B. W. Huebsch, 1924.

Arac, Jonathan. *Commissioned Spirits: The Shaping of Social Motion in Dickens, Carlyle, Melville, and Hawthorne*. New Brunswick, N.J.: Rutgers University Press, 1979.

Aristotle. *The Complete Works of Aristotle: The Revised Oxford Translation*. Rev. Jonathon Barnes. Princeton, N.J.: Princeton University Press, 1984.

Augustine of Hippo, Saint. *Confessions*. Trans. R. S. Pine-Coffin. London: Penguin, 1961.

Austin, Gilbert. *Chironomia*. London: Printed for T. Cudell and W. Davies, by W. Bulmer and Co., 1806.

Authorized Version of the Bible (King James), The. London: Robert Barker, 1611.

Bakhtin, Mikhail. *Rabelais and His World*. Trans. Heliene Iswolsky. Bloomington: Indiana University Press, 1984.

Banister, John. *The Historie of Man, Sucked from the Sappe of the Most Approved Anathomistes*. London: J. Daye, 1578.

Barber, C. L., and Richard P. Wheeler. "*Titus Andronicus*: Abortive Domestic Tragedy." In *The Whole Journey: Shakespeare's Power of Development*. Berkeley: University of California Press, 1986.

Barkan, Leonard. *The Gods Made Flesh: Metamorphosis and the Pursuit of Paganism*. New Haven, Conn.: Yale University Press, 1986.

———. *Nature's Work of Art: The Human Body as Image of the World*. New Haven, Conn.: Yale University Press, 1975.

Barker, Clive. "The Body Politic." In *The Inhuman Condition: Tales of Terror*. New York: Poseidon Press, 1986.

Bartrip, P. W. J., and S. B. Burman. *The Wounded Soldiers of Industry: Industrial Compensation Policy, 1833–1897*. Oxford: Clarendon Press, 1983.

Bartrip, P. W. J., and P. T. Fenn. "The Measurement of Safety: Factory Accident Statistics in Victorian and Edwardian Britain." *Historical Research: Bulletin of the Institute of Historical Research* 63, no. 150 (1990): 58–72.

Beckford, William. *Vathek*. London: Printed for J. Johnson, 1786.

Bell, Charles. *The Hand: Its Mechanism and Vital Endowments as Evincing Design*. 6th ed. London: John Murray, 1860.

Belsey, Catherine. "Emblem and Antithesis in *The Duchess of Malfi*." *Renaissance Drama* New Series 11 (1980): 115–34.

Benjamin, Walter. "On Some Motifs in Baudelaire." In *Illuminations*, edited by Hannah Arendt, translated by Harry Zohn, 155–200. New York: Schocken Books, 1969.

———. "The Storyteller." In *Illuminations*, edited by Hannah Arendt, translated by Harry Zohn, 83–109. New York: Schocken Books, 1969.

———. "The Work of Art in the Age of Mechanical Reproduction." In *Illuminations*, edited by Hannah Arendt, translated by Harry Zohn, 217–51. New York: Schocken Books, 1969.

Beowulf. Edited, with Introduction, Bibliography, Notes, Glossary and Appendices by Fr. Klaeber. 3d ed. Lexington, MA: D. C. Heath, 1950.

Bernstein, Richard. *Praxis and Action: Contemporary Philosophies of Human Activity*. Philadelphia: University of Pennsylvania Press, 1971.

Berry, Lloyd E., ed. *John Stubbs's Gaping Gulf, with Letters and Other Relevant Documents*. Folger Documents of Tudor and Stuart Civilization. Charlottesville: University of Virginia Press, 1968.

Bertillon, Alphonse. *Identification anthropometrique*. Melun, France: Imprimiere Administrative, 1893.

Blakeborough, Richard. *The Hand of Glory, and Further Grandfather's Tales and Legends of Highwaymen and Others*. London: Grant Richards, 1924.

———. *Wit, Character, Folklore and Customs of the North Riding of Yorkshire*. London: Henry Frowde, Oxford University Press, 1898.

The Bloody Hand, or the Fatal Cup. London: Stevens and Co. Circulating Library.

Bolton, Samuel. *The Arraignment of Errour*. London: G. Miller for A. Kembe, 1646.

Boorde, Andrew. *A Dyetary of Health*. Vol. 10. Early English Text Society. London: N. Trubner, 1870.

Boyes, Joseph H. *On the Shoulders of Giants: Notable Names in Hand Surgery*. Philadelphia: J. B. Lippincott, 1976.

Bradbrook, Muriel C. *Shakespeare and Elizabethan Poetry*. New York: Penguin Books, 1951.

———. "Two Notes upon Webster." *Modern Language Review* 42 (1947): 283–84.

Braunmuller, A. R. " 'Second Means': Agent and Accessory in Elizabethan Drama." In *The Elizabethan Theatre XI*, edited by A. L. Magnusson and C. E. McGee. Port Credit, Ontario: P. D. Meany, 1990.

Brayley, Frederic A. *Brayley's Arrangement of Finger Prints Identification and Their Uses for Police Departments, Prisons, Lawyers, Banks, Homes, Trust Companies, Steamship Companies, Secret Societies, Political Uses, and in Every Branch of Business Where an Infallible System of Identification Is Necessary*. Boston: The Worcester Press, 1910.

Brinkley, Alan. "Poverty, Depression, and War." In *The New American History*, edited by Eric Foner. Philadelphia: Temple University Press, 1990.

Brontë, Emily. *Wuthering Heights*. Ed. Pauline Nestor. London: Penguin Books, 1995.

Browne, Douglas, and Alan Brock. *Fingerprints: Fifty Years of Scientific Crime Detection*. London: George G. Harrap, 1953.

Bruckner, Wolfgang. "Hand und Heil im 'Schatzbehalter' und auf Volkstumlicher Graphik." *Anzeiger des Germanischen Nationalmuseums, Nurnberg* (1965): 60–109.

Bullokar, John. *An English Expositor*. Menston: Scolar Press, 1967.

Bulwer, John. *Chirologia: Or, the Natural Language of the Hand, and Chirono-*

mia: Or, the Art of Manual Rhetoric. Ed. James W. Cleary. Carbondale: Southern Illinois University Press, 1974.

Burke, Kenneth. *A Grammar of Motives.* New York: George Braziller, 1955.

Burrison, John A. *"The Golden Arm": The Folk Tale and Its Literary Use by Mark Twain and Joel C. Harris.* Atlanta: Georgia State College School of Arts and Sciences, Research papers, no. 19 (1968).

Bynum, Caroline Walker. *Fragmentation and Redemption.* New York: Zone Books, 1992.

Callinicos, Alex. *Making History: Agency, Structure and Change in Social Theory.* Ithaca: Cornell University Press, 1988.

Cannetti, Elias. *Crowds and Power.* Trans. Carol Stewart. New York: Farrar, Strauss, Giroux, 1973.

Care, Norman S., and Charles Landesman, eds. *Readings in The Theory of Action.* Bloomington: Indiana University Press, 1968.

Carlyle, Thomas. "Signs of the Times." In *Thomas Carlyle: Selected Writings,* edited by Alan Shelston, 59–64. Baltimore: Penguin Books, 1971.

Cassidy, Frederic G., ed. *Dictionary of American Regional English.* 3 vols. Cambridge, Mass.: Harvard University Press, 1991.

Chapel, Charles Edward. *Fingerprinting: A Manual of Identification.* New York: Coward McCann, 1941.

Cleary, James W. "John Bulwer: Renaissance Communicationist." *Quarterly Journal of Speech* 45 (1959): 391–98.

Cockeram, Henry. *The English Dictionarie of 1623.* New York: Huntington Press, 1930.

Collins, Wilkie. "The Dead Hand." In *Tales of Terror and the Supernatural,* edited by Herbert van Thal, 40–60. New York: Dover Publications, 1972.

Columbus, M. Realdus. *De re anatomica.* Venice, 1559.

Connor, R. D. *The Weights and Measures of England.* London: Her Majesty's Stationery Office, 1987.

Cooke, T. G. *The Blue Book of Crime.* 15th ed. Chicago: Institute of Applied Science, 1941.

———. *Fingerprints, Secret Service, Crime Detection.* 3d ed. Chicago: Fingerprint Publication Association, 1930.

Cortázar, Julio. "Estación del Mano." In *La Vuelta al día en ochenta mundos.* 2: 105–10. Madrid: Los Talieres Gráficos de Ediciones Castilla, 1970.

Crawford, Gary William. *J. Sheridan Le Fanu: A Bio-Bibliography.* Westport, Conn.: Greenwood Press, 1995.

Crooke, Helkiah. *Microcosmographia: A Description of the Body of Man. Together with the Controversies Thereto Belonging. Collected and Translated out of*

All the Best Authors of Anatomy, Especially out of Gasper Bauhinus and Andreas Laurentius. London: W. Jaggard, 1615.

Curtis, Mark. "The Alienated Intellectuals of Early Stuart England." In *Crisis in Europe, 1560–1660,* edited by Trevor Aston. London: Routledge, 1965.

Dalton, Michael, ed. *The Countrey Justice, Containing the Practise of the Justices of the Peace out of Their Sessions. Gathered, for the Better Helpe of Such Justices of Peace as Have Not Been Much Conversant in the Studie of the Lawes of This Realme. Classical English Law Texts.* London: Professional Books Limited, 1973.

Daly, Peter M., ed. *The English Emblem and the Continental Tradition.* New York: AMS Press, 1988.

———, ed. *The English Emblem Tradition.* Toronto: University of Toronto Press, 1988.

———, ed. *Index Emblematicus.* Toronto: University of Toronto Press, 1988.

Daston, Lorraine. "Historical Epistemology." In *Questions of Evidence: Proof, Practice and Persuasion Across the Disciplines,* edited by James Chandler, Arnold I. Davidson, and Harry Hartoonian, 282–89. Chicago: University of Chicago Press, 1991.

———. "Marvelous Facts and Miraculous Evidence in Early Modern Europe." In *Questions of Evidence: Proof, Practice and Persuasion Across the Disciplines,* edited by James Chandler, Arnold I. Davidson, and Harry Hartoonian, 243–74. Chicago: University of Chicago Press, 1991.

Davidson, Donald. "Action, Reasons, and Causes." *The Journal of Philosophy* 60 (1963): 685–700.

Defoe, Daniel. *Robinson Crusoe.* Ed. Michael Shinagel. New York: W. W. Norton, 1975.

Derrida, Jacques. "Heidegger's Hand." In *Deconstruction and Philosophy: The Texts of Jacques Derrida,* translated by John P. Leavey Jr. Edited by John Sallis, 161–96. Chicago: University of Chicago Press, 1987.

———. *Of Grammatology.* Trans. Gayatri Spivak. Baltimore: Johns Hopkins University Press, 1967.

———. "Signature/Event/Context." In *Margins of Philosophy,* translated by Alan Bass. Chicago: University of Chicago Press, 1982.

Dessen, Alan C., ed. *Titus Andronicus. Shakespeare in Performance.* Manchester: Manchester University Press, 1989.

Dickens, Charles. *Hard Times for These Times.* London: Oxford University Press, 1974.

Dollimore, Jonathan. *Radical Tragedy: Religion, Ideology and Power in the Drama of Shakespeare and His Contemporaries.* Brighton, Sussex: Harvester Press, 1984.

Dreiser, Theodore. "The Hand." In *Chains: Lesser Novels and Stories by Theodore Dreiser*, 43–63. New York: Boni and Liveright, 1927.

Du Boisgobey, Fortune Hippolyte Auguste. *The Lost Casket (La main coupée).* In *The Trans-Atlantic Series: Selected English and Continental Novels in Authorized American Editions*, translated by S. Lee. New York: G. P. Putnam's Sons, 1881.

Duncan, Ian. *Modern Romance and Transformations of the Novel: The Gothic, Scott, Dickens.* Cambridge, Mass.: Cambridge University Press, 1992.

Engel, William E. *Mapping Mortality.* Amherst: University of Massachusetts Press, 1995.

Engels, Frederick. "Introduction to Dialectics of Nature." In *Karl Marx and Frederick Engels: Selected Works.* 342–57. New York: International Publishers, 1968.

———. "The Part Played by Labour in the Transition from Ape to Man." In *Karl Marx and Frederick Engels: Selected Works.* 358–68. New York: International Publishers, 1968.

Evans, G. Blakemore, ed. *The Riverside Shakespeare.* Boston: Houghton Mifflin, 1974.

Fabricius ab Aquapendente, Heironymus. *De visione voci auditu.* Venice, 1600.

FACTS Promotional Brochure. New Delhi: CMC Limited, A Government of India Enterprise, 1990.

Faulds, Henry. "On the Skin-furrows of the Hand," Letter to the Editor, 28 October. *Nature* 22 (1880): 605.

Fell, Christine. "Some Domestic Problems." *Leeds Studies in English.* New Series 16 (1985): 59–82.

———. *Women in Anglo-Saxon England.* London: British Museum Publications, 1984.

"Fingerprinting: A Story of Science vs. Crime." *FBI Law Enforcement Bulletin* 40, no. 7 (July), 1971.

Florio, John. *The Essays of Montaigne done into English by John Florio, 1603. Tudor Translations.* London: David Nutt, 1893.

Foote, Robert D. "Fingerprint Identification: A Survey of Present Technology, Automated Applications and Potential for Future Development." *Criminal Justice Monograph* 5, no. 2 (1974).

Fowler, Elizabeth. "Civil Death and the Maiden: Agency and the Conditions of Contract in *Piers Plowman*." *Speculum* 70, no. 4 (October 1995): 760–92.

Freeman, Rosemary. Introduction to *A Collection of Emblemes, Ancient and Moderne: Quickened with Metricall Illustrations* by George Wither. Publications of the English Renaissance Text Society. Columbia: University of South Carolina Press, 1975.

Freud, Sigmund. "Fetishism." In *The Standard Edition of the Complete Psychological Works of Sigmund Freud*. Vol. 21. General editor James Strachey, translated by Joan Riviere. 149–57. London: Hogarth Press, 1955.

———. "The Uncanny." In *The Collected Papers of Sigmund Freud*. Vol. 4. Translated by Alex Strachey. London: The Hogarth Press and the Institute of Psycho-Analysis, 1956.

Furness, Horace Howard, ed. *The Variorum Shakespeare: Coriolanus*. Philadelphia: J. B. Lippincott, 1928.

Galambos, Louis. *The Rise of the Corporate Commonwealth: United States Business and Public Policy in the Twentieth Century*. New York: Basic Books, 1988.

Galen. *Galen on the Usefulness of the Parts of the Body (De usu partium)*. Trans. Margaret Tallmadge May. Ithaca: Cornell University Press, 1968.

Galton, Francis, F. R. S. *Finger Prints*. London: Macmillan, 1892.

Garber, Marjorie. *Shakespeare's Ghost Writers: Literature As Uncanny Causality*. New York: Methuen, 1987.

Gataker, Thomas. *A Good Wife God's Gift: A Wife In Deed: Two Marriage Sermons*. London: John Haviland for Fulke Clifton, 1623?

Gaule, John. *Pus-Mantia, the Mag-Astro-Mancer, or the Magicall-Astrological-Diviner Posed, and Puzzled*. London: Printed for Joshua Kirton, 1652.

———. *Select Cases of Conscience Touching: Witches and Witchcrafts*. London: Printed for Richard Clutterbuck by W. Wilson, 1646.

Giddens, Anthony. *Central Problems in Social Theory: Action, Structure and Contradiction in Social Analysis*. Berkeley: University of California Press, 1979.

Gifford, George. *A Dialogue Concerning Witches and Witchcrafts*, 1593. With an introduction by Beatrice White. London: Oxford University Press, 1931.

Gillman, Susan. *Dark Twins: Imposture and Identity in Mark Twain's America*. Chicago: University of Chicago Press, 1989.

Godfrey, Sima. "Lending a Hand: Nerval, Gautier, Maupassant and the Fantastic." *Romanic Review* 78, no. 1 (January 1987): 74–83.

Goldberg, Jonathan. "Hamlet's Hand." *Shakespeare Quarterly* 39, no. 3 (1988): 307–27.

———. *Writing Matter: From the Hands of the English Renaissance*. Stanford: Stanford University Press, 1990.

Greaves, John. *A Discourse of the Romane Foot*. London: M. F. for William Lee, 1647.

Green, Douglas. "Interpreting 'Her Martyr'd Signs': Gender and Tragedy in *Titus Andronicus*." *Shakespeare Quarterly* 40, no. 3 (1989): 317–26.

Guazzo, Brother Francesco Maria. *Compendium Maleficarum*. Trans. E. A Ashwin. London: John Rodker, 1929.

Haaker, Ann. "*Non sine causa:* The Use of Emblematic Method and Iconology in the Thematic Structure of *Titus Andronicus*." *Research Opportunities in Renaissance Drama*. Vol. 13 (1970): 143–68.

Hall, Wayne. "Le Fanu's House by the Marketplace." *Eire-Ireland: Journal of Irish Studies* 21, no. 1 (spring 1986): 55–72.

Harcourt, Glenn. "Andreas Vesalius and the Anatomy of Antique Sculpture." *Representations* 17 (winter 1987): 28–61.

Hart, H. L. A., and A. M. Honore. *Causation in the Law*. New York: Clarendon Press, 1959.

Harvey, William Fryer. "The Arm of Mrs. Egan." In *The Arm of Mrs. Egan and Other Stories*. 121–37. London: J. M. Dent and Sons, 1947.

———. "The Beast with Five Fingers." In *The Beast with Five Fingers: Twenty Tales of the Uncanny*, edited by Maurice Richardson, 19–47. New York: E.P. Dutton, 1947.

Hauff, Wilhelm. *Tales by Wilhelm Hauff*. Trans. S. Mendel. London: G. Bell and Sons, 1914.

Hawthorne, Nathaniel. "P.'s Correspondence." In *Mosses from an Old Manse. The Centenary Edition of the Works of Nathaniel Hawthorne*, edited by William Charvat. 10: 361–80. Columbus: Ohio State University Press, 1974.

Hazeltine, H. D. "Mortmain." In *The Encyclopaedia of the Social Sciences*, edited by Edwin R. Seligman. 40–50. New York: Macmillan, 1967.

Heidegger, Martin. *What Is Called Thinking?* Trans. Fred D. Wieck and J. Glann Gray. New York: Harper & Row, 1968.

Henry, Sir E. R. *Classification and Uses of Finger Prints*. London: His Majesty's Stationery Office, 1913.

Herodotus. *Herodotus*. Trans. William Beloe. Philadelphia: M'Carty & Davis, 1844.

Herschel, Sir William J. *The Origin of Finger-Printing*. London: Oxford University Press, 1916.

Hertz, Robert. *Death and the Right Hand*. Trans. Rodney Needham and Claudia Needham. Glencoe, Ill.: The Free Press, 1960.

Hildburgh, W. L. "Images of the Human Hand as Amulets in Spain." *Journal of the Warburg and Courtauld Institutes* 18 (1955): 67–89.

Hobbes, Thomas. *Leviathan*. Collier Edition. New York: Macmillan, 1962.

Hoover, J. Edgar. "Address Read by Inspector James S. Egan Before the Joint Meeting of the International Association of Chiefs of Police and the International Association for Identification." Hotel Sherman, Chicago, Ill., 1933.

———. "Detection and Apprehension." Address delivered before the Attorney General's Conference on Crime. Washington, D.C., 1934.

———. "Law Enforcement and the Citizen." Address delivered before the Chamber of Commerce of the State of New York, 1935.

———. "Modern Problems in Law Enforcement." 1935.

———. "The Role of Identification in Law Enforcement: An Historical Adventure." *FBI Law Enforcement Bulletin* no. 42 (March 1973).

———. Speech given before the International Association of Chiefs of Police. 1925.

Hopkins, Matthew. *The Discovery of Witches*. Norwich, Eng.: H. W. Hunt, 1931.

Hulse, Clark. "Wresting the Alphabet: Oratory and Action in *Titus Andronicus*." *Criticism* 21 (1979): 106–18.

Hunt, Maurice. "Webster and Jacobean Medicine." *Essays in Literature* 16, no. 1 (1989): 33–49.

Ingoldsby, Thomas [Richard Harris Barham]. *The Ingoldsby Legends*. London: Richard Bentley, 1869.

Jacobs, W. W. "The Monkey's Paw." In *Selected Short Stories*, edited by Hugh Greene, 31–42. London: The Bodley Head, 1975.

James, Heather. *Shakespeare's Troy*. Cambridge, Eng.: Cambridge University Press, 1997.

James, William. *The Principles of Psychology*. Vol. 2. New York: Dover Publications, 1950.

Jankowski, Theodora A. "Defining/Confining the Duchess: Negotiating the Female Body in John Webster's *The Duchess of Malfi*." *Studies in Philology* 87, no. 2 (1990): 221–45.

Jerome, Owen Fox. *The Hand of Horror*. New York: Edward J. Clode, 1927.

Jewett, William. "Hawthorne's Romanticism: From Canon to Corpus." *Modern Language Quarterly* 57, no. 1 (1996): 51–76.

Jordan, Constance. *Renaissance Feminism: Literary Texts and Political Models*. Ithica, N.Y.: Cornell University Press, 1990.

———. *Shakespeare's Monarchies: Ruler and Subject in the Romances*. Ithaca, N.Y.: Cornell University Press, 1997.

Kahn, Victoria. "Margaret Cavendish and the Romance of Contract." *Renaissance Quarterly* 50, no. 2 (1997).

Kaplan, Justin. *Mr. Clemens and Mark Twain*. New York: Simon and Schuster, 1966.

Kayser, Wolfgang. *The Grotesque in Art and Literature*. Trans. Ulrich Weisstein. Bloomington: Indiana University Press, 1963.

Kemp, Martin, ed. *Leonardo on Painting.* New Haven, Conn.: Yale University Press, 1989.

Kendall, Gillian Murray. " 'Lend Me Thy Hand': Metaphor and Mayhem in *Titus Andronicus.*" *Shakespeare Quarterly* 40, no. 3 (1989): 299.

Kiefer, Frederick. "The Dance of Madmen in *The Duchess of Malfi.*" *Journal of Medieval and Renaissance Studies* 17, no. 2 (1987).

King James I. *Daemonologie in Forme of a Dialogue, 1597, Newes from Scotland, 1591.* Facsimile reproduction. New York: E. P. Dutton, 1924.

Kittredge, George Lyman. *Witchcraft in Old and New England.* Cambridge, Mass.: Harvard University Press, 1929.

Knoper, Randall. *Acting Naturally: Mark Twain in the Culture of Performance.* Berkeley: University of California Press, 1995.

Knox, Dilwyn. "Ideas on Gesture and Universal Languages, c. 1550–1650." In *New Perspectives on Renaissance Thought*, edited by J. Henry and S. Hutton. London: Duckworth, 1990.

Korff, Gottfried. "From Brotherly Handshake to Militant Clenched Fist: On Political Metaphors for the Worker's Hand." English summary by Larry Peterson. *International Labor and Working-Class History* no. 42 (fall 1992): 70–81.

Lanham, Richard. *The Electronic Word: Democracy, Technology, and the Arts.* Chicago: University of Chicago Press, 1993.

Le Bot, Marc. *La Main de dieu, la main du diable.* Saint-Clement-la-Riviere: Fata Morgana, 1990.

Le Fanu, Joseph Sheridan. "Ghost Stories of the Tiled House." In *Best Ghost Stories of J. S. Le Fanu*, edited by E. F. Bleiler. 397–407. New York: Dover Publications, 1964.

———. "Some Odd Facts About the Tiled House—Being an Authentic Narrative of the Ghost of a Hand." In *The House by the Churchyard.* 53–58. Belfast: Appletree Press, 1992.

———. *Wylder's Hand.* New York: Carleton, 1866.

Lee, W. R. "Robert Baker: the First Doctor in the Factory Department." *British Journal of Industrial Medicine* 21 (1964): 85–93.

Leighton, Marie Connor. *The Hand of the Unseen.* London: Ward, Lock & Company, 1918.

Leneman, Leah. "Lives and Limbs: Company Records as a Source for the History of Industrial Injuries." *Social History of Medicine* 6, no. 3 (1993): 405–27.

Lévy, Maurice. *Le Roman "Gothique" Anglais, 1764–1824.* Toulouse: Association des Publications de la Faculté des Lettres et Sciences Humaines de Toulouse, 1968.

Liebler, Naomi. "Getting It All Right: *Titus Andronicus* and Roman History." *Shakespeare Quarterly* 45, no. 3 (1994): 263–78.

Locke, John. *Two Treatises of Government*. Cambridge, Eng.: Cambridge University Press, 1970.

Lomazzo, Giovanni Paolo. *Trattato dell' arte della pittura*. Trans. Richard Haydock. London, 1598.

Love, Harold. *The Culture and Commerce of Texts: Scribal Publication in Seventeenth-Century England*. Amherst: University of Massachusetts Press, 1993.

Lynch, Kathryn. " 'What Hands Are Here?' The Hand as Generative Symbol in *Macbeth*." *Review of English Studies* 39, no. 153 (1988): 29–38.

Macfarlane, Alan. *Witchcraft in Tudor and Stuart England: A Regional and Comparative Study*. New York: Harper & Row, 1970.

Macpherson, C. B. *The Political Theory of Possessive Individualism: Hobbes to Locke*. Oxford: Oxford University Press, 1962.

Maine, Henry Sumner. *Ancient Law: Its Connection with the Early History of Society and Its Relation to Modern Ideas*. New York: Henry Holt, 1906.

Marcus, Jane. "The Asylums of Antaeus: Women, War, and Madness—Is There a Feminist Fetishism?" In *The New Historicism*, edited by Harold Veeser. New York: Routledge, 1989.

Maupassant, Guy de. *Contes et Nouvelles, 1875–1884*. Vol. 2. Paris: Gallimard, 1974.

Maxwell, Richard C. Jr. "G. M. Reynolds, Dickens, and the Mysteries of London." *Nineteenth-Century Fiction* 32, no. 2 (1977): 196–97.

McCullough, Malcolm. *Abstracting Craft: The Practiced Digital Hand*. Cambridge, Mass.: The MIT Press, 1996.

McCormack, W. J. *Sheridan Le Fanu and Victorian Ireland*. Oxford: Clarendon Press, 1980.

McLuskie, Kathleen. "Drama and Sexual Politics: The Case of Webster's Duchess." In *Drama, Sex and Politics*, edited by James Redmond. Cambridge, Eng.: Cambridge University Press, 1985.

———. *Renaissance Dramatists*. New York: Harvester Wheatsheaf, 1989.

McLuskie, Kathleen, and Jennifer Uglow. *The Duchess of Malfi (Plays in Performance)*. Bedminster: Briston Classical Press, 1989.

Mehlman, Jeffrey. "A partir du mot 'unheimlich' chez Marx." *Critique* 31 (1975): 232–53.

Melden, A. I. *Free Action*. London: Routledge, 1961.

Melville, Herman. *Moby Dick*. New York: W. W. Norton, 1967.

Middleton, Thomas, and William Rowley. *The Changeling*. In *The New Mermaids*. New York: W. W. Norton, 1990.

Minsheu, John. *Ductoris in Linguas: The Guide into Tongues*. London: John Haviland, 1627.

Mitchell, Silas Weir. "The Case of George Dedlow." *The Atlantic Monthly* (July 1866): 1–11.

Moenssens, Andre. *Fingerprints and the Law*. Philadelphia: Chilton Book Company, 1969.

Montaigne, Michel de. *The Complete Essays of Montaigne*. Trans. Donald M. Frame. Stanford: Stanford University Press, 1958.

Morris, Wright. Foreword to *Pudd'nhead Wilson*. Signet Classic. New York: New American Library, 1964.

Moseley, Charles. *A Century of Emblems*. Aldershot, England: Scolar Press, 1989.

Moynahan, Julian. "The Politics of Anglo-Irish Gothic: Maturin, Le Fanu and 'The Return of the Repressed.' " In *Studies in Anglo-Irish Literature*, edited by Heinz Kosok, 43–53. Bonn: Bouvier, 1982.

Munk, William. *The Roll of the Royal College of Physicians of London*. Vol. I. 2d ed. 7 vols. London: The College, Pall Mall East, 1878.

Neill, Michael. "Amphitheatres in the Body": Playing with Hands on the Shakespearean Stage." *Shakespeare Survey* 48 (1995): 23–50.

Nerval, Gèrard de. *Sylvie / La Main Enchantée*. Paris: Le Livre Francais, 1924.

Newman, Karen. *Fashioning Femininity*. Chicago: University of Chicago Press, 1991.

Nussbaum, Felicity, and Laura Brown, eds. *The New Eighteenth Century: Theory, Politics, English Literature*. New York: Methuen, 1987.

O'Malley, C. D. *Andreas Vesalius of Brussels, 1514–1564*. Berkeley: University of California Press, 1964.

———. "Helkiah Crooke, M.D., F.R.C.P., 1576–1648." *Bulletin of the History of Medicine* 42, no. 1 (1968): 1–18.

———. "Origin of Pudd'nhead Wilson." *Literary Digest* 45 (26 October 1912): 740–41.

Paine, Albert Bigelow, ed. *Mark Twain's Notebook*. New York: Harper & Brothers, 1935.

Paradin, Claude. *Devises Heroiques*. Ed. Alison Saunders. Aldershot, England: Scolar Press, 1989.

Parker, Louis Napoleon. *The Monkey's Paw*, adapted from W. W. Jacobs, for *French's Acting Edition*. London: Samuel French, 1903.

Parker, Patricia. "Preposterous Reversals: Love's Labor's Lost." *Modern Language Quarterly* 54, no. 4 (December 1993): 435–82.

Passmore, John. *A Hundred Years of Philosophy*. Rev. ed. New York: Basic Books, 1966.

Patterson, Annabel. "Paradise Regained: A Last Chance at True Romance." *Milton Studies* 17 (1983): 187–208.

People v. Sallow. 165 NY Supp. 915, 924, Gen. Sess. 1917. 100 Misc. 447: 462–64.

Peters, Edward, ed. *Heresy and Authority in Medieval Europe.* Philadelphia: University of Pennsylvania Press, 1980.

Peters, R. S. *The Concept of Motivation.* London: Routledge, 1958.

Pinney, Thomas, ed. *The Essays of George Eliot.* London: Routledge and Kegan Paul, 1963.

Plowden, Edmund. *The Commentaries or Reports.* 2 vols. London: Printed by Catherine Lintot and Samuel Richardson, Law Printers to the Kings Most Excellent Majesty, 1761.

Porter, Enid. *Cambridgeshire Customs and Folklore.* London: Routledge and Kegan Paul, 1969.

Potter, Lois. *Secret Rites and Secret Writing: Royalist Literature, 1641–1660.* Cambridge, Eng.: Cambridge University Press, 1989.

Powers, Richard Gid. *G-Men: Hoover's FBI in American Popular Culture.* Carbondale: Southern Illinois University Press, 1983.

Prest, Thomas Peckett. *The Death Grasp; or, A Father's Curse.* London: E. Lloyd, 1842.

Radford, Edwin, and M. A. Radford. *The Encyclopaedia of Superstitions.* Ed. and rev. Christine Hole. London: Hutchinson, 1961.

Randall, Dale. "The Rank and Earthy Background of Certain Physical Symbols in *The Duchess of Malfi.*" *Renaissance Drama* 18 (1987): 171–203.

Ravenscroft, Edward. *"Titus Andronicus," or the Rape of Lavinia.* 1687.

Rider, John. *Bibliotecha Scholastica.* London: The Scholar Press, 1970.

Robbins, Bruce. "The Butler Did It: On Agency in the Novel." *Representations* 6 (spring 1984): 85–97.

———. *The Servant's Hand: English Fiction from Below.* New York: Columbia University Press, 1986.

Robbins, Russell Hope. *The Encyclopedia of Witchcraft and Demonology.* New York: Crown Publishers, 1959.

Roberts, K. B., and J. D. W. Tomlinson. *The Fabric of the Body: European Traditions of Anatomical Illustration.* Oxford: Clarendon Press, 1992.

Rogin, Michael. "Francis Galton and Mark Twain: The Natal Autograph in *Pudd'nhead Wilson.*" In *Mark Twain's "Pudd'nhead Wilson": Race, Conflict and Culture,* edited by Susan Gillman and Forrest G. Robinson, 78–81. Durham, N.C.: Duke University Press, 1990.

Roodenburg, Herman. "The 'Hand of Friendship': Shaking Hands and Other Gestures in the Dutch Republic." In *A Cultural History of Gesture,* edited by Jan Bremmer and Herman Roodenburg. Cambridge, Eng.: Polity Press, 1991.

Rowe, John Carlos. "Trumping the Trick of the Truth: The Extra-Moral Sense of Twain's *Pudd'nhead Wilson.*" In *Through The Custom-House.* Baltimore: Johns Hopkins University Press, 1982.

Sacks, Oliver. *The Man Who Mistook His Wife for a Hat.* New York: Harper and Row, 1970.

Salisbury, John of. *Policraticus: Of the Frivolities of Courtiers and the Footprints of Philosophers.* Trans. Cary J. Nederman. Cambridge, Eng.: Cambridge University Press, 1990.

Sawday, Jonathan. *The Body Emblazoned: Dissection and the Human Body in Renaissance Culture.* London: Routledge, 1995.

Scarry, Elaine. "Consent and the Body: Injury, Departure, and Desire." *New Literary History* 21, no. 4 (autumn 1990): 867–96.

———. "The Merging of Bodies and Artifacts in the Social Contract." In *Culture on the Brink: Ideologies of Technology,* ed. Gretchen Bender and Timothy Druckrey. Seattle: Bay Press: 1994.

Schmitt, Jean-Claude. "The Rationale of Gestures in the West: A History from the Third to the Thirteenth Centuries." In *A Cultural History of Gesture,* edited by Jan Bremmer and Herman Roodenburg. Cambridge, Eng.: Polity Press, 1991.

Scholz, Bernard F. " 'Ownerless Legs or Arms Stretching from the Sky': Notes on an Emblematic Motif." In *Andrea Alciato and the Emblem Tradition: Essays in honor of Virginia Woods Callahan,* edited by Peter M. Daly. New York: AMS Press, 1989.

Schumacher, E. F. *Small Is Beautiful: Economics as if People Mattered.* New York: Harper & Row, 1973.

Schupbach, William. *The Paradox of Rembrandt's "Anatomy of Dr. Tulp."* Medical History Supplement no. 2 (London: Wellcome Institute for the History of Medicine, 1982): 110.

Scot, Reginald. *The Discoverie of Witchcraft.* Arundel: Centaur Press, 1964.

Sedgwick, Eve Kosofsky. *The Coherence of Gothic Conventions.* New York: Arno Press, 1980.

Sewell, David R. *Mark Twain's Languages: Discourse, Dialogue, and Linguistic Variety.* Berkeley: University of California Press, 1987.

Seymour, St. John D., B.D. *Irish Witchcraft and Demonology.* Dublin: Hodges, Figgis, 1913.

Sherrington, C. S. *The Integrative Action of the Nervous System.* New Haven, Conn.: Yale University Press, 1906.

Simmel, George. "The Handle." Trans. Rudolph H. Weingartner. In *A*

Collection of Essays, edited by Kurt H. Wolff, 267–75. Columbus: Ohio State University Press, 1959.

Simpson, A. W. B. *A History of the Common Law of Contract: The Rise of the Action of Assumpsit*. Oxford: Oxford University Press, 1975.

The Skeleton Clutch; or, the Goblet of Gore. 1842.

Skocpol, Theda, and Kenneth Finegold. "State Capacity and Economic Intervention in the Early New Deal." *Political Science Quarterly* 97 (summer 1982): 255–78.

Skowronek, Stephen. *Building a New American State: The Expansion of National Administrative Capacities, 1877–1920*. Cambridge, Eng.: Cambridge University Press, 1982.

Smith, Adam. *The Theory of Moral Sentiments*. Oxford: Clarendon Press, 1976.

Sorell, Walter. *The Story of the Human Hand*. Indianapolis: Bobbs-Merrill, 1967.

Spector, Robert Donald. *The English Gothic: A Bibliographic Guide to Writers from Horace Walpole to Mary Shelley*. Westport, Conn.: Greenwood Press, 1984.

Spicer, Joaneath. "The Renaissance Elbow." In *A Cultural History of Gesture*, edited by Jan Bremmer and Herman Roodenburg. Cambridge, Eng.: Polity Press, 1991.

Stallybrass, Peter. "The Materiality of Reading c. 1450–c.1650." In *Anatomy of Readers in Early Modern England*, ed. Elizabeth Sauer and Jennifer Andersen. Philadelphia: University of Pennsylvania Press. Forthcoming.

———. "Reading the Body: *The Revenger's Tragedy* and the Jacobean Theatre of Consumption." *Renaissance Drama* New Series 18 (1987): 121–48.

Stepto, Robert B. "Distrust of the Reader in Afro-American Narratives." In *Reconstructing American Literary History*, edited by Sacvan Bercovitch. Cambridge, Mass: Harvard University Press, 1986.

Stone, Allucquère Rosanne. *The War of Desire and Technology at the Close of the Mechanical Age*. Cambridge, Mass.: MIT Press, 1995.

Strier, Richard. "Faithful Servants: Shakespeare's Praise of Disobedience." In *The Historical Renaissance: New Essays on Tudor and Stuart Literature and Culture*, edited by Heather Dubrow. 104–33. Chicago: Chicago University Press, 1988.

Summers, Montague. *The History of Witchcraft and Demonology*. New York: Alfred A. Knopf, 1926.

Taylor, Charles. *Sources of the Self: The Making of the Modern Identity*. Cambridge, Mass.: Harvard University Press, 1989.

Thompson, E. P. *The Poverty of Theory & Other Essays*. New York: Monthly Review Press, 1978.

Thompson, Stith. *Motif-Index of Folk-Literature: A Classification of Narrative Elements in Folktales, Ballads, Myths, Fables, Mediaeval Romances, Exempla, Fabliaux, Jest-Books and Local Legends.* Bloomington: Indiana University Press, 1956.

Thorndike, Lynn. "Chiromancy in Mediaeval Latin Manuscripts." *Speculum* 40, no. 4 (October 1965): 674–706.

Thorwald, Jurgen. *The Century of the Detective.* Trans. Richard Winston and Clara Winston. New York: Harcourt, Brace and World, 1964.

Tricomi, Albert. "The Aesthetics of Mutilation in *Titus Andronicus*." *Shakespeare Survey* 27 (1974).

Tucker, Robert C., ed. *The Marx-Engels Reader.* 2d ed. New York: Norton, 1978.

Twain, Mark. "How to Tell a Story." In *How to Tell a Story and Other Essays.* 3–12. New York: Harper & Brothers, 1897.

———. "Personal Habits of the Siamese Twins." In *Mark Twain's Works.* New York: Harper & Brothers, 1899.

———. *Pudd'nhead Wilson and Those Extraordinary Twins.* Ed. Sidney E. Berger. New York: W. W. Norton, 1980.

United States Department of Justice. *Fingerprints: Court Decisions.* Washington, D.C.: Division of Investigation, 1934.

———. *Fingerprint Identification: The Identification Division of the FBI.* Federal Bureau of Investigation, 1991.

———. "Press Release." Washington, D.C.: Federal Bureau of Investigation, 1964. Transcript provided by Printed Media, Office of Public Affairs, FBI.

Valverde de Amusco, Juan. *Historia de la composicion del cuerpo humano.* Rome: Impressa por Antonio Salamanca, y Antonio Lesrerdy, 1556.

Vesalius, Andreas. *De humani corporis fabrica libri septem.* Basel, 1543.

Vickers, Nancy. "Diana Described: Scattered Woman and Scattered Rhyme." *Critical Inquiry* 8 (1981): 625–80.

———. " 'This Heraldry in Lucrece' Face'." In *The Female Body in Western Culture: Contemporary Perspectives,* edited by Susan Rubin Suleiman. Cambridge, Mass.: Harvard University Press, 1985.

Wadsworth, Frank W. " 'Rough Music' in *The Duchess of Malfi*: Webster's Dance of Madmen and the Charivari Tradition." In *Rite, Drama, Festival, Spectacle: Rehearsals Toward a Theory of Cultural Performance,* edited by John J. MacAloon. Philadelphia: Institute for the Study of Human Issues, 1984.

Waith, Eugene. "The Ceremonies of *Titus Andronicus*." In *Mirror up to Shakespeare: Essays in Honour of G. R. Hibbard,* edited by J. C. Gray. Toronto: University of Toronto Press, 1984.

————. "The Metamorphosis of Violence in *Titus Andronicus*." *Shakespeare Survey* 10 (1957): 39–49.

Walpole, Horace. *The Castle of Otranto.* Oxford: Oxford University Press, 1996.

Wayne, Don E. "Drama and Society in the Age of Jonson: An Alternate View." *Renaissance Drama* New Series 13, no. 104 (1982): 103–29.

Webster, John. *The Duchess of Malfi.* Ed. John Russell Brown. London: Methuen, 1964.

————. *The Duchess of Malfi and Other Plays.* Ed. Rene Weis. Oxford: Oxford University Press, 1996.

————. *The White Devil.* Ed. John Russell Brown. New York: Manchester University Press, 1996.

Wentworth, Bert, and Harris Hawthorne Wilder. *Personal Identification: Methods for the Identification of Individuals, Living or Dead.* Boston: The Goreham Press, 1918.

Wharton, Edith. "The House of the Dead Hand." In *The Collected Short Stories of Edith Wharton,* edited by R. W. B. Lewis., 1: 507–29. New York: Scribner, 1968.

Whitelock, Dorothy. *History, Law and Literature in Tenth- and Eleventh-Century England.* London: Variorum Reprints, 1981.

Whitney, Geffrey. *A Choice of Emblemes.* Aldershot, England: Scolar Press, 1586; 1989.

Wiebe, Robert H. *The Search for Order, 1877–1920.* New York: Hill & Wang, 1967.

Wigger, Anne P. "The Source of Fingerprint Material in Mark Twain's *Pudd'nhead Wilson*." *American Literature* 28, no. 4 (1957): 517–20.

Wigmore, John Henry. *The Principles of Judicial Proof.* 2d ed. Boston: Little, Brown, and Co., 1931.

Willbern, David. "Rape and Revenge in *Titus Andronicus*." *English Literary Renaissance* 8, no. 2 (spring 1978): 159–82.

Williams, Bernard. "Moral Luck." *Moral Luck: Philosophical Papers, 1973–80.* Cambridge, Eng.: Cambridge University Press, 1981.

Williams, Linda. *Hard Core: Power, Pleasure, and the "Frenzy of the Visible."* Berkeley: University of California Press, 1989.

Williams, Patricia J. *The Alchemy of Race and Rights.* Cambridge, Mass.: Harvard University Press, 1991.

Wilson, Frank R. *The Hand: How Its Use Shapes the Brain, Language, and Human Culture.* New York: Pantheon, 1998.

Wilson, Luke. "Ben Jonson and the Law of Contract." *Cardozo Studies in Law and Literature* 5, no. 5 (1993): 281–306.

————. "Promissory Performances." *Renaissance Drama* New Series 25 (1994): 59–88.

————. "William Harvey's *Prelectiones*: The Performance of the Body in the Renaissance Theater of Anatomy." *Representations* 17 (winter 1987): 62–95.

Wilton, George Wilton. *Fingerprints: Fifty Years of Injustice.* Galashiels: A. Walker & Son, 1955.

————. *Fingerprints: History, Law and Romance.* London: William Hodge and Company, 1938.

————. *Fingerprints: Scotland Yard and Henry Faulds.* Edinburgh: W. Green & Son, 1951.

Wither, George. *A Collection of Emblemes, Ancient and Moderne: Quickened with Metricall Illustrations. Publications of the English Renaissance Text Society.* Columbia: University of South Carolina Press, 1975.

Wittgenstein, Ludwig. *On Certainty.* Trans. Denis Paul and G. E. M. Anscombe. Oxford: Basil Blackwell, 1977.

Wollock, Jeffrey. "John Bulwer and his Italian Sources." *Italia ed Europa nella linguistica del Rinascimento (Atti del convegno internazionale, Ferrara, 20–24 March 1991).* Ed. Mirko Tavoni. Modena: Franco Cosimo Panini, 1996. 2: 417–33.

Yates, Frances. *Astraea: The Imperial Theme in the Sixteenth Century.* London: Routledge & Kegan Paul, 1975.

Index

In this index an "f" after a number indicates a separate reference on the next page, and an "ff" indicates separate references on the next two pages. A continuous discussion over two or more pages is indicated by a span of page numbers, e.g., "57 – 59" and *passim* is used for a cluster of references in close but not consecutive sequence. Page numbers in parentheses following a note indicate the text page on which the author is quoted, e.g. 112n. 12(4). Page numbers in italics represent illustrations. Character names are entered in quotation marks followed by the title of the work in which they appear, e.g. "Lavinia" (*Titus Andronicus*).

Electronic labor, 208–9
Eliot, George, 3, 116–17, 147–50
    passim
Elizabethan drama, 11, 51–83 *passim*,
    86; "Ambidexters" in, 87–88;
    manual symbolism, 215n. 4
Elizabeth I, 218n. 6, 220n. 21
Emblems: emblem books, 43–51
    passim, 60–67 *passim*, 216n. 23,
    217n. 28, 219n. 11; tradition of,
    59, 65; fingerprints as, 176; severed
    hands as, 220n. 17;
Emperor v. Sahdeo, 229n. 10
"En Dextra Fides Que" (Withers), 67,
    68
Engels, Frederich, 15, 19, 121–27
    passim, 136, 144
English common law, 18, 213n. 19
English Dictionarie (Cockeram), 14
English Expositer (Bullokar), 14
English Gothic literature,
    development of, 126–31
English National Covenant, 24
Essentialism, 1–13, 26, 74–76, 207
"Études de Mains" (Gautier), 130–
    31
Eugenics, 168
Evolution, theory of, 124–29, 133,
    168–69
Exhumation, 100–1
Experience (double sense of), 144–
    45

Factories, labor injuries in, 138–41,
    188–89, 194, 226n. 39
Factory hand(s), 15, 112, 122
Familiars, 108–9. *See also* Witches
    and witchcraft
Fatalism, 133–35
Faulds, Henry, 166f, 170
FBI. *See* Federal Bureau of Investiga-
    tion Identification Division
"Fear of Being Touched, The"
    (Canetti), 111f

Federal Bureau of Investigation
    Identification Division (FBI), 17,
    159, 160–204 *passim*, 230n. 23,
    231n.34. *See also* Fingerprints and
    fingerprinting
Fenianism, 148
"Ferdinand" (*Duchess of Malfi, The*),
    94–98 *passim*, 104–9
Fetishism, 73–80 *passim*, 132
"Fiducia concors" (Paradin), 72
"Field hand," 15
Fingerprint Identification (Federal Bu-
    reau of Investigation), 163
*Fingerprinting: A Manual of Identifica-
    tion* (Chapel), 160–63
Fingerprints and fingerprinting, 16–
    17, 20f, 154–56, 160–204 *passim*,
    229n. 8, 231n. 34; and race, 160–
    66 *passim*, 175–79 *passim*, 180–94,
    197, 203, 230nn. 24,25; as legal
    evidence, 165–66, 200–1; forensic
    history of, 167–80; modern use
    of, 169–76, 228–29n. 6; and Fifth
    Amendment, 170–71; and self-
    possession, 180–94, 197; validation
    of, 180–81; possession of, 183,
    193; as involuntary confessions,
    194–204 *passim*; in detective
    stories, 228n. 5; as legal seals,
    233n. 50. *See also* Hoover, J. Edgar
Finger Prints (Galton), 160, 166
Fingers, dissection of, 40
Flexor-muscles, 33, 40ff, *41*, 45
Folklore: dead hand(s), as charms,
    99, 101ff, 222n. 16, 224n. 10; and
    severed arms, 3f, 198; Irish, 148,
    224n. 10; in law enforcement,
    160–63. *See also* Witches and
    witchcraft
Foote, Robert D., 181f
Forensic practice(s), 154–56, 159–
    204 *passim*, 228–29n. 6;
    bureaucratization of, 171–76
Fortune telling, 176, 184, 215n. 4,

Ownership (of self), 55, 76, 180–94, 197; and race slavery, 200, 203

Page, William, 57–58, 220n. 21
Palmistry *See* Chiromancy
Paradin, Claude, 61–63, 72, 83
Paraplegic limbs, 212n. 13
"Pardoner's Tale, The" (Chaucer), 232–33n. 45, 233n. 48
Parker, Louis Napoleon, 133–35
Parker, Patricia, 107
Parkin, Bella, 100
"Part Played by Labor in the Transition from Ape to Man, The" (Engels), 124–26
Passivity, 18–19
Passmore, John, 6, 212n. 10
Patient, 18, 45, 50
People v. Sallow, 170–71, 181, 201
Perkins, William, 102, 108
Perrott, Albert G., 181
Peter Pan (Barrie), 3
Phantom limbs, 188–89, 197
Pinney, Thomas, 147–48
Plowden, Edmund, 56
Policraticus (John of Salisbury), 11, 25–26, 54
Possession (of self), 55, 76, 180–94, 197, 203
Possessive individualism (theory of), 11–12, 55
Poverty of Theory (Thompson), 19f
Powers, Richard Gid, 230n. 23
Practical anatomy, 32f
Praxis. See Action and *praxis*
Prayer, hands in, 215n. 4
"Presence-at-hand," 211n. 8
Principles of Judicial Proof, The, 180–81
Prophecy, 113
Proprioception, 180–94, 203, 206; and theory of possessive individualism, 11–12, 55; and slavery, 167–

80, 194–204 *passim*; and amputation, 188–89, 194, 204; S. Weir Mitchell and, 188, 199–92
Prosthetics, 4, 94, 189f, 198, 212n. 15, 224n. 28; as metaphor for dispossession, 199–200; computers as, 209
Proxies (as agents), 88, 100, 108
Pudd'nhead Wilson (Twain), 16–17, 159, 160–67 *passim*, 178–204 *passim*, 228n. 4
Puns, use of hands in, 16, 57f; "Handlynge" puns, 34–38, 42, 46
Purpose *See* Intention and purpose

Race slavery, 10, 17, 21, 159, 165, 228n. 4; institutional control over, 166f; and character, 169, 178–80; and possession (of self), 180–94 *passim*, 197, 200–3; and labor relations, 190; and alienation, 199–200; and sociopolitical identity, 200. *See also* West case
Radcliffe, Ann Ward, 113f, 127, 156
Randall, Dale, 67–68
Reaching hand, and rejection, 117
"Ready-to-hand," 211n. 8
"Red-hand," 27
Religious iconography: medieval pointing hands, 9, 24–25, 71, 209, 219n. 12; God's hand, 28, 46–50 *passim*, 62, 103, 214n. 1, 217n. 27; Lazarus, raising of as motif, 118f; hands in prayer, 215n. 4
Remy, Nicholas, 98–99, 101
Renaissance anatomy, 28–40, 215n. 10
Renaissance genealogy, 80–82
Richard II (Shakespeare), 60
Rider, John, 14
Robbins, Bruce, 147, 152f, 224n. 17
Robbins, Russell Hope, 100ff, 108
Robinson Crusoe (Defoe), 20

Library of Congress Cataloging-in-Publication Data

Rowe, Katherine.
   Dead hands : fictions of agency, Renaissance to modern / Katherine Rowe.
      p.   cm.
   Includes bibliographical references (p.) and index.
   ISBN 0-8047-3385-6
      1. English literature—History and criticism. 2. Hand in literature. 3. Shakespeare,
   William, 1564–1616. Titus Andronicus.   4. Ghost stories. English—History and
   criticism. 5. Webster, John, 1580?–1625? Duchess of Malfi. 6. Twain, Mark,
   1835–1910. Pudd'nhead Wilson. 7. Agent (Philosophy) in literature. 8. Body,
   Human, in literature. 9. Death in literature.   I. Title.
   PR408.H35R69   1999
   820.9'375–dc21   99-39447

⊛ This book is printed on acid-free, archival quality paper.

Original printing 1999
Last figure below indicates year of this printing:
08   07   06   05   04   03   02   01   00   99

Typeset by BookMatters in 10.5/12.5 Bembo with Texas Hero display.